Laptops

2nd Edition

Visual

Sherry Kinkoph Gunter

WILEY

John Wiley & Sons, Inc.

About the Author

Sherry Kinkoph Gunter has written and edited oodles of books over the past 20 years covering a wide variety of computer topics, including Microsoft Office programs, digital photography, and web applications. Her recent titles include *Easy Microsoft Word 2010, Sam's Teach Yourself Facebook, 3E,* and *Microsoft Office 2008 for Mac Bible*. Sherry began writing computer books back in 1992, and her flexible writing style has allowed her to author for a varied assortment of imprints and formats. Sherry's ongoing quest is to aid users of all levels in the mastering of ever-changing computer technologies, helping users make sense of it all and get the most out of their machines and online experiences. Sherry currently resides in a swamp in the wilds of east central Indiana with a lovable ogre and a menagerie of interesting creatures.

Author's Acknowledgments

Special thanks go out to Aaron Black, for allowing me the opportunity to tackle this project; development editor Terri Edwards, for her dedication and patience in shepherding this project; to copy editor Scott Tullis, for ensuring that all the i's were dotted and t's were crossed; to technical editor Vince Averello, for skillfully checking each step and offering valuable input along the way; and finally to the production team at Wiley, for their talents in creating such a helpful, much-needed, and incredibly good-looking book. Also, special thanks to Matty, for his love and support, and for always providing much needed humor.

How to Use This Book

Who This Book Is For

This book is for the reader who has never used this particular technology or software application. It is also for readers who want to expand their knowledge.

The Conventions in This Book

① Steps

This book uses a step-by-step format to guide you easily through each task. **Numbered steps** are actions you must do; **bulleted steps** clarify a point, step, or optional feature; and **indented steps** give you the result.

② Notes

Notes give additional information — special conditions that may occur during an operation, a situation that you want to avoid, or a cross-reference to a related area of the book.

③ Icons and Buttons

Icons and buttons show you exactly what you need to click to perform a step.

④ Tips

Tips offer additional information, including warnings and shortcuts.

⑤ Bold

Bold type shows command names or options that you must click or text or numbers you must type.

⑥ Italics

Italic type introduces and defines a new term.

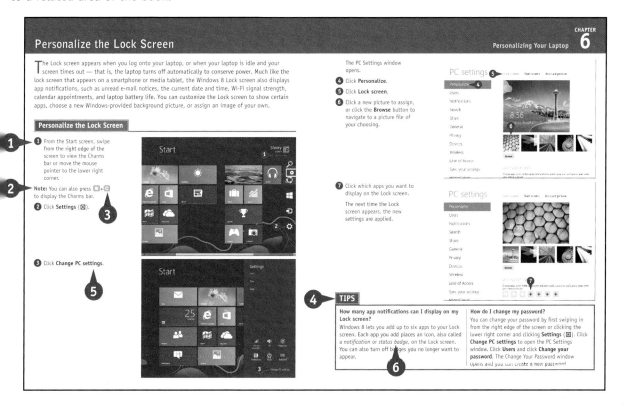

Table of Contents

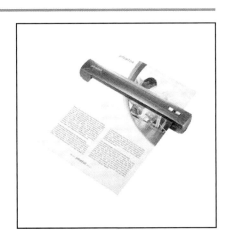

Chapter 4   Setting Up Your New Laptop

Chapter 5   Exploring Windows 8

Table of Contents

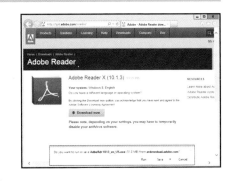

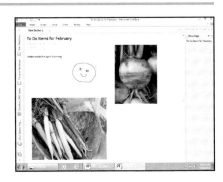

Chapter 9   Managing Computer Files and Folders

Chapter 10   Connecting to a Network

Chapter 11   Exploring the Internet

Table of Contents

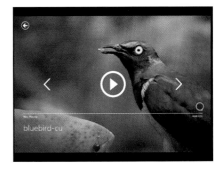

Chapter 15 Managing Laptop Power

Chapter 16 Maintaining Your Laptop

Chapter 17 Keeping Your Laptop Secure

CHAPTER 1

Introducing Laptops

Portable computers, referred to as *notebooks* or *laptops*, began as a great tool for people who travel and want to take their computer along. Today, laptops with high-end displays and huge processing power are taking over the desktop, as well. Laptops are lighter and more durable than ever before, making them a practical choice for most computing needs.

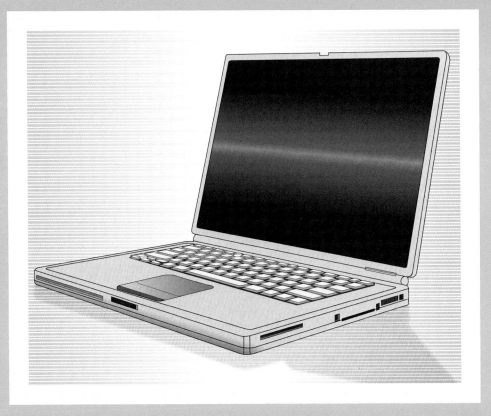

Study Laptop Anatomy

aptop computers are very similar to their desktop counterparts. Both contain a hard drive and other hardware, use an operating system, run software, and save files. Both can be connected to peripheral devices such as printers. However, key differences exist. Laptops, which are designed for portability, are much more compact. Desktops require an external keyboard and mouse, these features along with a monitor are built into laptops. Finally, laptops run on a battery, whereas desktops require an electrical outlet.

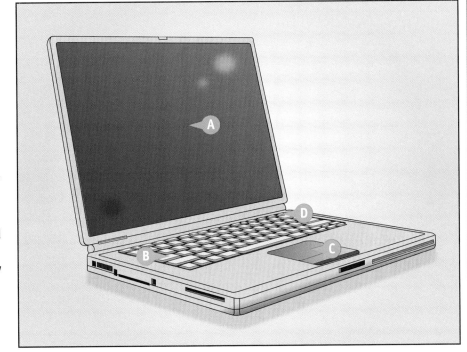

A Monitor

The monitor on a laptop is typically made of a soft-to-the-touch, and somewhat fragile, liquid crystal display. Some monitors even swivel.

B Keyboard

Keyboard configurations vary based on the size of the laptop, with larger laptops having a separate number pad and smaller ones embedding number pad functionality within the regular keys.

C Touchpad Pointing Device

Laptops feature a built-in pointing device — usually a touchpad, as shown here. You move your finger over the pad to move the mouse pointer on your screen.

D Function Keys

Most laptops have preassigned functions for these aptly named function keys. Typical uses are for muting the speakers or accessing the Internet.

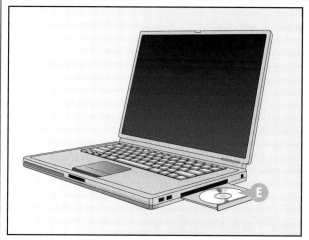

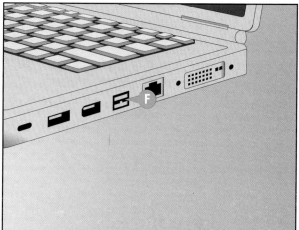

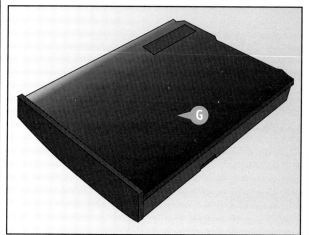

ⓔ DVD Drive

Most laptops include a DVD drive, although some still feature a CD drive. The location of these drives varies by model.

ⓕ Slots and Ports

Located along the sides of most laptops are slots and ports for plugging in peripheral devices, such as a printer or USB drive.

ⓖ Battery

A battery usually slots into the bottom of a laptop. This battery needs to be recharged on a regular basis.

ⓗ Power-Cord Connector

To recharge your battery, you plug in your laptop using a power cord connector.

Review Types of Laptops

Different manufacturers build a wide variety of laptops with a large range of prices and features. Unlike desktops that let you add a new screen or keyboard, laptops have major components built in, so choosing one that meets your needs is important from the start. For example, if you plan on using your laptop at home or at the office, a general purpose laptop works just fine. But if you plan to use your laptop strictly for video games or movie viewing, you may want a laptop built just for these types of tasks.

General Purpose Laptops

Casual users find general purpose laptops meet their basic computing needs. These types of laptops are perfect for using at home or office, allowing users to browse the web, perform basic software tasks, work with music and digital image files, and watch movies. General purpose laptops fall in the midrange price area, above budget laptops, but are not as feature-heavy as the higher-end laptops.

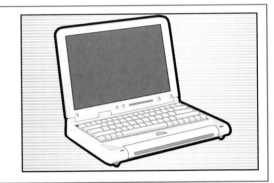

Budget Laptops

Budget laptops generally have all the general features you may need without the extra processing power or graphics performance that higher-end models offer. Naturally, laptops in this category are a bit less expensive than general purpose laptops. These go-to notebooks are an economical option for students or new computer users. Although not as feature-packed, budget laptops are often heavier than ultra-thin models.

Gamer Laptops

If you enjoy playing computer games, a gamer laptop offers the power and performance needed to handle all the graphics that game play requires. Gamer laptops are generally heavier even than budget laptops, featuring larger monitor screens, better speakers, and blazing fast graphics cards. They also have state-of-the-art networking features so you can play games online. This type of laptop often rivals the performance of desktop computers.

Multimedia Laptops

If you are looking for a laptop to handle numerous gadgets, such as an MP3 player, digital camera, or camcorder, a multimedia laptop is your best bet. Pricier than regular laptops, multimedia notebooks include features for television viewing/recording, video editing, music storage and inventory, and all the processing power needed to handle your gadgets. This includes bigger storage capacity, a faster graphics card, and faster processing speed.

Ultra-Thin Laptops

Although all laptops are meant for easy transport, ultra-thin laptops are designed to be lighter and easier to carry than regular laptops, especially if you travel by plane or car. Weighing less than four pounds, they tend to feature not as much battery life than some of the heavier laptops. Everything is a bit smaller on this type of laptop, including the keyboard and screen, but still efficient enough to handle computing tasks such as slide presentations, web surfing, and more.

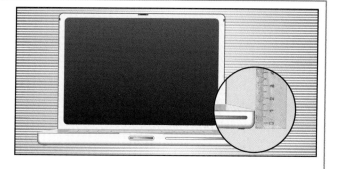

Netbooks

Netbooks are scaled-down laptops designed specifically for connecting to the Internet. Much smaller in size and processing power than other laptops, they do not have DVD/CD drives or many ports and slots for peripherals. They also feature less data storage and graphics capabilities. Netbooks can support simple software tasks. If you are looking for a lightweight computer just to perform e-mailing and web surfing tasks, consider a netbook.

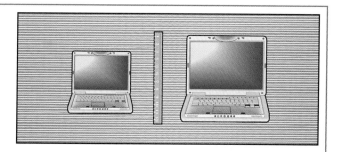

Explore Microprocessors

A microprocessor, called a *processor* for short, is an important part of a laptop and can make a big difference in its performance. A microprocessor incorporates most or all of the functions of a computer's central processing unit, or *CPU*. Microprocessor manufacturers are constantly working to improve them. Newer microprocessors offer more processing power, handle multiple tasks concurrently, generate less heat, and require less power to operate, all important capabilities for laptop computing.

What a Microprocessor Does

A microprocessor acts as the brain of the computer, handling data, performing calculations, carrying out stored instructions, and so on. Microprocessors, which are integrated circuits composed of millions of transistors, can perform many instructions per second, such as mathematical equations, calibrations, data storage, display updates, and so on. A microprocessor is housed on a tiny silicon wafer base, or *chip*, where some or all of the functions of a computer's central processing unit (CPU) are integrated.

Microprocessor Design

A microprocessor incorporates functions of the CPU onto an integrated circuit, or chip. An integrated circuit is a tiny electronic circuit composed of millions of transistors situated on a silicon wafer. This circuit consists mainly of semiconductor devices — that is, components that make use of the electronic properties of various semiconductor materials (primarily silicon).

Clock Rate

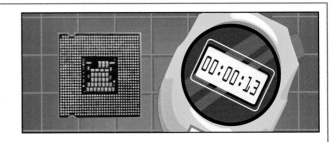

The clock rate of your processor reflects how quickly your laptop can complete a clock cycle, or *click*, which is the smallest unit of time a device recognizes. The higher the clock rate, the faster your computer can operate and the more instructions the microprocessor can execute per second. You will often see a clock rate, also known as *clock speed*, expressed in gigahertz. A microprocessor may execute several instructions in a single clock cycle.

Explore Power Options

Laptops have to carry their power supply with them when you take them on the road. They do this in the form of batteries that typically plug into the bottom of the computer. Laptop batteries come in various types, depending on the notebook manufacturer. The time you can run your laptop on a charged battery is called the *battery life,* and this varies from laptop to laptop. You must charge your laptop battery on a regular basis.

Battery Life

Batteries provide a certain number of hours of battery life, or operating time. The average laptop battery offers anywhere from two hours to four hours of battery life. The life of the battery is affected by whether the laptop is being used or is on standby mode, and by the size of the laptop monitor, with large displays draining power more quickly than smaller ones.

Types of Batteries

There are several types of laptop batteries, with the most popular type being the lithium ion (Li-ion). Li-ion batteries hold a charge longer than earlier types such as nickel cadmium (NiCad) or nickel-metal hydride (NiMH). Some laptops also feature secondary alkaline batteries to power internal clocks or keep the laptop running while the main battery is changed. For best performance, Li-ion batteries are the standard today.

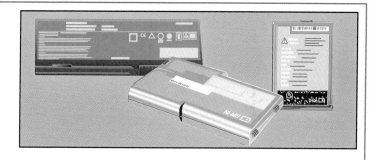

AC Power

If you use your laptop at home or office rather than on the road, you can plug it into an electrical outlet and run the computer off electricity all the time. However, laptops used for more than a few hours this way can become overly warm, which can adversely damage or interfere with your computer's "health." To avoid this, invest in a specially made laptop pad to help disperse unwanted heat.

Understanding Hard Drives

Your laptop computer can have several drives, with all but the hard drive removable or external. A *hard drive*, also called a hard disk drive, is a device inside your laptop for storing and retrieving digital data, such as software programs, files, photos, and music. Hard drives have been essential components of computers since the late 1950s. Improvements in design, manufacture, and performance made hard drives the standard in personal computers of the 1980s. Today's hard drives can store several gigabytes or even terabytes of data.

Hard Drive History

The first hard drive (1956) was about the size of a very large vending machine, weighing over 1 ton. Made up of magnetically coated, stacked platters it could store around 5 megabytes of data and took more than 100 milliseconds to access it. Over the years, hard drives became smaller and more efficient. Now a hard drive can weigh as little as .1 pound (about 48 grams) and can retrieve stored data in a few milliseconds. Future hard drives may evolve to have no moving parts and utilize laser technology like a DVD.

The Hard Drive Disk

An internal hard drive is actually a spinning hard disk inside the laptop that records data magnetically onto the disk. The term "hard" was applied to distinguish the disk from softer floppy disks that were used to store data on thin film. An arm with a magnetic head moves over the hard disk to read or write data on the disk as it spins. Data can also be erased, although the magnetic data pattern may remain on the drive after you have erased it.

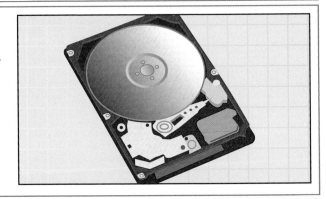

How Data Is Stored

Data is stored in files as a series of bytes in a sector on your hard drive. Each sector can contain a certain number of bytes. These bytes may be located in various sectors of the drive. Because bytes are spread across multiple sectors, those files are said to be *fragmented*, which take longer to load. When you format a disk, you are creating the track and sector structure along with a file allocation table used for retrieving the data.

Read/Write Heads

In addition to the hard platter that forms a hard drive, your laptop contains an "arm" that holds read/write heads. When you access data, whether by opening a program or opening a file, the read/write heads move across the hard drive, looking for the required bytes that make up the program or file. The heads operate very closely to the magnetic surface of the disk

without physically touching the disk, aided by the air flow that the spinning of the disk produces.

Partitions

You can create partitions on a hard drive that essentially break it up into two or more hard drives. You may do this to run different operating systems on the same computer. You may also create a partition to foster the appearance of having multiple hard drives for file management purposes or to accommodate multiple users. Creating additional partitions also

enables you to separate your data from your operating system; that way, in the event your operating system is damaged, your data remains safe.

Hard Drive Capacity

Hard drives today have a certain capacity for storing data, measured commonly in gigabytes (GB) and terabytes (TB). Older laptops can max out in megabytes (MB). Today's hard drives have grown to 160GB at the low end or 500GB or greater at the high end, with recent models packing as much as 2TB. The more you need to store and the more programs you need to run, the larger-capacity hard drive you should look for in a laptop.

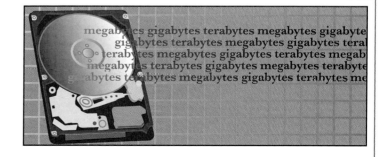

Understanding Types of Data Storage

In addition to a hard drive, you can also utilize other types of data storage on your laptop. Most laptops also have a disc drive for inserting a CD, DVD, and/or Blu-ray disc into it to store data on the disc. Other data storage options include USB Flash drives and portable external hard drives you can plug into the laptop.

Using the Disc Drive

Just about every laptop, with the exception of netbook-type laptops, feature a disc drive into which you can insert various storage media. These storage media include compact discs (CDs), digital versatile discs (DVDs), and Blu-ray discs. Depending on your disc drive's setup, you may be able to read data on and write data to all three of these types of storage media.

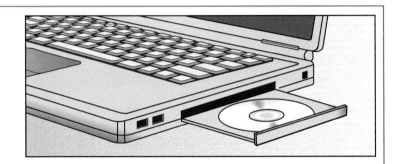

Storing Data on CD

Nearly all disc drives support the use of compact discs, or CDs — hard plastic disks on which you can store data, music, or images. CDs can typically store up to 700MB of data. To read from or write to a CD, your laptop must have a CD drive with the appropriate support (read, write, or read/write).

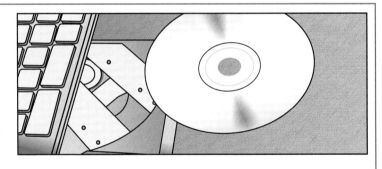

Storing Data on DVD

DVDs are similar to CDs, but with more storage capacity. A single-layer DVD can store 4.7GB of data, whereas a dual-layer DVD can store twice that. DVDs come in several formats, including DVD+, DVD−, and DVD+/−. DVDs also come in readable, writeable, and read/write format. Your laptop's disc drive must explicitly support a DVD format for you to be able to use that type of DVD.

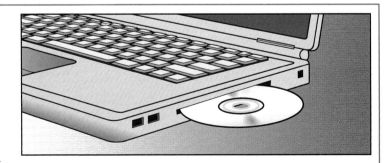

Storing Data on Blu-ray

The name Blu-ray stems from the blue-violet laser used to read and write to this type of disc. A single-layer Blu-ray disc can store 25GB of data, more than five times the storage capacity of a standard DVD disc, and a double-layer disc can store twice that. This storage format, designed to enable the recording, playback, and rewriting of high-definition video, is expected to supersede the DVD format.

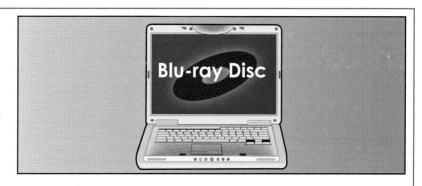

Flash Drive

A flash drive, also referred to as a USB stick or pen drive, is smaller than a pack of gum but can hold a huge amount of data. Plugging a flash drive into a USB port is like adding a second hard drive. Flash drives come with differing amounts of storage space, from 64MB to 256GB.

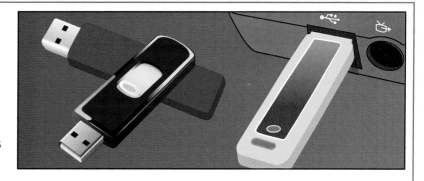

External Hard Drive

If you need to store large amounts of data — for example, to back up your system — you can buy an external hard drive. External hard drives have storage capacities of many gigabytes or even terabytes. An external hard drive can be connected to your laptop via its FireWire or USB port.

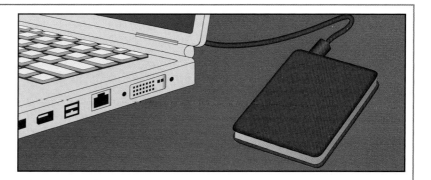

Understanding Types of Slots and Ports

You can use the various slots and ports built into your laptop to connect peripheral devices to it, such as a printer, a mouse, a keyboard, an extra monitor, headphones, a microphone, a digital camera, and more. Most of these slots and ports are located on the sides or back of the laptop. In addition to using the slots and ports built into your laptop to connect peripheral devices, you can also connect these devices to ports and slots in a docking station. You can then plug your laptop into the docking station to access the peripheral devices.

USB Port

You can use a universal serial bus (USB) port to connect a wide variety of devices, from a flash drive for data storage to a printer or digital camera. Devices that can be connected via USB are generally Plug and Play — that is, you need not restart your computer to use them after connecting them via a USB cable. And Windows can automatically install many USB devices when you connect them, requiring no additional input from you.

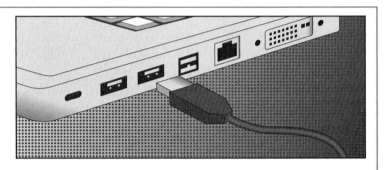

Memory Card Reader

A memory card is a small, removable digital storage device used in many electronic gadgets such as digital cameras, MP3 players, and so on. Many laptops feature memory card readers — small slots into which you can insert a memory card. You can then view the contents of the memory card, and even use the memory card as an external storage device to save data on your laptop.

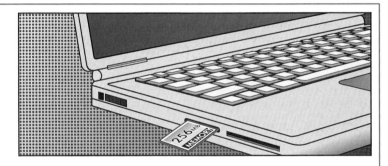

Monitor Port

Some laptop computers include a monitor port. If you want to connect an external monitor to your laptop — for example, to show a presentation on a larger screen or if you use a dual-monitor system in your workflow — you can connect a standard monitor cable into the laptop's monitor port.

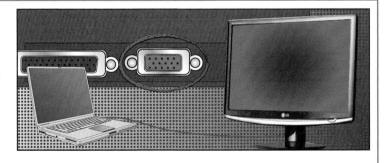

Ethernet Jack

You use an Ethernet jack to connect your computer to a router that controls your local area network (LAN) through a coaxial or fiber-optic cable. You can also use an Ethernet jack to establish a high-speed connection to the Internet. You simply plug the Ethernet cable into the Ethernet jack on your laptop, and then connect the other end of the cable to a high-speed modem.

Modem Jack

Although most people use an Ethernet cable or a wireless signal to access the Internet, there may be times when you must use a phone line. In the event you are required to use a phone line to dial up your Internet connection, you can plug a phone cable into the modem jack to pick up a signal.

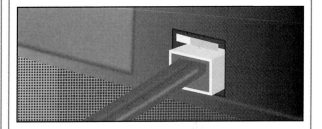

PC Card Slot

The PC card, also called the PCMCIA card (short for Personal Computer Memory Card International Association, the group of industry-leading companies that defined and develop the standard), was originally another type of storage card but ultimately expanded to house other devices such as network cards and modems. Many laptops include slots for PC cards.

Headphone and Microphone Jacks

If you want to use headphones to listen to music from your computer, you plug them into the headphone jack. Alternatively, you can use this jack to plug in computer speakers. You use the microphone jack to plug in a microphone. You might use a microphone, for example, to communicate with others using a video chat application.

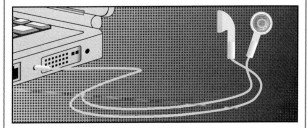

CHAPTER 2

Shopping for a Laptop

You can find many styles of laptops on the market, from those designed to be lightweight and portable to heavy desktop models with large screens and hefty keyboards. Today's laptops are designed for better durability and longevity, and the prices for laptops vary widely. This chapter is where you discover all the key factors involved when choosing the perfect laptop for your needs and your pocketbook.

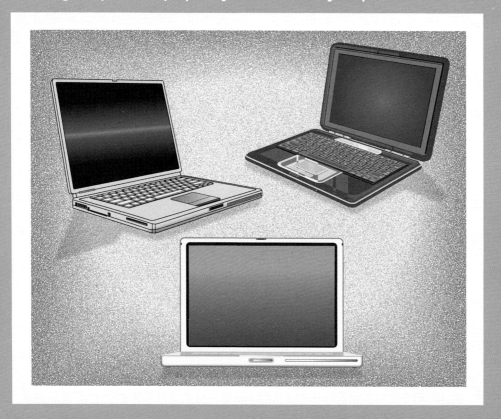

Choose an Operating System

An *operating system*, or *OS*, is the software that makes your computer work. It comes preinstalled on any computer you buy, and your laptop cannot operate without it. When buying a laptop, one of the considerations you must make is what operating system you want to use. The OS graphical user interface, or GUI, is one way to distinguish systems. A GUI helps users to interact with the computer's functions and features, offering clickable icons, menus, and other elements. You may have a preference based on your previous computing experience, or you may be ready to learn another operating system.

What Does an Operating System Do?

A computer's operating system (OS) runs all of your computing tasks, including software you install. Operating systems also help the computer to interact with other hardware devices, such as printers and external hard drives. In addition, the OS helps you manage your folders and files. OS security features help to keep your computer and data safe. You can use maintenance tools supplied by your operating system to repair or troubleshoot problems with your hardware and software. Popular operating systems today include Windows, Macintosh, and Linux.

Which Version Should I Buy?

Operating systems are updated every few years, and so you should be sure that your laptop comes with the most current version. Around the time a new system is released, stores often sell off machines with the older system at enticing prices. If you buy a used laptop, you may also be buying an older operating system. You should compare features of the different versions to be sure that the newest system is worth the extra money.

Upgrading Your Operating System

At some point in time, manufacturers stop supporting an older operating system. If you buy a laptop with an older version of an operating system and you want to upgrade to the latest version, go to a computer store or the manufacturer's website and look for an upgrade version. The upgrade version costs much less than the full product.

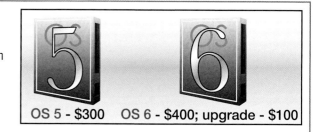

OS 5 - $300   OS 6 - $400; upgrade - $100

Microsoft Windows

The most popular operating system in the world today is Windows from Microsoft. Based originally on DOS (Disk Operating System) programming, Windows 8 is the most current version of this operating system, which is built into computer models from a wide variety of manufacturers, including Dell, Gateway, and Toshiba. Windows comes in several versions designed for home or business users. Check the features in each product to be sure that you get the one that meets your needs. The rest of this book focuses on the Microsoft Windows OS.

Apple Macintosh

Second in popularity to Microsoft Windows, Apple's Macintosh operating system is based on Unix and BSD (Berkeley Software Distribution). Apple was the first to develop a graphical user interface. Originally, the Macintosh was geared more towards personal computing, but today it is widely regarded for its exceptional graphic capabilities and easy-to-use interface, making it a popular choice for people in the graphics, photography, and video industries. Mac notebooks are generally more expensive than Windows-loaded laptops. Mac OS X is the latest version of this operating system.

Linux

Linux is an open OS, meaning no one company is responsible for it, sharing development and support among partnering companies and individuals. As an open-source OS, programmers are free to write and edit code, and share the programs with others. A bit more technical than Windows or Mac, the Linux OS is comparable to Unix. Linux is also a free operating system.

Select a Microprocessor

Choosing a microprocessor, also known as the CPU or *processor* for short, is an important part of deciding which laptop is right for you. As discussed in Chapter 1, a microprocessor is a tiny chip in your laptop that controls performance, speed, and memory. The microprocessor is the brains of your computer, enabling it to process data, calculations, and more. Because the microprocessor is such an integral part of your computer, it is important to know what to look for to end up with a laptop that meets your needs.

Microprocessor Types

With today's dual-core chips, laptops are more powerful than ever. Older computers utilized single-core chips which did not use power efficiently. Intel introduced the Core 2 Duo, which offered two processors in one chip, enhancing overall performance. Future processors will likely include numerous core chips. When shopping for a laptop, look for an Intel Core i7 or an AMD Phenom II, or comparable processor. If you are on a budget, consider an AMD Turion II or an Intel Core i3.

Clock and Bus Speed

Another aspect to consider in microprocessor shopping is internal speed, specifically clock speed and bus speed. Clock speed refers to the speed at which the processor runs, measured in megahertz (MHz) or gigahertz (GHz). Faster clock speeds are a must if you want to use your laptop for gaming or multimedia tasks. Bus speed, also measured in MHz or GHz, is the speed at which the processor communicates with the computer system. With either speed, look for a larger number for better performance.

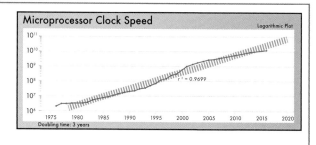

Cache Size

Processors utilize a small bit of internal memory, called a *cache*, which stores and feeds instructions or data to help the computer run efficiently. Unlike the cache found on your hard drive, processor cache is described in levels of accessibility to the chip. L1 cache is located on the same chip as the processor, whereas L2 and L3 caches are usually on a separate RAM chip. The bigger the cache size, the better the computer's performance.

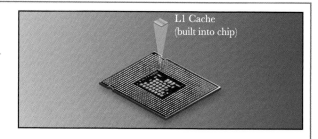

Choose the Right Weight

aptops started out as portable computing devices for people who traveled regularly. Today, you can find ultraportable laptops that weigh as little as a pound. These laptops offer a smaller display and keyboard size, but have the advantage of a longer battery life. You can also buy laptops that weigh as much as 18 pounds. These larger models often include multimedia features and larger screen sizes. In fact, these models are so full featured, many people have adopted them for use in lieu of a desktop computer. When it comes to choosing the right weight for your laptop, you need to compare portability against performance.

Portability

If you need a laptop for use while on the road, consider a lighter-weight model. Be aware, however, that there can be a trade-off in features and price when you buy a very lightweight laptop. A one- or two-pound laptop may be more expensive, and may be less able to handle larger programs or run at faster speeds. In contrast, a larger portable laptop may offer more speed or features, but it may be difficult to carry on long trips.

Stay-at-Home Laptops

Some people use laptops at home in lieu of a desktop computer. Even larger laptops, which boast 17- or even 20-inch screens, take up less space than a computer tower, and plugging external devices into them is easier without having to crawl around on the floor or move a heavy tower. Although weight is less of an issue for stay-at-home laptops, consider whether you might want to carry such a computer from room to room or out of the house.

Rugged Laptops

Some laptops are marketed for their durability. If you work in an industry in which your laptop may be subjected to a harsh physical environment, a rugged laptop may be for you. Their keyboards are sealed to prevent water damage, and they can withstand more variation in temperature, as well as the effects of shock, vibration, drops, and fire. They can also function near electromagnetic transmissions, such as from power generators. Not surprisingly, rugged laptops are heavier than traditional models.

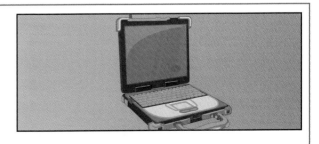

21

Choose the Best Battery

Because laptops carry their power supply in the form of a rechargeable battery, batteries are an important feature to consider. The amount of time you can run your laptop on a charged battery is called the *battery life*, which varies from laptop to laptop. The battery life represents the number of hours your laptop can operate on a fully charged battery before being recharged. Some manufacturers claim up to 5–7 hours of work time on their battery, but this may not take into effect the power drainage caused by common computing activities.

Battery Life

Look for a laptop with a Lithium-ion (Li-ion) battery. Laptops with NiMH or NiCad batteries, though great in their day, are older technologies not suitable for today's computing tasks and hardware. Lithium-ion batteries have the longest life spans — about 500 charges — but even they eventually wear down. As batteries wear down, they no longer hold a charge as long, or they may fail to fully charge. Some laptops even feature a second battery expansion slot, which can double battery life.

What Affects Battery Life?

Various issues affect battery life. One is whether the laptop is being used or is on standby mode. Another is how long the laptop takes to power down or power up. In addition, having a larger monitor with higher resolution or one used at a higher brightness setting can drain a battery faster. Fortunately, laptop PCs have several tools for prolonging battery life, from dimming the screen display to automatically switching to a standby mode when not in use.

Add a Second Battery

The easiest way to stretch the time you have to work on your laptop is to carry a spare battery. When the first one runs low, simply swap it out. Some laptops are designed with quick swapping in mind, enabling you to simply eject the spent battery and insert the spare, without even shutting down your system. Others require that you power-down first. You can expect to pay from $90 to $200 for a spare battery.

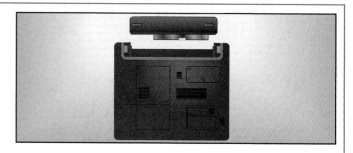

Compare Monitor Display Sizes

Laptop displays range in size from 12 inches or less — perfect for portability — to 17 or even 20 inches. These larger monitors are ideal for handling graphics and animations, a must for gaming or multimedia tasks. In addition to varying in size, laptop monitors can also vary in image quality. Which monitor is right for you depends on how many hours you will spend in front of it and what functions you need to perform. When choosing a monitor, you should keep both size and image quality in mind.

Note that laptop monitors are notoriously fragile. Avoid scratching them or submitting them to extreme temperatures.

Display Sizes

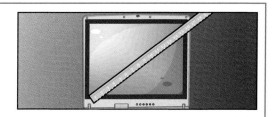

As a general rule, the larger the screen, the better the image quality, but the lower the portability. If you mainly need to check e-mail or type a few memos on the road, a smaller monitor might be adequate. However, if you spend hours reading reports, studying graphs, and viewing high-end graphics, a larger monitor is best. Netbooks average around 12 inches, whereas ultra-thin laptops average 14–16. If you want a laptop as a desktop replacement, choose a 17–19-inch screen.

Display Quality

Laptop monitors vary widely in quality. When researching laptop monitors, you will hear various terms, such as backlit and reflective, active matrix and passive matrix, and TFT. Generally speaking, TFT, active matrix, backlit displays are superior. A monitor's screen resolution indicates the number of pixels that form an image on the screen; the higher the numbers, the crisper the display. Look for a screen resolution of at least 1024 × 768 pixels — higher if you use graphics-intensive applications.

Screen Types

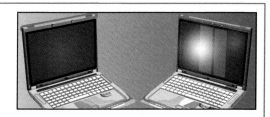

Most laptops utilize LCD (liquid crystal display) panels; however, some offer glossy displays, and others offer anti-glare displays. Anti-glare screens have a special coating to help cut down on glare from external light sources, making them ideal for outside usage. Glossy screens are brighter, yet more reflective, making them better for indoors. If glare is an issue for your purposes, look for a laptop with the appropriate display. Some laptops even have monitors that swivel, turning the laptop into a tablet for watching movies or giving a presentation.

Assess Graphics Capabilities

The graphics card is a circuit board inside your laptop that controls what appears on your laptop's monitor. The graphics card is also called the video card, video adapter, display adapter, graphics accelerator card, or graphics processing unit. The graphics card is particularly important when playing games or running animations. Laptops that can handle the graphics and animations that appear in many computer games tend to have powerful graphics cards along with large screens with a high resolution, a lot of memory, and fast processors. These come with a high price tag, but for a dedicated gamer or multimedia designer, they may be worth it.

Graphics Cards

Graphics cards contain a graphics processing unit (a GPU) with a specific speed and amount of memory. For most users, the graphics card that comes installed on a laptop is sufficient. For users who intend to use their laptop for graphics-rich applications such as design or animation software or games, a graphics card with more speed and memory may be required.

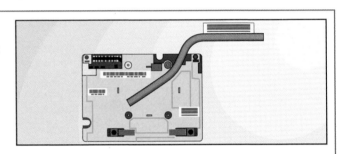

Considerations

If you are a hardcore gamer or plan to use your laptop to handle 3-D graphic work, a top-of-the-line graphics card is essential. However, a high-end graphics card is not necessary on a laptop that will be used primarily for such tasks as checking your e-mail or using a word processing program. Note that your graphics card must be a good match for your CPU. A very powerful graphics card with a slower or older CPU would be a waste.

Brands of Graphics Cards

Three manufacturers of graphics cards dominate the market: Intel, AMD, and NVIDIA. Intel owns the low-end category, offering a line of graphics cards integrated into the manufacturer's motherboard chipsets. If you plan to use your laptop primarily to check e-mail or work with a word processing program, this type of graphics card is adequate. If, however, you plan to use your laptop for gaming or working with 3-D graphics, an AMD and NVIDIA graphics card may be a better choice.

Explore Wireless Capabilities

With wireless technology, you can use your laptop to connect to the Internet using a wireless network — without cable connections or a phone line. These wireless networks exist in many locations, including hotels, airports, libraries, schools, businesses, cafes, and more. If you plan to take your laptop on the road, the ability to connect to wireless networks while traveling, or at your destination, can be very important. As you shop for a laptop, you should make sure that it includes the hardware components necessary to use a wireless network. You will quickly find that a laptop without this capability is much less useful than one that has it!

How Wireless Works

A special piece of equipment called a *wireless router* broadcasts a radio-based signal, which is received by computers in the router's vicinity (assuming those computers have the appropriate hardware installed). Specifically, computers need to have a wireless card installed to access the wireless signal. Computers with the necessary hardware can use the signal for two-way communication. The transmission speed varies depending on the quality of the connection and the quality of the wireless card installed in the laptop.

Wireless Protocols

There are various wireless technology protocols. These include Bluetooth and Wi-Fi, also referred to as 802.11. This technology enables you to connect wirelessly to the Internet. Within the Wi-Fi protocol are several versions, including 802.11a, which operates at 54 megabits per second (Mbps) and has an indoor range of 115 feet; 802.11b, which operates at 11 Mbps but has an indoor range of 125 feet; and 802.11g, which operates at 54 Mbps with an indoor range of 125 feet. In addition, the most recent version, 802.11n, operates at 150 Mbps with an indoor range of 250 feet. 802.11n offers significant increases in data throughput and link range, without requiring additional bandwidth or transmission power.

Finding Wireless Networks

Many restaurants, hotels, airports, libraries, bookstores, and other public places offer wireless hot spots — that is, areas where you can use your laptop to connect to a wireless router and access the Internet for free or for a small fee. In addition, you can subscribe to various wireless services from popular providers such as T-Mobile, Verizon, and so on to pick up their signal when you travel.

FREE WIFI HERE

Determine Memory and Storage Needs

Memory and data storage are two considerations for any laptop purchase. Your computer needs a certain amount of *random access memory*, or *RAM*, to run programs and load files. More RAM can also help your computer run faster. Your laptop can read from and write to RAM more quickly than to other types of computer storage. Your computer also needs to be able to store data. You store data on a hard drive as well as on external storage media, such as CDs, DVDs, flash drives, and external hard drives. Make sure any laptop purchase includes enough memory and storage to accomplish your computing tasks.

RAM

The more RAM, or *memory*, your system has, the faster items load on your computer. All programs, including the operating system, use memory while they run. RAM exists on an integrated circuit memory chip, which is rated by its maximum clock rate (how quickly it can request data to appear) measured in megahertz (MHz). Its memory size is measured in megabytes 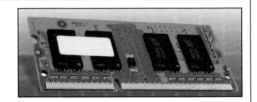 (MB), gigabytes (GB), or terabytes (TB). RAM comes in several varieties, including static RAM (SRAM), dynamic RAM (DRAM), synchronous dynamic RAM (SDRAM), and double data rate SDRAM (DDR SDRAM). At the minimum range, look for a laptop with at least 2GB. For optimal performance, choose 4GB, and for best performance, choose 8GB or greater.

Hard Drive Capacity

Hard drives have a certain capacity for storing data, measured in gigabytes (GB) or terabytes (TB). You should buy a hard drive with enough capacity to handle your day-to-day data storage needs. Today, a 160GB hard drive is pretty much the minimum standard, and most have between 250 and 750GB of storage. The more files you need to store and the more programs you need to run, the larger-capacity hard drive you should get.

Basic Requirements

Windows 8 requires at least 1GB of system memory (RAM) for the 32-bit version of the operating system and 2GB of system memory (RAM) for the 64-bit version. Windows 8 also requires 20GB of available space on the hard drive to function. In reality, however, minimum requirements for operating systems are not adequate for a smooth computing experience. When purchasing a new laptop, you should opt for one with additional RAM and hard drive space.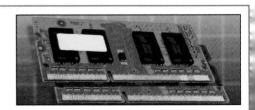

Everyday Use

If you plan to use your laptop on a day-to-day basis, and if it fits in your budget, you should look for a computer with a Windows Experience Index rating of at least 2.0, and preferably 3.0. Bumping up your RAM to 3GB helps ensure your laptop does not get bogged down. In addition, you may want to opt for a larger hard drive — say, 200GB — especially if you want to store a significant number of photos, songs, or videos on your computer.

Power Users

You may need to run several programs at once (called *multitasking*). For example, you may want to check your e-mail while running a Microsoft PowerPoint slide show presentation and opening a word processing document. In this case, opt for a laptop with a Windows Experience Index rating of at least 3.0, and preferably 4.0. In addition, you may want more memory — 4GB should do the trick. And you will almost certainly want a larger hard drive.

Graphics and Gaming

For the graphics professional or hardcore gamer, a Windows Experience Index rating of at least 5.0 ensures that any high-end games or graphics applications run without a hitch. And again, you will want yet more memory and an even larger hard drive than a power user would require — 5GB of RAM and a 500GB hard drive should suffice.

External Data Storage

You should also look for a laptop that has a DVD drive for storing data, such as digital pictures and movies. Most laptops feature a read/write DVD/CD drive. Blu-ray drives are another way to store data and watch movies, especially if you want HD video playback. USB ports are required if you want to store data to removable disk drives, flash drives, and other peripheral storage devices.

Compare Keyboard and Mouse Features

You can input data into your laptop using a keyboard and a pointing device. Unlike desktop systems, laptops have built-in keyboards and pointing devices, called *touchpads*. You are not limited to using these, however, and you can plug in external input devices such as a corded or wireless mouse, if you prefer. "Test driving" laptop keyboards at a local store is a good idea to see what sort of layouts work best for your own needs.

Laptop Keyboards

The keyboard on laptops can vary from those that are condensed for space — depending on function keys to provide full functionality — to expansive, desktop-style keyboards with number pads and special shortcut keys. Your choice of keyboard is mostly related to the size and weight of the laptop you need. Larger laptops feature full-size keyboards that duplicate the keyboards used with desktop computers. The only thing that might be missing is the 10-key number pad.

Keyboard Differences

If you are purchasing a regular size laptop, the keyboard elements are still about the same as a regular desktop keyboard. Traditional keyboard keys are close together and feature slanted edges. However, on the ultra-thin laptops, the keyboards are condensed to accommodate the smaller laptop size. Called chiclet keyboards, they feature straight-edged square keys spaced apart to help decrease the likelihood of pressing a neighboring key when typing.

Choosing a Keyboard

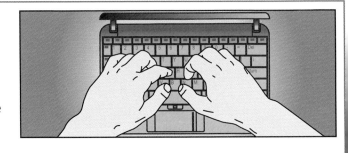

One of the most important features of a laptop is how the keyboard feels to you. As mentioned previously, if possible, try out the keyboard before you buy. If you are buying your laptop online, try to find a comparable laptop from the same manufacturer in a brick-and-mortar store to test in person. The feel of the keys under your hands, the heat on your wrists as you rest them on the laptop case, and the size of the keyboard should all be important factors in your choice of laptop.

Laptop Touchpads

Laptops have a touchpad or touch-sensitive control pad for interacting with the computer much like you would with a mouse. Also called a pointing device, the flat surface of the trackpad enables you to move your finger on the pad and track the cursor simultaneously on-screen. You can also tap your finger on the pad to click an area on-screen. Touchpad sizes vary. When reviewing laptops, be sure to test the touchpad functions.

Touchpad Differences

Some laptop touchpads are quite wide and others are quite compact. Extra room on a touchpad can make a difference to some users as they perform everyday tasks. You will also note the difference in the surface material surrounding the touchpad. The material differs from the actual touchpad so your fingers can tell by feel where the touchpad begins and ends. Some touchpads also feature multi-touch sensitivity, which means you can use two or more fingers to activate gesture-based commands.

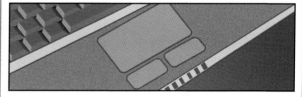

Mouse Options

Laptops have all integrated mouse devices into touchpads so that you can function without adding on equipment when you go on the road. However, if you still prefer the feel of a regular mouse, you can attach a wireless mouse through a USB port to add more traditional mouse functionality to your laptop. You can also attach a regular corded mouse to your laptop if you have a more permanent or solid surface where your laptop sits.

Pointing Sticks

Some laptops, such as ultra-compact netbooks, feature a pointing stick as an alternative to touchpads. Pointing sticks resemble an isometric joystick. Pointing sticks are often located in or near the bottom row of keyboard keys (called the home row) or below the touchpad and feature an orange or blue rubber cap. Like joysticks, you use your finger to move the stick and track a cursor on-screen. Older laptops sometimes featured trackballs that operated in a similar fashion.

Consider Extra Features and Add-Ons

When you are ready to buy your laptop, you will find that many stores and manufacturers offer a mind-boggling array of extra features and add-ons to choose from. Before you buy, make sure you fully explore what is available and which items are priorities for your own computer needs. Selecting the best options for your needs can help keep the price down and get you the system you want.

Preinstalled Software

Trial versions of programs, such as Microsoft Office, are usually preloaded on new computers. However, some free programs may also be included. Look for a basic productivity suite, such as Microsoft Works, that includes word processing, spreadsheet, database, and electronic calendar programs. It may save you time and money to have the manufacturer install other programs when configuring your system. Also, look for the most current version of an operating system; if a new release is imminent, consider waiting for its release or buying a new version-compatible model.

Expandability

Although accessing the inside of your laptop and changing out hard drives or swapping out the monitor display is next to impossible, you can expand certain features to ensure that your current system serves your future needs. Look for several USB slots where you can add memory modules or network adapter cards. You also need these slots to add peripherals such as an external DVD drive or printer.

Extra Connectors

If you plan on using your laptop on the road, carrying along cables and adapters can help you stay connected. If a wireless network is not available, you may need to bring along a phone cable. If you are traveling with additional peripheral devices, such as a printer, extra USB connectors are essential. Overseas travel requires electric adapters for your charger. If you plan on sharing data between your laptop and desktop computer, a data transfer cable is handy.

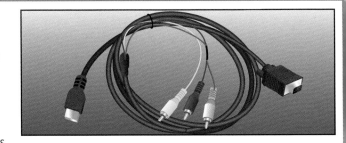

Cooling Pads

The bottom of a laptop heats up when you use it and can be quite uncomfortable sitting on your actual lap, not to mention the wear and tear of heated hardware on the laptop itself. Cooling pads use fans to cool the area under the laptop. Some pads plug in right into your laptop, whereas others have to be plugged into an electrical outlet. Some cooling pads also raise your laptop to provide airflow underneath.

Docking Stations

Docking stations can turn a portable laptop into a desktop computer solution without a lot of extra cabling. A laptop slots into the station, which contains a good supply of expansion slots, keyboard and mouse connectors, and USB slots. You can leave your peripherals plugged into the docking station and just place your laptop into the station to be up and running quickly. You might also consider a port replicator, which provides connections for peripherals, but without expansion boards or slots for storage devices.

PC Cards and Flash Drives

You can add-on PC cards for extending laptop memory, or for adding input/output devices such as data/fax modems or sound cards for gaming enhancement. Purchasing flash drives, or sticks, that plug into your laptop's USB slot for storing pictures, music, and other files and folders is also a good idea. If you plan on using a digital camera with your laptop, look for additional memory cards you can use to swap out digital photos. Make sure the laptop supports the memory card type your camera uses.

Laptop Case

A laptop case can help you carry your laptop easily while on the road, but it also serves a more important purpose. A case protects your computer from dents, scratches, and more serious damage if you drop it. Laptop cases come in many styles, from the standard briefcase to lightweight padded sleeves. If you are a student user, you may find laptop backpacks and messenger bag cases more in line with your on-the-go lifestyle.

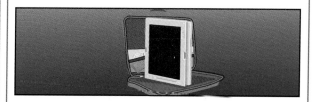

Make a Shopping List

When you are ready to buy your laptop, start by assembling a shopping list of all the features you are looking for in a notebook computer. Decide which operating system you want and think about how you plan on using the laptop; at work, at home, on the road, or all three. Prioritize exactly which features and components are a must and which are just nice to have. It might help to establish a list of required features and a wish list of features that are desirable, but not absolutely necessary.

Set a Budget

Start by asking yourself how much you have available to spend on a laptop; set a budget and stick with it. Laptops are generally more expensive than desktop computers, but you can still find some nice bargains, especially if you are just looking for a basic model. You can expect to spend several hundred on the low end or several thousand on the high end. The good news is that laptop prices are falling. You can expect a general all-purpose laptop to run around $500–$600 in price. Multimedia and gaming laptops are $800 and up.

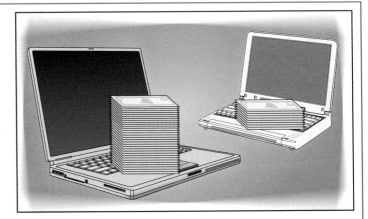

Do Your Homework

One way to arm yourself with knowledge before purchasing a laptop is to check various advice sites on the web. For example, sites like laptopadvisor.com, cnet.com, and notebookreview.com, offer extensive reviews and recommendations. You should also check out online forums with postings from other users of the laptop model you want to buy. You can conduct a search online to find out whether other users have had trouble with the machine or if they are happy with their purchase.

LaptopReview.com

Compare hundreds of laptop by price, brand, speed, power, and versatility. Updated daily with links to the best prices by the best sellers

Start now!

Find the Best Laptop

The price of your laptop depends on several factors. You are the only person who can decide which features are most important to you and what your budget should be. With such a wide variety of options, however, choosing the right laptop is no easy task. Even when you decide on a specific model, you must then decide whether you want to buy it in a store or through an Internet retailer. Thankfully, lots of online resources you are available to help you, including tips to help you narrow down your choices.

Consider the Source

You can often have a less expensive laptop custom made by a company that builds products from parts they obtain from different sources. You can even buy a computer from an auction site, such as eBay; in this case, you would be dealing with individuals or small businesses unfamiliar to you, although many are quite reputable. Price should be weighed against your comfort with the seller and his or her ability to support you after the sale.

10.1" Mini Laptop Wifi Camera White

One-day shipping available

Returns: Accepted within 30 days

$139.99   28d 10h 35m

Free Shipping

Comparison Shop

To get the most bang for your buck, take time to comparison-shop between stores and online retailers. Test drive the laptop at a brick-and-mortar store to get a feel for the laptop's weight and how the main components, such as keyboard and touchpad, work. If you know other laptop owners, ask them what sort of computers they have and whether they are happy with their choices. Also check online forums to see what other users recommend.

> Posted today, 3:35 P.M.
>
> I just bought the new StarSpeed Laptop for Gamers, and wanted to post a review.
> First off, realise that when StarSpeed says, "All the computer you'll ever need for gaming," that does NOT mean right out of the box. It actually means, "All the computer you'll ever need for gaming" AFTER you've bought about $650 worth of extras. It will run only the most basic game with the simplest graphics.

Warranties

Many laptops are backed by one-year parts and labor warranties, and some stores offer additional warranties. Warranties are limited, however, and do not cover accidents. Be sure to ask what the warranty covers and what it does not. A good rule of thumb to follow is that if a warranty costs more than 15 percent of the laptop price, you are better off spending the money on upgrades or backup drives to extend the life of the machine.

This warranty covers design and manufacturing defects for a period of 1 (one) year, plus parts and labor for 90 days.

CHAPTER 3

Adding Peripherals and Accessories

This chapter looks at all the different options you can explore to add onto your laptop or enhance your laptop's life.

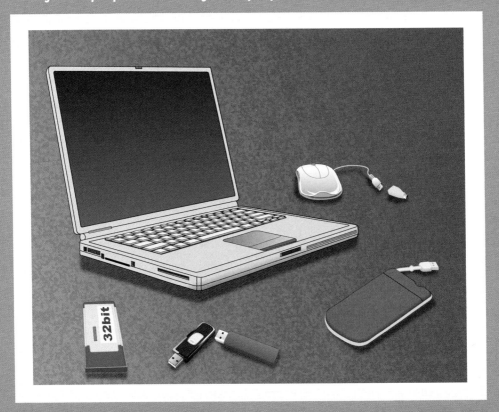

Get Extra Cables

Just like their desktop counterparts, laptops can utilize connectors to add on peripherals and connect to networks. In such cases, your laptop may require connectors like USB cables, data transfer cables, or travel adapters. It never hurts to have some extra connectors on hand for different purposes. Take a moment and familiarize yourself with the various types of connectors you may need with your own computing tasks.

Data Transfer Connectors

Data transfer connectors let your laptop communicate with other devices, such as an external keyboard or mouse. The most common type of data transfer connector these days is the USB connector. Just about every laptop sold has USB ports or slots for connecting peripheral devices. The most common USB connector is type A, but some devices, such as external hard drives, may use type B connectors. Some devices may utilize a mini-USB or micro-USB connector or jack. When adding devices, make sure your computer has a slot or port for the connector or you will have to buy an extra cable to make the transition.

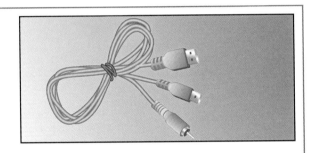

Audio/Video Connectors

If you plan on using audio or video equipment with your laptop, you will need special cables for carrying audio and video signals to and from the computer. Most peripherals come with the necessary connectors, but you may need extras. For example, if you want to give a slide show presentation using your laptop and a projector, you need cables to connect to the projector and/or stereo speakers. Most laptops feature a video port, such as an S-video, VGA, or High Definition (HDMI) port, which lets you output video to another monitor through a video cable, as well as a jack for outputting sound to an external speaker.

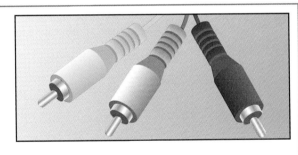

Travel Adapters

If you travel internationally, you need different adapter cables that enable you to connect to the electrical power supply. Be sure to do your research and find out exactly what type of adapter you need to plug into the wall for a particular country. If you try plugging in your laptop power cord without the necessary adapter, you can seriously damage your computer.

Add Input Devices

Your laptop comes with a mouse and keyboard built-in, but sometimes you may want to work with a different input device. A variety of input devices are available on the market today, ranging from a typical desktop mouse or keyboard to pointing devices, pens, and gaming controllers. By definition, an input device is any piece of hardware that allows you to interact with the computer, providing data and signals. You may need different devices for different sorts of tasks, such as a wireless mouse or a joystick for games.

Keyboards

If your laptop keyboard is too compact for the type of tasks you want to perform, you can always add on another. For example, you may prefer a standard desktop computer keyboard, an ergonomic keyboard, or even a wireless keyboard. You might also try a virtual keyboard, which is a small device that projects a keyboard on a flat surface using laser technology. Lots of keyboards connect through a USB cable, making it easy to plug into any of the USB ports on your laptop. You can also add wireless keyboards that use either a USB connector box or cable-free Bluetooth technology.

Mouse

The touchpad area of your laptop allows you to perform typical mouse tasks, such as pointing and clicking, using your finger. If you prefer the touch and feel of a traditional desktop mouse, you can hook it up to your laptop using a USB port. A wireless mouse is typically a bit smaller than a traditional mouse and uses a transmitter plugged into a USB port to send and receive mouse signals without the need for a cable.

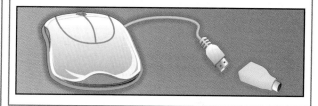

Gaming Joysticks

If you are using your laptop to play computer games, you may need a game controller or joystick to enhance the experience. These types of input devices offer additional controls that let you interact with a game, such as buttons or triggers for firing virtual weapons or levers for moving the pointer in different directions.

Other Input Devices

Tablet computers utilize a stylus or pen to write directly on the screen and interact with the computer. For example, a graphic or drawing tablet uses a pressure-sensitive input device that mimics a pen or pencil. There are also a variety of input devices tailored to users with physical challenges, such as braille keyboards. Even a microphone can act as an input device using speech recognition. Other types of hardware, such as digital cameras and scanners, are also classified as input devices, but are more specific in their focus.

Add External Storage Devices

In addition to your laptop's internal hard drive, you can use external storage devices to store data. For example, you may want to use an external storage device to back up important files, house large digital libraries, or run programs. In the past, floppy disks and Zip disks were used to store backup data. Today, external storage devices range in size and storage capacity, and adding portable, affordable storage to your laptop is easier than ever.

External Hard Drives

External hard drives are just like your laptop's internal hard drive, but operate outside of your computer through a cable, typically plugged into a USB port. Generally compact in size and box-like in appearance, you can find external hard drives that offer up to several terabytes of storage. Some even have their own cooling fans. Most external hard drives can use used with laptop or desktop computers.

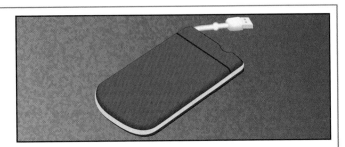

Flash Drives

Also called *thumb drives* or *key drives* because of the small size, flash drives plug into your laptop's USB port and offer a compact way to store data in a portable fashion. Small enough to hook onto a keychain, flash drives are also called *jump* or *stick drives*, and you can use them to transfer data from one computer to another or back up files, even software. You can find flash drives in a wide variety of shapes and colors. They also offer a range of storage capacity, from just a few gigabytes to a terabyte.

Memory Cards

Memory cards, also called *smart cards*, are another way to store and transfer data. Flatter and smaller than flash drives, memory cards are commonly used with digital cameras, printers, mobile phones, and laptops. Memory cards store 2GB or more of data, depending on the card. Memory cards measure about 2 × 3 inches in size.

PC Cards

Before the popularity of smaller memory cards, PC cards were common among laptops. Also called *PCMCIA cards*, PC cards are the size of a credit card and fit into a PC card slot on the laptop. PC cards were used to insert added memory, sound, or modem functionality. PC cards come in three types. Type I cards are used for memory devices, type II cards are used for input/output devices,

such as data/fax components. Type III cards are used for mass storage devices. Some laptops still offer the larger slot for such cards. Most, however, use the smaller memory card sizes instead.

Writable CD and DVDs

If your laptop has an optical CD or DVD drive, you can use discs to store data. Using the laptop's software, you can burn data to a disc, but only if the optical drive supports recordable (CD-R or DVD-R) or re-recordable (CD-RW or DVD-RW) formats. Most laptops sold today have a DVD combo drive, which means it can read, write, and rewrite CD and DVD media. Optical discs are perfect for storing digital media, files, and programs.

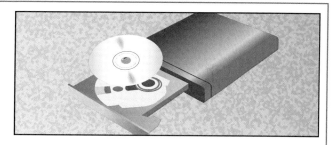

Online Storage

Another option is to store your data online. You can find numerous services that let you back up your data online, usually for a fee. Online data can be accessed anywhere using an Internet connection and any computer. With the advance of *cloud computing* — a general term for delivering hosted services over the Internet — you can also use the Internet to perform other computer tasks, such as accessing software, e-mail, photos, and videos.

Find the Right Laptop Case

You can use a laptop case to help you carry your laptop everywhere you go. After investing in a laptop, a case is an essential part of protecting your new computer. It protects the laptop from dents, scratches, and inclement weather, as well as more serious damage that can occur if the laptop is dropped. A case also makes the laptop easy to carry around. Laptop cases come in all kinds of price points, so you should do a little research and comparison pricing to see which type is right for you. Just remember, replacing a laptop is more expensive than buying a sturdy bag!

Briefcases

Commuters and travelers often find that sturdier briefcase-type cases work well for porting around a laptop. Clamshell-style cases, which open like a suitcase, offer a hard cover, typically metal, aluminum, or leather. If you prefer a softer case, look for one that includes lots of padding. Sturdier cases, such as those made from leather, may add a little weight to your load, but they can also offer better protection. Nylon finishes are less expensive, but not as durable.

Laptop Sleeves

Laptop sleeves are generally very thin, soft covers that slide over the laptop, helping to keep off dust or dirt, and offer protection from scratches. You may want to use a sleeve in addition to a regular laptop case to help keep the laptop safe from minor damage that can occur from the act of inserting or removing a laptop from a case. Sleeves offer no extra storage capacity for cables or other devices.

Messenger Bags and Backpacks

Although more casual in appearance, messenger bag cases are great for students and people who do a lot of walking to and from work. Messenger bags sling across the chest with a strong, durable strap. Smaller outer or inner pockets offer additional storage for cables or storage media. Backpack cases offer hands-free travel with two strong straps and lots of storage options. Leather materials offer greater durability over nylon. Both messenger bag and backpack styles are more comfortable, yet less sophisticated looking.

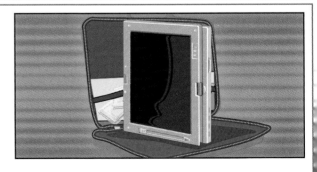

Using Cooling Pads

You can use cooling pads to help enhance your laptop's lifespan and overall computing experience. The inner workings of your laptop produce a lot of heat, and because all the components are housed in a tight area, the airflow is minimal. Excessive heat buildup can damage a laptop, and usually a laptop's internal fan is not enough to remove the heat produced over extended periods of use. A cooling pad, also called a *cooling base*, is a great accessory to help extend the life of your investment.

How Do Cooling Pads Work?

When you work with your laptop on your actual lap, you quickly notice how warm the bottom of the unit becomes; laptops generate a lot of heat. If you sit with it on your lap for too long, it can burn your legs. Cooling pads use fans to cool the area under your laptop. Some pads plug right into your laptop, whereas others have to be plugged into an electrical outlet. Some cooling pads also raise your laptop off the surface of a desk to provide airflow underneath, further cooling the laptop chassis. Other pads use no fans at all.

Types of Cooling Pads

You can find several types of cooling pads on the market. Active coolers are ones that use a power supply to operate fans for cooling. The power supply may be the laptop itself or an electrical outlet. Passive coolers require no power source; rather, they are made from organic materials, such as a crystalized salt compound, that work by absorbing heat as well as helping to raise the laptop off a surface. As the laptop heats up, the cooling pad's organic materials melt into a gel-like form within the pad and solidify again when not in use.

Portable Cooling Pads

Active coolers come in two types: fixed and foldable. Fixed laptop cooling pads are made of one-piece construction and lower power consumption, typically plugging into a wall outlet. Foldable cooling pads are easy to transport and store because they plug into your laptop. They are relatively quiet and use very little battery power from the computer. A cooling pad that plugs into your laptop usually offers an additional USB port to replace the one the cooling pad uses.

Cooling Pad Tips

Cooling pads come in different sizes to accommodate different laptops, so look for one that fits your computer. Make sure it does not block any airflow ports on the computer. Keep in mind what type of surface you primarily use your laptop on; some cooling pads are more suited for actual laptop usage than others. If you cannot afford a cooling pad at this time, be sure to use your laptop on a hard surface and avoid blocking airflow vents. Do not put your laptop directly onto soft surfaces, such as upholstery or a bed, which can restrict airflow to the device's vents and cause the unit to overheat quickly.

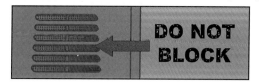

DO NOT BLOCK

Using Docking Stations

Docking stations can turn a portable laptop into a desktop computer solution without a lot of extra cabling. More and more people are using their laptops in place of desktop computers in the home or office environment. You can use a laptop docking station to create all the functionality of a typical desktop scenario, attaching to printers, a mouse, scanners, and other computer hardware. Docking stations provide a fixed spot to connect to all the devices you need and position the laptop to take advantage of a desktop workspace.

How Docking Stations Work

Docking stations do just as their name implies, they allow laptops to dock into a fixed spot. A laptop slots into the station, which contains a good supply of expansion slots, keyboard and mouse connectors, and USB ports. You can leave your peripherals plugged into the docking station, and then just place your laptop into the station to be up and running. You can angle the laptop in the station to create the best viewing elevation of the screen.

Port Replicators

A port replicator is similar to a docking station, in that it provides connectors for peripherals, such as a mouse, monitor, or printer all in one convenient location. However, unlike a docking station, a port replicator does not include slots for expansion boards or storage devices. The laptop does not dock so much as just connect everything from one spot from the port replicator.

Docking Station Features

Docking stations vary in price and features. Some include built-in coolers for your laptop. Depending on the model, docking stations can allow you to dock your laptop without powering it down first. Others require you to put the laptop in sleep mode first, or turn it off completely before connecting to the dock. You can also find mobile docking stations that operate in vehicles, thus creating a mobile field office in your car or truck.

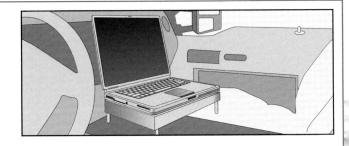

Add a Printer or Scanner

Need to print from your laptop or scan images? You can add a printer or scanner to your laptop that connects through a serial or USB cable, depending on the type of connection the device supports. Portable printers and scanners can help you when you are on the road, or you can use any desktop printer or scanner you may have at home or in the office, just as long as you have the necessary connectors and drivers installed.

Portable Printers

Portable printers are small and lightweight, typically using thermal or inkjet technology. Inkjet printers spray tiny droplets of ink onto paper to create a printout, whereas thermal printers require special paper. Portable thermal printers weigh around 1 pound, and inkjet portables are 2 pounds or more. Some portables even come with their own battery option instead

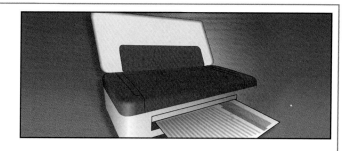

of tapping into your laptop's power supply. You can also find laptop printers that print from handheld devices or wirelessly from the laptop.

Other Types of Printers

Other types of printers include laser printers and photo printers. Laser printers use a laser beam and toner cartridges to produce a printout, unlike inkjet printers that spray liquid ink drops. Digital photo printers are great for printing out pictures. Regardless of the type of printer, be sure to compare features and add-ons, like ink and paper, to choose a printer that meets your needs.

Scanners

Portable scanners let you digitize documents on the go. You can find sheet-fed portable scanners as well as handheld scanners that enable you to scan business cards to build a contacts list. You can use a scanner to create a file, such as a PDF file, easily accessible by most computers. Scanners usually require a USB port to connect to your laptop.

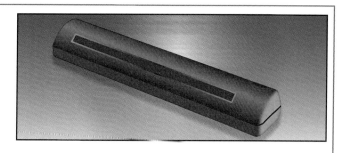

Add Security Items

Because your laptop is portable, you can carry it wherever you go. Although certainly convenient, it also puts you at risk of having your laptop stolen or having others access your private information. Security is a must for any laptop user, and not just creating passwords and firewalls, although those are very important security aspects. If you travel a lot, you may need locks, alarms, or sensors to keep your computer safe.

Cable Locks

One of the most common security devices for a laptop is a security cable. Taking advantage of the security lock slot found on most laptops, the cable allows you to connect the laptop to an object, such as a desk or chair. Cable locks come with keys or combination locks, and can help prevent snatch-and-grab theft. To determine whether your laptop has a lock slot, look for a

Universal Security Slot (USS) or Kensington Slot (K-lock), a round hole on the side or back of the laptop with a lock icon next to it. The end of the cable lock goes into this slot and clicks to lock.

Alarms

You can add proximity or motion alarms that produce attention-getting alarm sounds whenever the laptop is moved out of range or picked up. You can also insert USB or PC card alarms that sound off if anyone unplugs the cable or card from the laptop. You might also invest to have a tracking device installed on your laptop for an annual fee, which may help you recover a stolen laptop.

Fingerprint Sensors

Fingerprint sensors are used to restrict access to data on your laptop. Some laptop manufacturers build fingerprint sensor technology right into the palm-rest area of their laptops. If yours is not equipped with one, you can buy a USB fingerprint sensor device that uses a small camera to capture and upload an image of your fingerprint to your computer, which checks it against a stored fingerprint.

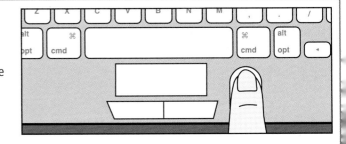

Add Headphones

Adding headphones to your laptop is easy to do, and ensures you can listen to music, movies, and other media while you travel. Just about every laptop offers built-in speakers which allow you to listen to music, movies, online audio, and other digital sounds. However, when you travel or use the laptop in a crowd, you may not want everyone to hear your selections. You can use your laptop's headphone jack to add a pair of headphones to your computing experience and keep your listening private.

Headphone Styles

You can choose from a variety of styles when selecting headphones. Inexpensive clip-on, earbud, and ear-canal headphones use small plugs that fit in your ear. Earpad-style headphones fit over your ear, placing a small speaker next to your ear canal. Full-size headphones are similar to earpad models, but have slightly larger pads that cover your ears completely, like earmuffs. For listening to your laptop in noisy areas, like an airport, full-size headphones work best to block ambient noise. If the environment is less noisy, the other styles work fine.

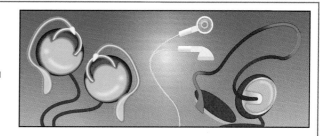

Wireless Headphones

Wireless headphones use a base that transmits a signal in addition to the receiving headphones. Because of this set up, they are probably less suited to travel with your laptop because the base itself is somewhat bulky to carry. Bluetooth wireless headphones, however, do not require cables or a base to connect, instead using your laptop's built-in Bluetooth technology. Wireless reception is sometimes poor, so wireless headphones are best suited for when your laptop is in a quieter area, such as at home.

Connect a Headphone

To connect your headphones, look for a headphone jack along the front or side of your laptop. Try not to confuse the headphone jack with the microphone jack. You may see a tiny headphone symbol next to the port. Plug the end of the headphone cable into the jack. If you want to use external speakers with headphones, you need a splitter, or "Y" adapter, to plug into the jack.

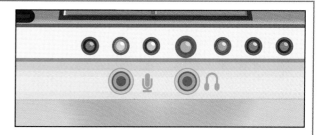

Add Portable Accessories

In addition to the peripherals and items already described in this chapter, you can also add other accessories to your laptop. Depending on your needs, there are dozens of devices you can connect to your laptop to add on to your computing experience. For example, you may want to connect your laptop to an external monitor for a presentation, or attach a web camera if your laptop did not already come with one. Here are three useful devices you may want to consider for your own laptop.

Portable Webcam

You can use a webcam to create a video feed in real time to broadcast online or conduct an online chat or video conference. Some laptops come with built-in webcams, others do not. You can easily add one using your laptop's USB port. When shopping for a webcam, look for one that can take at least 2.0-megapixel images, at a resolution of at least 640 × 480, and that offers auto-focusing and automatic light adjustment. Some cameras include motion sensing, which turns your webcam into a security system.

Laptop Power Inverter

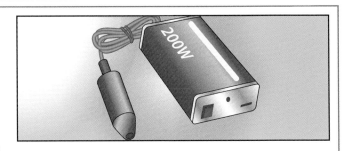

If you use your laptop on the road, you might consider adding a power inverter. It converts a 12v DC power source, such as the type found in your car, and turns it into an AC power source that laptops and other plug-in devices use. Most even include an adapter for plugging into airplane receptacles in the business class section of a plane. If you have room in your laptop case, you may want to carry an inverter in case you forget to charge your laptop.

USB Laptop Light

If you use your laptop on the go and lighting is an issue, particularly if you are trying to type on the keyboard in low light levels, consider adding a USB laptop light. It plugs into your USB port and you can bend the flexible gooseneck lamp to shine where you want it on the keyboard. Some even offer a built-in dimmer control so you can adjust the brightness level. Laptop lights use very little power from your laptop battery and are a good accessory to keep in your laptop case for an emergency.

Add Memory

After using your laptop for a while, you may decide you need more memory, known as *RAM*. Upgrading RAM can help your laptop run better, your software load faster, and reduce the amount of heat the machine produces. Adding or changing internal laptop parts is no easy task, especially for someone with little computer experience. However, today's newer laptops are designed so that users can upgrade memory with minimum problems. Always check with your laptop's manufacturer for details about adding RAM before attempting any internal changes.

Types of RAM

RAM chips are very affordable these days, and one of the few upgradeable parts on a laptop. The first thing you need to do is determine what kind of RAM is compatible with your system. Laptops have a limited amount of memory, and you need to check the maximum capacity to determine whether you can upgrade. Depending on what you want to do

with your laptop, such as play more video games, you may need several gigabytes.

Upgrade Steps

Before you do any work on a laptop's inner parts, you need to turn the computer completely off and unplug it from any power sources. You should also remove the battery. You can find a memory compartment door on the underside of the computer. Using the appropriate screwdriver, you can remove the door and look inside. Most laptops have two

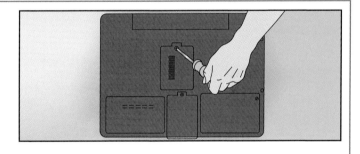

slots for RAM, and if both are full, you must replace one with the new chip.

Add a RAM Chip

Chips are held down by little ejector clips and usually pop in and out. Check with your manufacturer for details about adding or removing chips. Typically, to add a new chip, you move it over the slot and gently push it down to lock it in place. To remove an existing chip, press an ejector clip that holds the RAM module in place. After you add or replace the

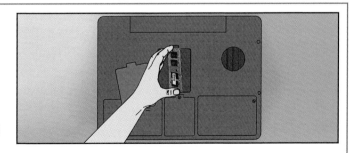

RAM chip, you can close up the memory compartment door and turn on the computer. The laptop should automatically recognize the extra memory.

CHAPTER 4

Setting Up Your New Laptop

This chapter guides you through the basic setup tasks to help you get everything ready to go.

Understanding Laptop Basic Operations

If you have never owned a laptop computer, you should take a moment and familiarize yourself with how the computer opens and closes, find out where all the plugs, slots, and ports are located, and learn how to care for the laptop screen. If this is your first time setting up the laptop, be sure to read all the materials enclosed with the new computer, including how to open and close it. Laptops are designed to be portable and sit on your lap when necessary, but most users find a solid surface, like a desk or table, is the best place to work with the computer.

Laptop Chassis

All laptops have two main parts of the body hinged in the back to connect them. The top of your laptop is the screen. When closed, the screen inside is protected. The bottom portion of the unit, often called the *chassis*, contains the inner workings of your computer, such as the CPU, motherboard, and memory chips. The keyboard is housed on the exterior of the bottom of the laptop body and is revealed when you open the laptop.

Learn How to Open the Laptop

Depending on the manufacturer, your laptop may open by simply lifting the top front edge. Some laptops have a latch on the front of the chassis with a slider mechanism that you must slide to release the top of the computer. Look along the front of your laptop to see what sort of mechanism is in place. If you find a slide button, slide it and pull up the laptop lid.

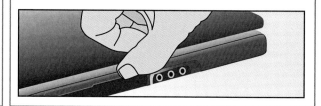

Practice Closing the Laptop

If you have powered down the computer or not turned it on yet, you can simply close the laptop lid/screen. If you have started the computer, closing the screen may just put your laptop to sleep. Most laptops go into sleep mode when you close the lid, also called *standby mode*. This keeps some parts of the computer working, but on very low power. Your laptop may automatically turn itself off after 30 minutes or more in sleep mode.

Care for the Screen

Laptop screens are typically liquid crystal displays, or LCD for short. They are somewhat soft to the touch, and unfortunately can be damaged rather easily. For that reason, be careful not to scratch, poke, or somehow dent the screen or it may become unusable. Having your manufacturer replace the screen or buying and installing a replacement yourself can be expensive.

Connect Cables and Peripherals

After unwrapping your new laptop, you can start plugging in all the cables and hooking up any peripheral devices you want to add, such as external hard drives or a home printer. You can use cables, such as USB cables, to connect peripheral devices to the ports and slots found around the perimeter of the laptop unit. If you access the Internet through a phone line or cable line, you can attach it to your laptop to establish an Internet connection.

Attach Devices

The most common type of connection used for peripheral devices these days is a USB cable. Most laptops come with at least two or three USB ports so you can connect several devices at the same time. You can also use USB ports to plug in flash drives for copying files or backing up data. External monitors and printers may use a different type of connector and plug into a monitor or printer port on the laptop.

Internet Connection

Laptops commonly feature a jack for plugging in a phone line or Ethernet cable. If you use a phone line to access a modem or DSL account, you can use this jack to make your connection. An Ethernet jack looks much like a phone jack found in a wall, although slightly bigger. If you use a wireless router or a wireless connection to the Internet, Windows 8 can help you establish the connection when you start the computer.

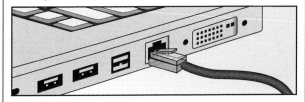

Memory Card Slots

You can use your laptop's memory card slots to upload data from a digital camera or another computer. For example, you can transfer data from another computer onto a memory card and copy the data into your own laptop from the card reader slot. If your laptop supports the same memory card as your digital camera, you can upload photos using the card; otherwise, you need the appropriate card reader to attach to your laptop for photo uploads.

Digital Video Camcorders

If you want to use a digital video camcorder with your laptop, you need an IEEE 1394 port on your laptop, also called a *Firewire* port. An IEEE 1394 port is designed especially for high-speed data transfer. Not all laptops feature this port, however, and if you did not shop for such a port, you may be able to use a PC card connection instead. Check with your camcorder manufacturer to learn more.

Charge the Battery

If you are using your laptop at your home or office, you can power it by plugging it into an electrical outlet. If, however, you are on the road, you can run your laptop on battery power. Keeping your battery charged is essential. Most laptop batteries can run for two to four hours, depending on the laptop's setup. When the battery runs down, you can recharge it by plugging your laptop back into an electrical outlet using the cord that came with it. (The time it takes for a laptop battery to recharge varies; consult your user manual for details.)

Charge the Battery

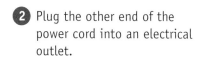

1 Plug the power cord into the appropriate slot on your laptop.

2 Plug the other end of the power cord into an electrical outlet.

Note: If you travel globally, find out what type of electric adapter you will need in your destination country. Without such an adapter, you could seriously damage your laptop if you attempt to plug it into a wall outlet to charge the battery.

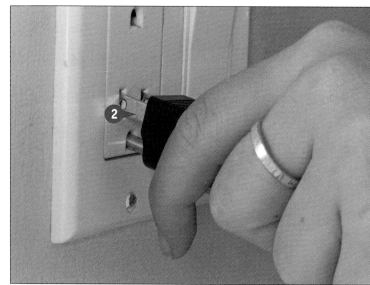

Turn the Laptop On

Y̲ou should take a moment to get used to how your laptop computer powers on; look for a power button somewhere above the keyboard keys. Laptop manufacturers typically put the power button in a corner of the computer. When you power-on your laptop, the operating system displays a Welcome screen. If multiple user accounts are set up on your laptop, you are prompted to select the user account you want to use. Depending on that account's settings, you may also be prompted to enter a password. (You can learn how to password-protect your laptop in Chapter 17.)

Turn the Laptop On

1 Open the laptop.

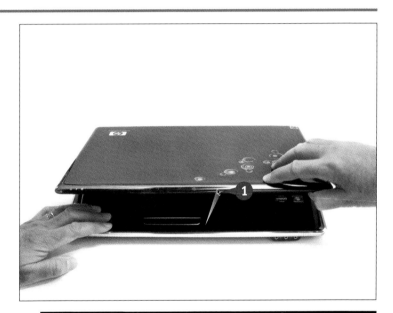

2 Press the power button.

In a few moments, the computer boots up and your operating system's Welcome screen appears.

Using a Touchpad

You can use your laptop's touchpad as a built-in computer mouse. The touchpad is a pointing device that delivers full mouse functionality, enabling you to move the mouse pointer as needed and tap to make selections, choose commands, and perform other important tasks. Also called a trackpad, the touchpad is a flat surface that detects finger contact; you move your finger to move the mouse pointer on-screen. A touchpad may also feature two large buttons you can press to perform traditional left- and right-mouse-button functions such as making a selection (left) or revealing a context menu (right).

Using a Touchpad

1 Place your finger on the touchpad.

Note the position of the mouse pointer on your monitor.

2 Slide your finger around the touchpad.

Note how the mouse pointer moves on the screen.

3 Press the left button.

The action that occurs depends on the location of the mouse pointer when you pressed the button.

4 Press the right button.

A context menu appears.

Explore a Wireless Mouse

I f you find a traditional mouse easier to use, you can purchase a wireless mouse. Many people have difficulty getting used to a touchpad or other pointing device on their laptops. A wireless mouse is a natural addition to any laptop. It does not require cables, it is lightweight, and it replaces the sometimes awkward touchpad with the familiar functionality of the desktop mouse. Several wireless mice are on the market, including ones made especially for laptops. These are smaller than desktop mice, making them easy to bring with you when you travel with your laptop.

The Elements of a Mouse

Mice come in different styles, but most include a right and left button and a scroll wheel. The left button is used for clicking on the screen, such as in a file to position your cursor, or for clicking and dragging to select objects and text. The right mouse button is used to display shortcut menus. You can roll the scroll wheel to scroll through windows.

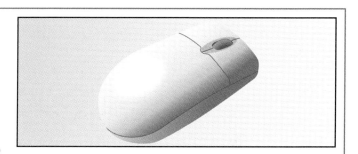

How a Wireless Mouse Works

When you purchase a wireless mouse, you also receive a transmitter that plugs into your laptop's USB port. When you plug in the transmitter, the Windows operating system typically detects it and installs the necessary software, called a *driver*, for the transmitter and mouse to work. When in use, the wireless mouse then overrides the built-in mouse function. You can also add a Bluetooth mouse that requires no transmitter, using your laptop's built-in Bluetooth technology instead.

Choose the Mouse

You can find a wireless mouse specifically designed for laptop users. They are smaller than a traditional mouse, and easily fit in a small space such as a pocket of a laptop bag. Higher-priced versions of wireless mice may feature an extended range and greater precision. You can find a wireless laptop mouse for under $10, or as high as $70.

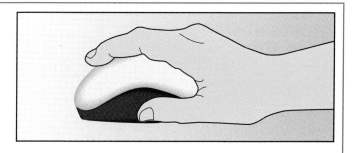

Get to Know the Keyboard

One of the most important features of a laptop is how its keyboard feels to you. Laptop keyboards can vary from those condensed for space — that depend on function keys to provide full functionality — to expansive, desktop-style keyboards with number pads and special shortcut keys. Your choice of keyboard is most directly related to the size and weight of laptop that you need. In addition to the alphanumeric keys that you press to enter text, laptops often include specialized keys, as discussed here.

Modifying Keys

Several keys on your keyboard are used to modify actions. For example, **Shift**, **Ctrl**, and **Alt**, when pressed with another key, modify how that key works. As an example, pressing **Ctrl**+**C** copies the selected text or object in a file, and pressing **Ctrl**+**V** pastes the copied text or object. These combinations of keys are called *keyboard shortcuts*. You can use many of these keys in conjunction with clicking your mouse to perform certain actions.

Navigation Keys

If you find it difficult to maneuver with the touchpad, you can use the various navigation keys to move your cursor around. Pressing **End** moves the cursor to the end of the current line. Pressing **Home** moves the cursor to the beginning of the current line. Pressing **Page up** or **Page down** moves the cursor up one page or down one page, respectively. And pressing the directional keys **↓**, **↑**, **←**, and **→** moves the cursor down, up, left, and right.

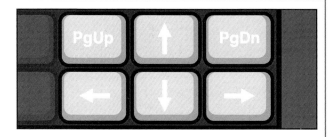

Function Keys

Function keys are available on all laptop keyboards to provide shortcuts to functions in programs. Function keys marked **F1** to **F12** initiate different actions, depending on the program in which you are working. On a laptop, where space is at a premium, you often find a key labeled **Fn**; by pressing this key along with a function key, you can initiate a different function than you would by pressing the function key alone.

Escape Key

Pressing **Esc** stops a current action. This key acts as a shortcut for clicking a No button, Quit button, Exit button, Cancel button, or Abort button, making it useful if you want to back out of an action or leave a dialog box or other input screen without saving an entry. Pressing **Esc** is also a common shortcut for clicking the Stop button found in many web browsers.

Caps Lock Key

Pressing **Caps lock** toggles the Caps Lock feature on and off. With Caps Lock on, anything you type appears in uppercase. With Caps Lock off, everything you type is lowercase, and you need to press **Shift** to capitalize a letter. On many keyboards, a small light indicates when the Caps Lock feature has been toggled on. Note that toggling on the Caps Lock feature does not affect nonletter keys, such as number keys or punctuation keys.

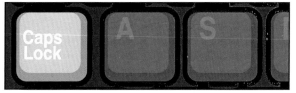

Keys for Cursor Placement

Enter starts a new paragraph in a document, or accepts an entry in a dialog box. **Spacebar** is used to add a space between letters in a sentence. Press **Del** to delete a selected object or text. Press **Backspace** to move your cursor back one character or space. Press **Insert** to switch from Overtype mode to Insert mode. Press **Tab** to advance the cursor to the next tab stop or the next field in a dialog box.

The Embedded Numeric Keypad

All keyboards feature a row of number keys along the top; however, it makes entering a lot of numbers difficult. For this reason, most keyboards include a numeric keypad on the far right, which is laid out similarly to a calculator to speed number entry. On laptops, the numeric keypad is embedded within the keyboard on the rightmost side. When you turn on the Num Lock feature (**N**umlk) or the appropriate function-key combination, those keys turn into numeric-keypad keys.

Connect a Printer or Hardware Device from Windows

With Windows, connecting printers, scanners, webcams, and other hardware to your laptop is a snap. In most cases, after you connect the device to your laptop via the appropriate port, Windows locates the software it needs to interact with the device (called a *driver*) online and installs it with no input from you. If Windows is unable to install a driver, it generally notifies you and offers suggestions on what steps to take next. You can manually start a wizard to set up any hardware you connect. To learn more about working in Windows 8, see Chapter 5.

Connect a Printer or Hardware Device from Windows

1 Plug in your printer or hardware device and turn it on.

2 Swipe from the right edge of the screen to view system commands or move the mouse pointer to the lower right corner.

3 Click **Settings** (⚙).

4 Click **Change PC settings**.

The PC Settings screen appears.

5 Click **Devices**.

6 Click **Add a device**.

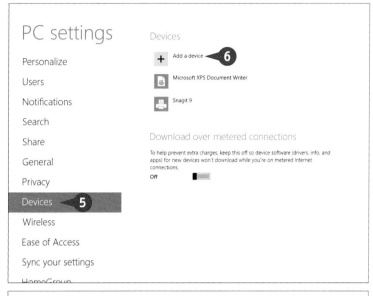

Windows launches the Add a Printer Wizard and tries to recognize the plugged-in device.

If Windows cannot find your device, you can click the **Not finding what you are looking for?** link to access a help window with more information about adding the device.

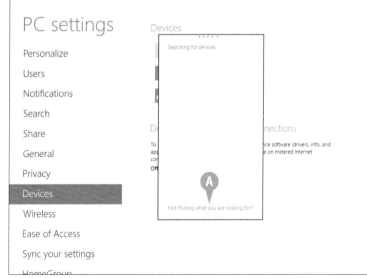

TIP

What do you do if the wizard fails to set up your hardware?
In most cases, Windows 8 installs the necessary drivers for your hardware automatically when you connect a printer or other device to your laptop. If it fails to do so, and if stepping through the Add a Device Wizard does not resolve the problem, you may need to obtain the necessary drivers from the manufacturer of your device. The easiest way to do this is to visit the manufacturer's website and download the driver. Alternatively, if the device came with a CD or DVD, that disc likely contains the necessary drivers to run the device with your laptop.

CHAPTER 5

Exploring Windows 8

Most new laptops you purchase today have the Windows 8 operating system preinstalled. Windows 8 enables you to run programs, manage files, surf the Internet, and more. Unlike previous versions of the operating system, Windows has undergone significant changes in look and feel, as well as operation. Learning your way around the new environment is the first step to laptop productivity.

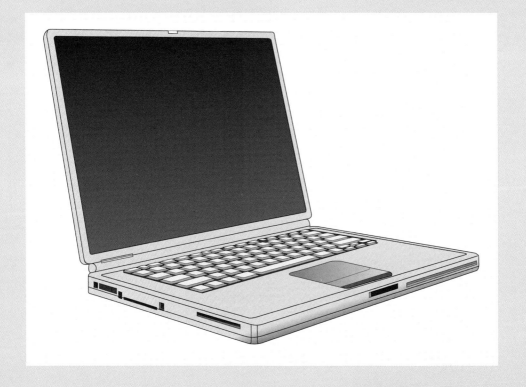

W indows 8 is a newly redesigned operating system that shares similarities with the innovative designs featured on smartphones and media tablets. The interface gives users quick access to apps, notifications, files, and more. Windows 8 is also designed to work on a variety of devices, ranging from laptops and desktops to tablets. Using new touchscreen technologies, you can swipe, zoom, slide, and tap to interact with apps and desktop elements, as well as utilize the traditional mouse and keyboard methods.

Lock Screen

Much like the lock screen on your smartphone, the Windows 8 Lock screen provides basic information at a glance, such as the date and time. It also displays system notifications, such as number of e-mail messages waiting for you, your network connection status, and battery life status. You can see the Lock screen at startup, or when the laptop

goes into sleep mode when idle. Press `Spacebar` or `Enter`, move the mouse, or touch the screen to wake it up.

Account Log On

If your laptop account is locked, Windows 8 displays a logon screen where you can enter your password to access the computer. Simply type your password and press `Enter` or position the mouse pointer over the `→`. As soon as you complete this procedure, Windows 8 opens the Start screen. You can learn more about creating passwords in

Chapter 17. Learn how to add user accounts in Chapter 6.

Windows 8 User Interface

The Start screen features the new Windows 8 UI (user interface). A *user interface* is the way in which people interact with their computing device, usually offering various ways to input data and activate commands. The Windows 8 interface gets its name from the design language created by Microsoft,

featuring big typography and groups of common elements. The Windows 8 interface mimics the look and feel of smartphone screens.

Navigate with Gestures

Windows 8 is designed to take full advantage of the rising popularity of touchscreen technologies. With touch-enabled computer screens, laptop users can interact directly with the screen rather than rely on a keyboard or pointing device. You can point your finger and touch the screen to swipe left, right, up, or down to move items or the entire screen. Called *gestures*, you can pinch in or out to zoom your view, or tap to select items on-screen.

Navigate with Keyboard and Mouse

If you do not happen to own a new touchscreen laptop, you can still use the new Windows 8 features and tools, just not as "hands on" as those with touch-enabled screens. You can use the mouse to perform similar actions, such as clicking and dragging or clicking to select, or use the keyboard navigation keys.

Apps

In previous renditions of the Windows operating system, small apps helped you accomplish simple computer tasks. Called *accessories*, these smaller apps included programs such as WordPad, Paint, Calculator, and Notepad. Those accessories are still around, and the new Windows 8 interface offers even more of them. Windows 8 apps present themselves as tiles on the Start screen, and include such functions as Mail, Calendar, Messaging, and Photos, just to list a few. (*Apps* and *programs* are both software, but apps are smaller and typically single purpose programs.)

Desktop

If you have worked with previous Windows operating systems, you will be glad to know the traditional Windows desktop is still around. The desktop holds shortcut icons, folders, and other items, plus features a taskbar at the bottom of the screen displaying notifications, open programs, and common apps, such as File Explorer and Internet Explorer. Gone, however, is the Start menu. You can now start programs from the Windows 8 Start screen.

Charms Bar

Hidden at the far right side of the screen, the Charms bar, a vertical opaque bar with large icons, called *charms*, represents categories. The Charms bar offers quick access to commonly used features and actions, such as searching, sharing files, and accessing computer settings. Click a Charm to view the associated options, features, and links.

If your laptop is sporting a touch-enabled screen, you can take advantage of the new Windows 8 navigation techniques. The Windows 8 Start screen is designed especially for touchscreen technology; you can swipe, tap, double-tap, and pinch using gestures you perform directly on the screen. If your laptop has a regular monitor, you can still use the mouse and keyboard to get around. Even if you do not have a touch-enabled screen, you can always buy one and plug it into your laptop as a peripheral device.

Gestures

Touch gestures are actions you perform directly on a touch-enabled screen using a finger or stylus. Designed to be intuitive, you can perform many basic moves without having to think about it. Most gestures are single-stroke, which means you typically use your index finger and your thumb together or separately to navigate around the screen to select commands and perform computer tasks. Touch gestures are already quite common with smartphones and tablets, so adding them to PC usage is the next logical step.

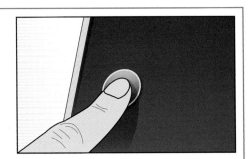

Touch Gestures

Gesture	Description
Tap	A tap represents the left-click of a mouse.
Double-tap	A double-tap represents a double-click of the left mouse button.
Hold	The user presses and holds on the screen.
Flick	The user moves a finger very quickly across the screen to initiate scrolling.
Swipe	Similar to a flick, but longer in duration and distance.
Pan	The user can press and hold on the screen and then drag the finger left or right, representing a mouse move event.
Pinch	Pinch in or out to zoom your view in or out.

Log On to Windows 8

You can use the Windows 8 logon screen, also called the Lock screen, to access your laptop's operating system. A logon screen is where you type your username and password. The new Windows 8 Lock screen includes a customizable background image, plus a separate overlay detailing your laptop's battery status, network status, and e-mail notifications. You can customize the Lock screen by adding other apps that show quick details and notifications, such as the weather or scheduled appointments.

Log On to Windows 8

1 Type your username.

2 Type your password.

3 Press **Enter**.

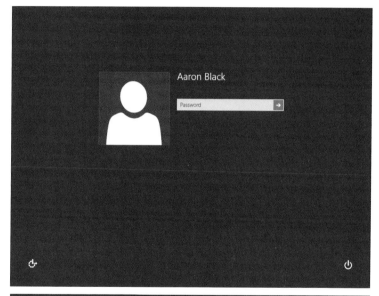

A Windows logs you on and displays the Windows 8 Start screen.

The Start screen is new to Windows 8. Borrowing similarities from the smartphone screen layout and design, the Windows 8 Start screen displays programs as *tiles* that can move around the scrollable screen, individually or in groups. You can pin items to the screen, hide tiles from view, move tiles, turn on live notifications within the tiles, and more. You can also use the edges of the screen to summon previously opened programs, computer settings, and an App bar, and you can zoom your view in and out to view groups of tiles.

A App Tiles

Programs are represented as app tiles on the Start screen. You can click a tile to launch the app. You can right-click a tile to display the App bar at the bottom of the screen with additional controls for the app.

B Account Picture and Controls

Your user name and account picture appear here. You can change user accounts or change your picture using this area.

C Scroll Bar

If you move your mouse to the bottom of the screen, you can scroll left and right using the scroll bar that appears. Touchscreen users can just swipe left and right to scroll.

D Zoom

Click the icon in the lower right corner to zoom your view of the Start screen in or out. Touchscreen users can pinch in or out to zoom.

Access the Windows 8 Start Screen

The Windows 8 Start screen is the jumping off point for all your computer activities. It offers much more than just tiles. The edges of the Start screen activate different functions. Swipe the left edge, or position your mouse pointer there, to display a thumbnail listing of recently used apps; just tap or click a thumbnail to reopen the program. If you swipe or pause the mouse over the right edge, the Charms bar appears. Swipe or pause over the bottom of the screen to display a scrollbar, or right-click this area to display an App bar of related commands.

Access the Windows 8 Start Screen

1 Tap the bottom left corner or hover the mouse over the corner.

Windows displays the Windows 8 Start screen thumbnail.

2 Click the thumbnail image.

Note: You can also press .

Windows switches you to the Windows 8 Start screen view.

Note: To learn more about personalizing the screen, see Chapter 6.

Launching a Windows 8 app is as simple as a click. In fact, that is all it takes — a single click of the mouse or tap of the screen, if your laptop uses touchscreen technology. The Windows 8 Start screen displays two groups of default apps and programs. Each square or rectangular tile represents a program or app — the term *app* refers to small programs. Windows 8 installs with several apps you may find useful, such as the Calendar app for keeping track of appointments, or the Messaging app for sending instant messages.

Launch Windows 8 Apps

1 Display the Windows 8 Start screen.

Note: You can press ⊞ to quickly switch to the Start screen.

2 Click the app tile you want to open.

Note: To learn more about customizing app tiles, see Chapter 6.

Windows opens the app in a full window.

If you open a program, Windows opens it on the desktop.

Find an App

Using new search technology, finding an app is as easy as typing its name. In fact, that is exactly how you find it. When you start typing while on the Start screen, Windows 8 immediately switches you to an Apps screen and attempts to guess at what you might be typing. Possible matches are listed in a pane on the left side of the screen, and a scrollable pane of apps and programs appears on the right. When you find the one you want, click it to open it.

Find an App

1 Display the Windows 8 Start screen.

Note: You can press ⊞ to quickly switch to the Start screen.

2 Start typing the name of the app.

The Apps window appears, listing search results.

3 You can continue typing to narrow down the selection.

4 Click the app you want to open.

Windows opens the app.

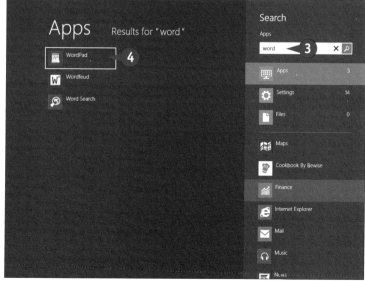

Shop for Apps

You can add all sorts of apps to Windows 8. You can use the Store app to shop online for more apps. The Microsoft Store features free, paid, and trial versions of apps. Apps at the Store are divided into categories and groups. You can view details about an app, and in some cases, try the app. You can also rate and review apps you have downloaded; adding your own input can help others learn more about an app. You can even search for specific apps.

Shop for Apps

1 Display the Windows 8 Start screen.

Note: You can press ⊞ to quickly switch to the Start screen.

2 Click the **Store** app tile.

The Store app window appears.

3 You can scroll through the store to peruse the featured apps and app groups.

4 Click an app to learn more about it or download it.

Note: You cannot purchase software programs, such as Microsoft Word or Adobe Photoshop, from the Store, only apps.

Work with the Charms Bar

You can use the new Charms bar, so named because of its charm-like icons, to find commonly used commands and features, such as sharing, search, and settings. The bar is hidden by default on the far right edge of the screen. You can use touchscreen technology to swipe to the right and view the bar, or you can move the mouse to the right edge and pause. When the Charms bar appears, it takes up the vertical edge of the screen, with each charm representing a category or feature. When you activate a charm, an additional pane or screen appears.

Work with the Charms Bar

1 Swipe the right side of the screen or move the mouse pointer to the far right or bottom right corner and pause.

Note: You can also press ⊞+C to display the Charms bar.

A Windows displays the Charms bar.

2 Click a charm.

Windows opens the associated panel with more options, settings, and links.

Work with the App Bar

lthough hidden most of the time, you can display an App bar to view additional controls pertaining to the app or task you are performing with Windows 8 apps or the Start screen. For example, if you are viewing contacts with the People app, the App bar displays a button for editing a contact. The App bar appears across the bottom of the screen, usually displaying buttons or commands you can click to activate more features or functions. You can toggle the App bar on or off.

Work with the App Bar

1 Swipe the bottom of the screen or press ⊞+Z.

Windows displays the App bar.

2 Click the button you want to activate.

A In this example, the Apps window opens.

B You can right-click an app from the Apps list to open the App bar with additional options, such as pinning or unpinning the app.

Note: If you display the App bar in another app, different options appear on the bar.

Access PC Settings

If you are looking for computer settings, such as where to change your password or how to check your network or battery status, look at the Start screen's PC Settings. The makers of Windows 8 have placed common settings and features on the PC Settings screen so you can easily access them when you need them. These commonly used settings include personalizing settings, a search tool, wireless settings, and more. Whenever you are looking for a particular feature, such as where to change a password, check the PC Settings window.

Access PC Settings

1 Swipe to the right side of the screen or move the mouse pointer to the far right or bottom right corner and pause to display the Charms bar.

2 Click **Settings** (⚙).

3 Click **Change PC settings**.

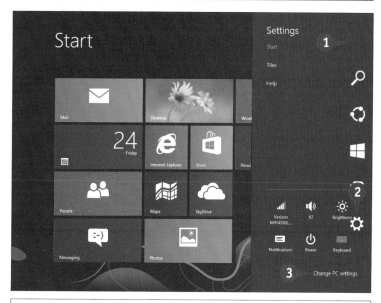

The PC Settings window appears.

Ⓐ Settings are grouped into categories listed here.

4 Click a category.

Ⓑ A list of corresponding settings, options, or features appears.

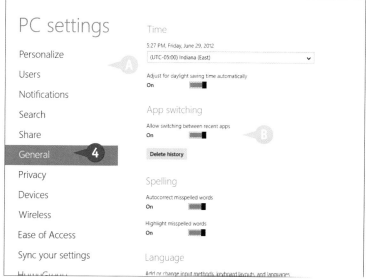

Y ou can pin items to the Start screen so that they are easy to find and use again later. You can pin folders, programs and games, contacts, and more. For example, if you use a certain Windows accessory all the time, like NotePad, you can pin it to the Start screen so you can always access it with a single click. Or if you constantly refer to a particular client, you can pin his or her contact info from the People app to the Start screen. Not all items can be pinned, but quite a few can.

Pin Items to the Start Screen

1 Locate the item you want to pin and right-click it.

Note: You may need to press ⊞+ℤ to display an App bar for the item you want to pin.

2 Click **Pin to Start** (📌).

Depending on the item, such as a contact, you may have to specify which name to pin.

Note: You can pin items from the Apps screen or from the desktop.

Note: To pin an item from the Desktop view, such as a program, right-click and click **Pin to Start**.

🅐 Windows pins the item to the Start screen. To access the item, click it.

Note: You can also pin some items to the desktop taskbar. When you right-click an item in File Explorer, for example, you can click the **Pin to Taskbar** command.

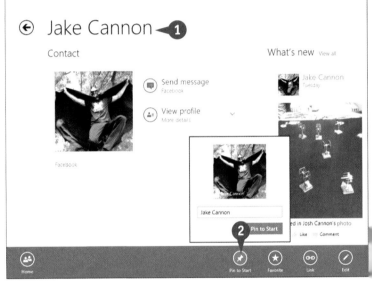

Shut Down Windows 8

You can shut down your laptop when you are no longer using it and conserve battery power. Windows 8 power controls are tucked away in the Settings category, which you can access through the Settings charm; navigate to the controls through the Charms bar located on the far right side of the Start screen. You can choose from three options. Sleep simply turns off most of the computer's power, but keeps some items running in the background. Restart turns your laptop off and on again, clearing out memory. Shut Down turns your laptop completely off and powers down.

Shut Down Windows 8

① Swipe to the right side of the screen or move the mouse pointer to the far right or bottom right corner to display the Charms bar.

② Click **Settings** (⚙).

The Settings pane appears.

③ Click **Power** (⏻).

④ Click a power option.

Windows 8 carries out your request.

A lthough much has changed in the new Windows 8 operating system, the desktop remains fairly the same as it has in previous versions. The desktop is hidden from view when you first start your laptop, and the Start screen is the default screen you see. To view the desktop, you can click the Desktop tile located among the app tiles, or press a keyboard shortcut key (⊞+D always summons the desktop into view). You can easily switch back and forth between the desktop and the Start screen as needed.

Access the Desktop

1 From the Windows 8 Start screen, click the **Desktop** tile.

Note: You can also press ⊞+D to switch to the desktop.

A Windows switches you to Desktop mode.

Note: See the next section to learn more about the Windows desktop elements.

Note: You can press ⊞ to return to the Windows 8 Start screen at any time.

Get to Know the Windows Desktop

You can use the desktop to launch programs, access files, and locate system tasks and settings for Windows 8. The desktop also enables you to keep track of what programs you have running, switch among those programs, and close them as needed. The taskbar at the bottom of the desktop screen displays important information about your computer's operation. Familiarizing yourself with the various components of the Windows 8 desktop can help you learn how to navigate your computer system.

A Desktop Shortcuts

Double-click a shortcut icon to a program or file to launch it. To create a shortcut, right-click the item in the Start menu or File Explorer, click **Send To**, and then click **Desktop (Create Shortcut)**.

B Taskbar

By default, the taskbar displays icons for all programs you have open. The taskbar features icons for launching Internet Explorer and File Explorer.

C Notification Area

This area displays information about your computer, such as whether it is connected to a wireless network. It also displays alert icons if your system is in need of attention.

D Internet Explorer

Click this icon to open the traditional Internet Explorer window for viewing web pages.

E File Explorer

Click this icon to open the Explorer window for viewing and working with computer drives, files, and folders.

F Work Area

Windows 8 displays any programs, folders, and files that you open in the large work area portion of the desktop.

You can use the File Explorer window, formerly called Windows Explorer, to view your computer's content, such as personal files, system files, programs, and more. Computer data, especially content created by users, is stored in files and folders. By default File Explorer offers four default folders you can use to add your own files, such as pictures, music, videos, and documents. You can also use File Explorer to view other storage media, such as external hard drives, USB flash drives, and so on. You can learn more about managing computer files and folders in Chapter 9.

View Your Computer's Contents

1 From the Windows 8 Start screen, click the **File Explorer** tile. If you are viewing the desktop, you can click the **File Explorer** icon (▨) on the taskbar.

Note: You can also press ▨+▣ to open the Explorer window.

The File Explorer window opens on the desktop.

Ⓐ View content by clicking the drive or folder name.

Ⓑ The File Explorer Ribbon groups tools and commands in tabs.

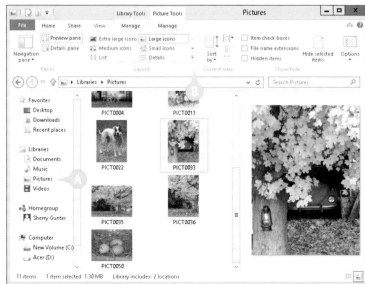

Empty the Recycle Bin

ou can use the Recycle Bin to delete files on your computer. Any time you select a file and press the Delete key, Windows moves the item into the trash bin. The Recycle Bin has been a part of the Windows operating system since its inception. You can drag files over to the Recycle Bin on the desktop and drop them, a process that offers a graphical representation of removing unwanted files; you can open the Bin later and complete the removal process. All deleted files remain in the Bin until you finally remove them permanently.

Empty the Recycle Bin

1 Double-click the Recycle Bin icon ( ) on the desktop.

Note: To switch to Desktop view, press + .

A A list of deleted files appears here.

B To restore a file to its original location, select it and click **Restore the selected items** ( ).

2 Click **Empty Recycle Bin** ( ).

The files are permanently removed.

Note: It is good practice to delete unwanted files on a regular basis to free up space on your computer.

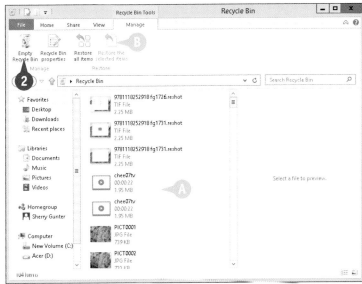

View Mobility Settings

Windows 8 includes many laptop-specific settings. As you might guess, many of these settings relate to conserving power — something especially critical when you must use a battery to power your PC. For example, you can reduce the brightness of the laptop display to minimize power usage. Other settings pertain to connecting to the Internet via wireless access points, synchronizing your laptop with another PC, and giving presentations. To make it easy to access all these laptop-specific settings, Windows has a special window called Windows Mobility Center. You access this window through the Windows 8 Control Panel.

View Mobility Settings

① Right-click the bottom left corner, or press **Ctrl**+**X**.

② Click **Control Panel**.

The Control Panel window appears.

③ Click here and change the view to **Small icons**.

④ Click **Windows Mobility Center**.

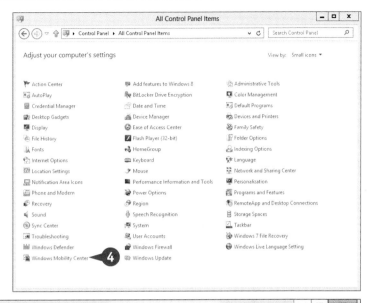

The Windows Mobility Center window appears.

Ⓐ You can make adjustments to the settings as needed.

⑤ Click the **Close** button () to close the center.

Note: An even faster way to open the Windows Mobility Center window is to right-click the power icon (🔋) in the taskbar's notification area and select **Windows Mobility Center** from the menu that appears.

TIP

What are the Ease of Access settings?
Located in the PC Settings window, the Ease of Access group of settings offers several tools you can apply to make your laptop easier to use. For example, you can make onscreen items bigger, adjust the screen contrast, change cursor thickness, and more. To display the Ease of Access settings, display the Charms bar (⊞+ C), press **Settings**, then **Change PC Settings**. Next, click the **Ease of Access** category.

Y ou can use the Windows 8 help files to learn more about features, settings, and controls. With an online connection, you can quickly view help pages from the Microsoft website within a navigable Help and Support window on the desktop. You can use the window to browse through a collection of help topics, view featured topics, or contact Microsoft support. The help pages often have links to other pages, tutorials, video clips, and step-by-step instructions among the various topics. If you do not find the topic you need, you can use the Search box to conduct a search.

Find Help

1 From the Windows 8 Start screen, type **help**.

Windows opens the Apps screen.

2 Click **Help and Support**.

Note: You can also click a Help icon (⊘) to learn more about the option or feature.

The Windows Help and Support window opens on the desktop.

Ⓐ To search for a specific keyword or words, type them in here and press Enter .

3 Click **Browse help**.

Ⓑ A list of Help topic categories appears.

4 Click a category.

5 Click a subcategory.

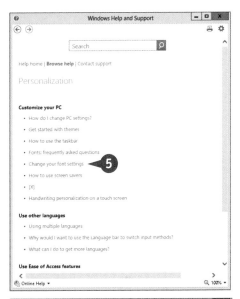

The Help and Support window displays your selected topic.

You can click a link to learn more about a topic.

You can use the navigation buttons (⊖ and ⊕) to move back and forth between topics.

6 When finished using Help, click **Close** (x).

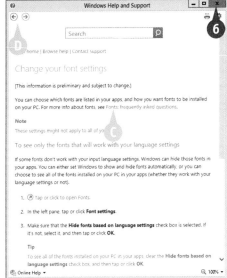

TIP

How do I find more support?
If you click the **Contact support** link at the top of the help pages, you can view a list of additional links you can explore online for more assistance. You can use these links to access Microsoft forums, find online videos and articles, or give your own feedback about a topic.

CHAPTER 6

Personalizing Your Laptop

Windows 8 offers a variety of customization options you can use to change how the operating system looks and works for you. You can customize the Start screen, the desktop background, add an account picture, edit the live tiles, and more. This chapter shows you how to utilize a few personalizing techniques to help you tailor your laptop to the way you work.

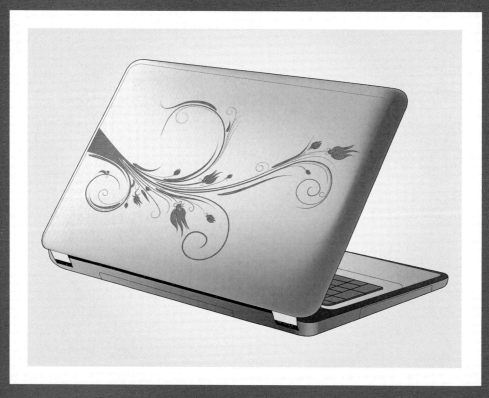

Change the Screen Resolution

You can change your laptop's screen resolution to adjust sharpness, text and image size. With a higher screen resolution, onscreen elements appear sharper. In addition, they are smaller, meaning that more items fit on the screen. With a lower resolution, items on your screen may appear less crisp, but larger and easier to see. Items on a screen with a resolution of 1024 × 768 appear much larger than in a screen with a resolution of 1600 × 900. The screen resolution setting is largely a matter of personal taste, but larger monitors often require a higher screen resolution.

Change the Screen Resolution

1 Display the Windows 8 desktop (click the **Desktop** app on the Start screen or press 🪟+🄳).

2 Right-click on the desktop.

3 Click **Screen resolution**.

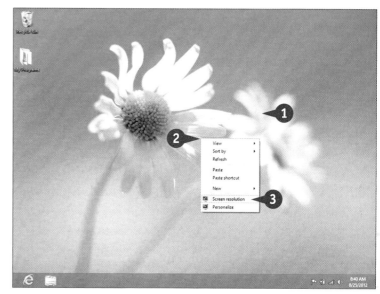

The Screen Resolution window appears.

4 Click the **Resolution** ▾.

5 Drag the **Resolution** slider (▭) to the desired resolution.

6 Click **OK**.

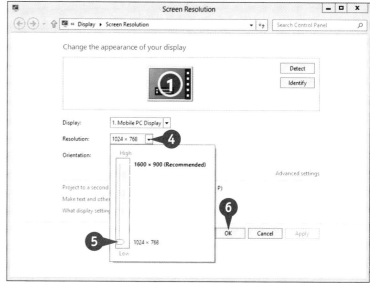

Windows prompts you to confirm the change.

7 Click **Keep changes**.

Windows changes the screen resolution.

TIP

Can I add a second monitor to my laptop?

If your laptop features a monitor port, it should support the addition of an external monitor. If so, you add an external monitor by following these steps:

1 Power down your laptop.

2 Connect the monitor to your laptop using a standard monitor cable.

3 Plug the monitor into an electrical power source.

4 Turn on the monitor.

5 Restart your laptop.

Windows should detect the monitor and install any necessary drivers.

Change Your Account Picture

The Windows 8 Start screen includes an account picture. The first time you use your laptop, the picture may be a generic placeholder image, but you can change it at any time. You can insert an image from your computer or take a new one with your laptop's webcam. You can also create a new picture using any of the picture-taking apps you have installed. To learn more about adding pictures to your laptop, see Chapter 13.

Change Your Account Picture

1 From the Start screen, click your account name in the upper right corner.

2 Click **Change account picture**.

The PC Settings screen appears.

3 To use an existing picture on your laptop, click **Browse**.

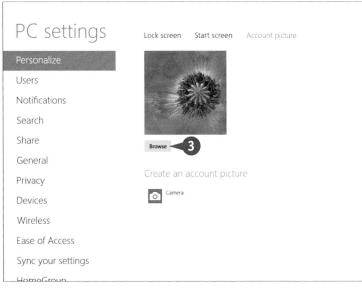

The Files screen appears.

④ Click **Files**.

⑤ Click the folder containing the picture file you want to use.

Windows displays the folder contents.

⑥ Click the image.

⑦ Click **Choose image**.

Windows assigns the new image as your account picture.

TIP

How do I use the webcam to take a picture?
If your laptop has a built-in webcam, or you have one attached to your laptop, you can easily use the device to take an account picture. To take a picture with the webcam, click the **Webcam** button in the PC Settings window and click the screen to take a picture. You can then crop it as you want; drag a crop corner (☐) or edge. Click **OK** (◉) to finish, or click **Retake** (◉) to try again. To cancel, click the navigation arrow (◉) to return to the PC Settings window.

Customize the Start Screen

You can customize the Windows 8 Start screen by changing the background design or color. By default, Windows 8 uses a preassigned design and color scheme. One way to customize the screen is to select another color scheme for the Start screen background. The background design choices are subtle variations of bubbles and swirls, or you can opt for a plain background without a design pattern. You can also choose another color scheme to apply, which changes command text colors and background color. Personalizing the Start screen colors does not affect the desktop screen.

Customize the Start Screen

1 From the Start screen, swipe the right edge of the screen or move the mouse pointer to the lower right corner.

Windows displays the Charms bar.

Note: You can also press ⊞+**C** to display the Charms bar.

2 Click **Settings** (⚙).

3 Click **Change PC settings**.

The PC Settings window opens.

4 Click **Personalize**.

5 Click **Start screen**.

The Start Screen options appear.

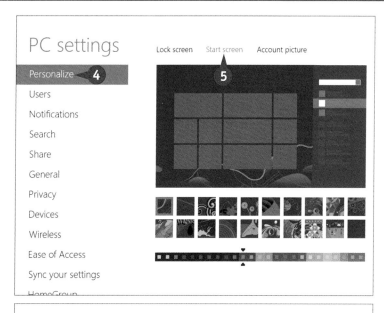

6 Click a background.

7 Click a background color.

Windows changes the Start screen design and colors.

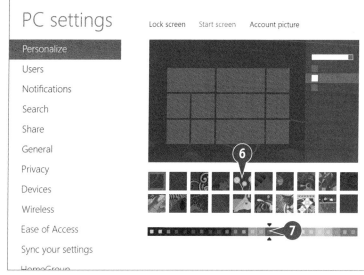

 TIP

How do I remove an app from the Start screen?
To remove an app, right-click the app. This places a check mark in the corner of the app tile and opens the Apps bar at the bottom of the screen. Next, click the **Unpin from Start** button (). Windows 8 removes the app from the Start screen, but the app is still available for use at any time. To find it, just start typing in the app name from the Start screen. Windows opens the Apps screen and lists any matches. To repin it, right-click the app name and choose **Pin to Start** ().

Personalize the Lock Screen

The Lock screen appears when you log onto your laptop, or when your laptop is idle and your screen times out — that is, the laptop turns off automatically to conserve power. Much like the lock screen that appears on a smartphone or media tablet, the Windows 8 Lock screen also displays app notifications, such as unread e-mail notices, the current date and time, Wi-Fi signal strength, calendar appointments, and laptop battery life. You can customize the Lock screen to show certain apps, choose a new Windows-provided background picture, or assign an image of your own.

Personalize the Lock Screen

1 From the Start screen, swipe from the right edge of the screen to view the Charms bar or move the mouse pointer to the lower right corner.

Note: You can also press ⊞+C to display the Charms bar.

2 Click **Settings** (⚙).

3 Click **Change PC settings**.

The PC Settings window opens.

4 Click **Personalize**.

5 Click **Lock screen**.

6 Click a new picture to assign, or click the **Browse** button to navigate to a picture file of your choosing.

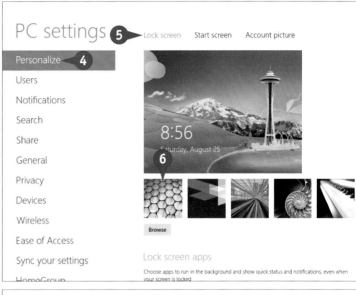

7 Click which apps you want to display on the Lock screen.

The next time the Lock screen appears, the new settings are applied.

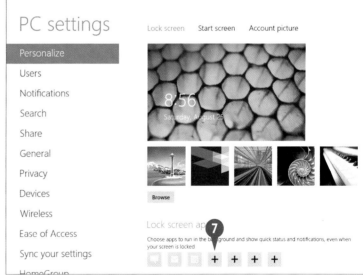

TIPS

How many app notifications can I display on my Lock screen?

Windows 8 lets you add up to six apps to your Lock screen. Each app you add places an icon, also called a *notification* or *status badge*, on the Lock screen. You can also turn off badges you no longer want to appear.

How do I change my password?

You can change your password by first swiping in from the right edge of the screen or clicking the lower right corner and clicking **Settings** (⚙). Click **Change PC settings** to open the PC Settings window. Click **Users** and click **Change your password**. The Change Your Password window opens and you can create a new password.

Customize Start Screen Tiles

Apps are represented as tiles on the Windows 8 Start screen, and you can customize the tiles to suit your personal taste. There are two types of tiles: Windows 8 app tiles, which you can download from the Windows Store, or non-Windows 8 tiles representing programs you install from other sources. You can move tiles around just by dragging and dropping them, or you can drag them over to other groups. You can also name groups, pin or unpin tiles, change their size, or access other options.

Customize Start Screen Tiles

Name a Group

1 To name a group, first click the **Zoom** button (⊞).

Note: To create a new group, move the tile outside of the current group and drop it in a new area on the Start screen.

2 Right-click the group you want to name.

A check mark appears in the upper right corner of the selected group.

3 Click the **Name group** button (⊘).

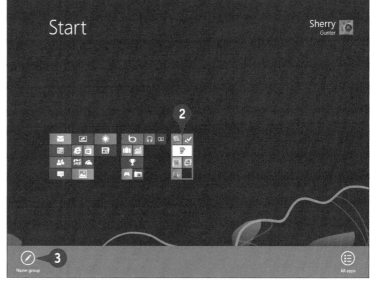

A box for naming the group appears.

4 Type a name for the group.

5 Click **Name**.

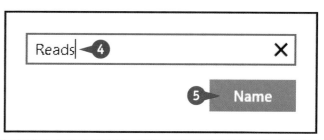

A The new group name appears above the group of tiles.

Note: To zoom back again to normal tile size, just click or tap the screen.

TIPS

Why are my app tiles different?
Several default Windows 8 tiles appear on the Start screen when you first start using your laptop. As you work with your laptop, apps may be added or removed. The tiles for Windows 8 apps, including ones you download from the Windows Store, are rectangular in shape and very colorful in design. Non-Windows 8 app tiles appear as simple squares with the name of the app and a small icon.

How do I un-name a group of tiles?
To remove a group name, follow the same steps listed in this section and click the clear button (✕) in the naming box. This clears the existing entry. Click the **Name** button to save the changes.

continued ▶

Customize Start Screen Tiles (continued)

Many of the Windows 8 tiles you add are live, which means they display current information. For example, the Weather app displays the current temperature for your location. You can turn the live tile feature on or off to customize your Start screen. You can also turn a live tile off again and revert to its original design or icon.

You can resize some of the Windows 8 tiles, when applicable. To find out if a tile is resizable, display the tile's options in the Apps bar. If it is, the Smaller or Larger options appear and you can resize the tile.

Customize Start Screen Tiles (continued)

Turn Live Tiles On

1 Right-click the tile.

A A check mark appears in the corner of the tile.

Windows opens the Apps bar.

2 Click the **Turn live tile on** (⊙) button.

B The tile is now live and current; in this example, a new photo appears in the Photo app's tile.

Note: To turn the live tile off again, repeat these steps, this time deselecting the live tile option.

Resize a Tile

1 Right-click the tile you want to resize.

C A check mark appears in the corner of the tile.

Windows opens the Apps bar.

2 Click the **Smaller** (⊡) or **Larger** (⊡) button.

D Windows resizes the tile.

<hr>

TIPS

How do I add an app to the Start screen?

To add an app, you first have to find it. You can start typing the app name while viewing the Start screen to open the Apps search screen. When the correct app appears, right-click the app name and then click the **Pin to Start** button (⊡). Windows immediately adds a tile for the app to the Start screen.

How do I change the arrangement of groups on the Windows 8 Start screen?

You can click the Zoom button (⊞) to zoom your view, then position the mouse pointer over the group to select it. Next, drag it to a new location and drop it where you want it to go.

Add a New User Account

If you share your laptop with one or more people, such as family members, you can create different accounts for each user. With different accounts, each user can customize his or her own settings and preferences, add apps, and control files. Windows 8 offers two different types of user account: Microsoft account or local account. A local account works only on that particular computer, whereas a Microsoft account works through the Cloud to sync your settings with other computers you log into.

Add a New User Account

1 Swipe in from the right edge of the screen or click the bottom right corner.

2 Click **Settings** (⚙).

3 Click **Change PC settings**.

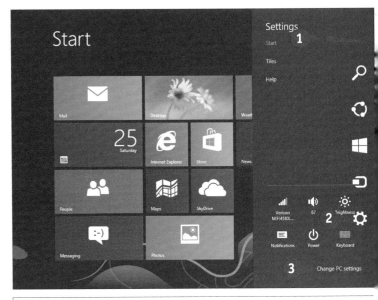

The PC settings window appears.

4 Click **Users**.

5 Click **Add a user**.

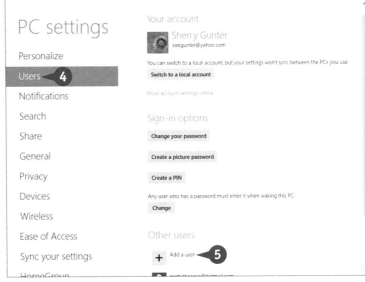

The Add a User window opens.

6 Type the e-mail address to associate with the account.

7 Click **Next**.

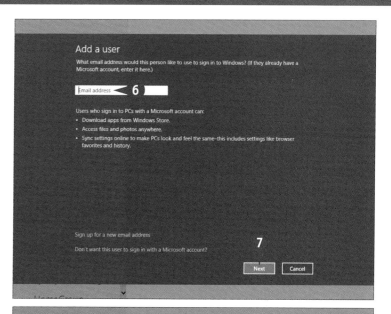

8 Click **Finish**.

The new user must log onto the Internet to finish creating the new account.

TIP

Can I edit a user account?
You can use the Control Panel to edit an account, add more user accounts, or remove accounts you no longer need. To access the Control Panel, right-click the lower left corner of the screen and choose **Control Panel** from the pop-up menu that appears. In the Control Panel window, click the **Add or remove user accounts** link under the **User Accounts and Family Safety** heading. Within the Control Panel, you can find additional settings for administering accounts, credentials, and parental controls.

Change the Desktop Background

In addition to the Windows 8 Start screen, you can also customize the classic Windows desktop background. Your laptop features a default background, but you can choose a different image or set of images. One option is to select from the Windows 8 predesigned backgrounds; alternatively, you can choose from your own photos. A third option is to obtain images online to use for your desktop background.

Change the Desktop Background

1 Right-click an empty area of the desktop.

2 Click **Personalize**.

Note: To display the desktop at any time, press ⊞+D or click the Desktop app on the Start screen.

The Personalization window appears.

3 Click **Desktop Background**.

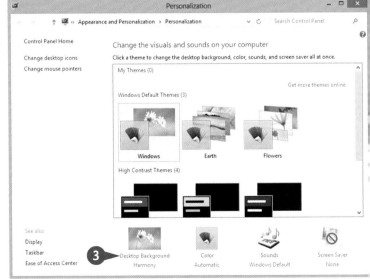

The Desktop Background window opens.

4 Click the **Picture location** ⊡ and select **Windows Desktop Backgrounds.**

Ⓐ To choose from your own images, click **Browse,** locate your photo folder, and then click **OK.**

5 Click the image you want to use as the desktop background.

6 Click the **Picture position** ⊡ and select how the image(s) should appear on-screen.

Ⓑ If you have selected multiple images, click the **Change picture every** ⊡ and select how often the pictures should change.

Ⓒ To display multiple images in random order, select the **Shuffle** option.

7 Click **Save changes.**

Ⓓ Windows changes the desktop background.

8 Click the **Close** button (✕) to close the Personalization window.

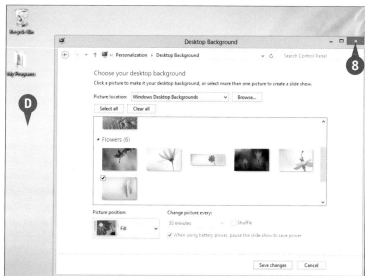

TIP

How to I turn on a screen saver?

Setting a screen saver — that is, a still or animated picture that appears on your laptop's screen when the pointing device and keyboard have been inactive for a prescribed period of time — prevents others from viewing your desktop when you are away from your laptop. To turn off the screen saver and again view the Windows desktop, simply use your pointing device or press a key on your keyboard. You choose a screen saver from the Screen Saver Settings dialog box; to open it, right-click a blank area of the desktop, click **Personalize**, and click **Screen Saver** in the Personalization window.

Set the Date and Time

You can use the Control Panel to set the correct date and time. For example, you may need to adjust the time if you change time zones while on the road. The desktop screen shows the current time in the taskbar, whereas the Start screen displays the time when you display the Charms bar or the Lock screen. You can use the Control Panel to adjust the date and time, as needed. The Control Panel is your central dashboard for setting laptop and operating system controls.

Set the Date and Time

1 Right-click the bottom left corner of the screen.

2 Click **Control Panel**.

The Control Panel window appears.

3 Click **Clock, Language, and Region**.

The Clock, Language, and Region window opens.

4 Click **Set the time and date**.

The Date and Time dialog box opens.

5 Click **Change date and time**.

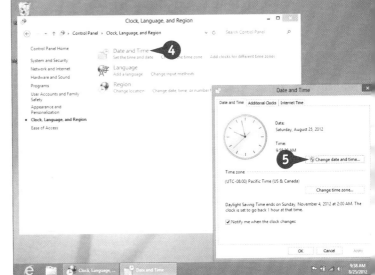

The Date and Time Settings box appears.

⑥ To change the date, click a new date on the calendar.

⑦ To change the time, click the hands or type a time.

⑧ Click **OK**.

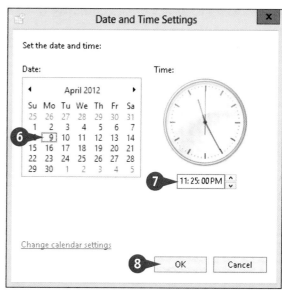

Windows applies the new settings.

⑨ Click the **Close** button (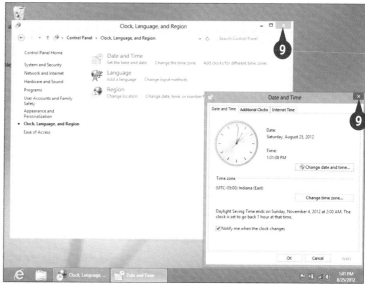) for each remaining open window to exit.

TIPS

How can I change the time zone?
The Date and Time dialog box shown in the section above also features a **Change time zone option**. Click this button to display a Time Zone Settings dialog box where you can specify a time zone and apply Daylight Saving Time, if applicable.

Can I add a larger clock to my desktop?
The Windows operating system comes with several useful gadgets you can add to the desktop, one of which is a clock. To access the clock gadget, open the Control Panel as described in this section's steps, but instead of clicking the **Set the time and date** link, click the **Add the Clock gadget to the desktop** option. This opens the Gadget window, and you can drag the Clock gadget onto the desktop.

Adjust Laptop Volume

You can adjust your laptop volume using several different methods. Some laptops include a volume control located directly on the laptop chassis, typically along the side or front, which allows you to adjust the volume manually. You can also use the Windows operating system to turn your laptop's speaker volume up or down. You can adjust volume from the Start screen or from the desktop screen.

Adjust Laptop Volume

Adjust Volume from the Start Screen

① From the Start screen, swipe from the right edge of the screen or move the mouse pointer to the lower right corner.

Windows displays the Charms bar.

Note: You can also press ⊞+C to display the Charms bar.

② Click **Settings** (⚙).

③ Click **Volume** (🔊).

Note: You can also use the keyboard (Fn) key along with the designated volume keys (↑ and ↓) to adjust speaker volume.

④ Drag the slider up or down to adjust the volume level.

You can press Esc or click anywhere to deselect the option.

Note: You can also adjust volume from the Windows Mobility Center. From the desktop taskbar, right-click the battery meter icon (🔋) and choose **Windows Mobility Setting**.

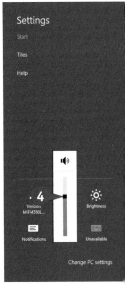

Adjust Volume from the Desktop

1 From the Desktop screen, click the **Speakers** icon ( ) on the taskbar.

2 Drag the slider ( ) up or down to adjust the volume level.

Windows adjusts the volume.

Mixer

TIPS

How do I mute the laptop speakers?
You can click the **Mute** button ( ) in the Speaker volume control on the Desktop taskbar to mute your laptop speakers. The button toggles on and off. The Start screen has no Mute button.

How do I use headphones with my laptop?
You can plug headphones into your laptop's headphone jack located along the side or front of your laptop. When headphones are plugged in, your computer's audio is audible only through the headphone jack; others cannot hear what you are listening to.

Working with Software

Computers are not much use without software — the programs that tell a computer what to do, such as create documents, organize images, or play games. Although not all programs operate in exactly the same way, many do share common tools and features, as outlined in this chapter. Learning the basics of working with programs is an essential part of mastering your laptop.

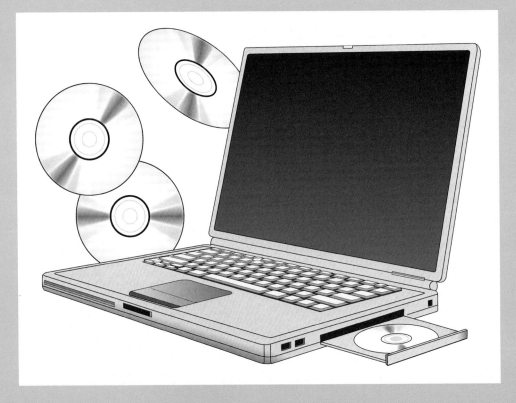

Understanding Software

Software programs provide the instructions for telling a computer what to do and how to do it. Unlike hardware, which encompasses all the physical items associated with a computer (hence the description "hard" in its name), software works behind the scenes as coding, procedures, and functions (it cannot be touched, therefore "soft" is more appropriate to the name). Software is commonly referred to as *programs* or *applications*. Software designed for a specific task, such as checking the weather or adding numbers, is called an *app*. Windows 8 comes with programs and apps you can use to enhance your computing experience.

Types of Software

The software installed with Windows 8 comes in two types: system apps and application software. System apps are tools for managing computer resources, such as utilities for defragmenting a hard drive or backing up data. Application software, also called *end-user programs*, help you create data files and perform special tasks and functions, like building text documents or playing games. Windows 8 also features smaller applications, or *apps*, with more singular focus, such as checking the weather or sending an e-mail.

System Apps

System apps refer to operating system and utility programs. These programs often work behind the scenes to help you to configure, maintain, or optimize your laptop. For example, Windows 8 includes several utilities for helping you maintain laptop performance and tackle important management tasks, such as freeing up disk space, backing up data, or updating your operating system. Even the Windows Control Panel is a system app. You can learn more about using Windows 8 system apps in Chapter 16.

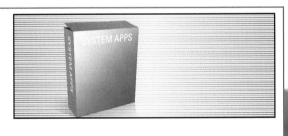

Application Software

End-user programs, or application software, help you to perform tasks. Most applications revolve around a particular function, such as creating documents or managing a database. You can find programs for just about everything you want to do on a computer, such as creating slide shows, editing digital photographs, or crunching numbers in a spreadsheet. Popular categories of apps include word processing, accounting, graphics and illustration, video editing, desktop publishing, content access, and entertainment, just to name a few.

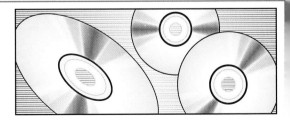

Windows 8 Apps

Windows 8 offers a variety of built-in apps ready to go on the Start screen. For example, you can use the Mail app to send and receive e-mail messages or the Calendar app to keep track of appointments. You can use the Photo app to view images on your laptop or through online services. The Music and Video apps are powered by Zune, part of Microsoft's digital media market.

Windows 8 Accessories

Windows 8 also includes a variety of accessory apps, many carried over from previous versions of the operating system. You can use the WordPad app, for example, to accomplish simple word processing tasks, such as writing and formatting a letter. For even simpler note taking, you can use Notepad. You can use Sticky Notes to place yellow note squares directly on your desktop. Other accessories include Calculator, Paint, Snipping Tool, and Windows Media Player.

Popular Software

Thousands of programs are available on the market today; different ones target different operating systems and different tasks. You may recognize many of the major players, including the Microsoft Office suite that features Word, Excel, PowerPoint, and Access. Word, for example, is one of the most popular word processing programs on the market. Other types of popular software include antivirus tools, tax software, media players, personal finance software, and photo and video editing tools.

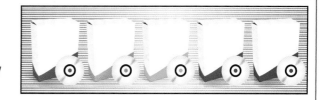

Shopping for Software

You can find software for your laptop in stores and online. Windows 8 makes it easy to shop for apps from its online marketplace using the Store app. Or you can also shop for software elsewhere on the web and download it directly onto your laptop. Software prices range from high-end to freeware — software offered free of charge. When shopping for software, make sure it suits your operating system. Check the system and compatibility requirements before purchasing.

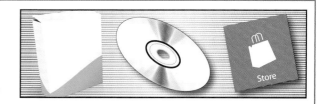

Install a Program

Few people limit themselves to using only the programs that came installed on their laptop. Odds are, over time you will want to install additional programs. Windows 8 is designed to make this as easy as possible. The ins and outs of installing a program differ by program. Some programs are downloaded from the Internet, others from a CD or DVD. And the precise steps required are as different as the programs themselves. Do not let this deter you from installing programs on your laptop. Windows 8 is designed to guide you step by step through the installation process.

Install a Program

1 From the product's website, click the link for the program that you want to download.

Internet Explorer displays a prompt bar.

2 Click **Run** when prompted.

Windows downloads the file. Depending on the file size and connection speed, it may take a few minutes or longer.

Note: If you are installing from a CD or DVD, Windows will likely recognize the software for installation and display the appropriate prompts to begin. If it does not, try double-clicking the setup file to begin installing.

A An installation or setup wizard appears, a tool for installing programs, and depending on your program, the steps may differ from what you see here.

3 Click **Install** or **Next**.

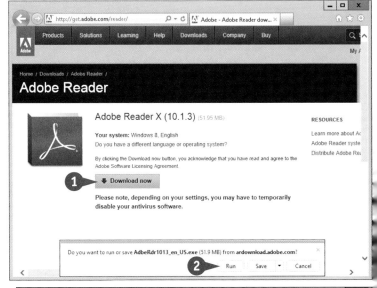

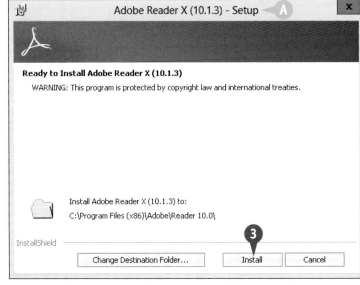

B The setup or installation wizard begins installing the files.

Some programs may require additional input from you before completing the installation. You may need to click **Next** to continue.

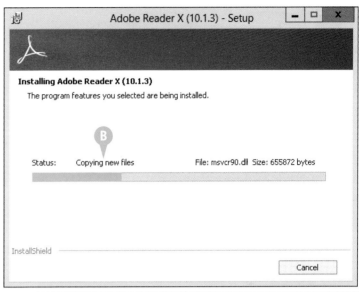

C The installation or setup wizard informs you when setup is complete.

4 Click **Finish**.

D Depending on the program, Windows may add a shortcut icon on the desktop or on the Windows 8 Start screen, or both.

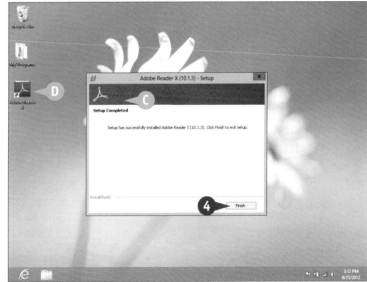

TIPS

How do I uninstall a program I no longer want?
To uninstall a program, right-click the lower left corner of the screen and click **Control Panel**. In the Control Panel window, click **Uninstall a Program** under Programs. The Programs and Features window opens. Click the program you want to remove. Click **Uninstall**. Windows prompts you to confirm the removal of the program. Click **Yes**. The program is removed.

How do I download an app from the Store?
You can use the Store app on the Windows 8 Start screen to look for more apps to download. From the Start screen, click the **Store** tile. When you browse through the offerings and find something you want, click it and click **Install**. Windows downloads and installs the app for you, then prompts you when the process is complete.

Open and Close a Program

Before you can begin working with a program, you must instruct Windows to launch it. When you do, Windows starts the program and opens its program window. You can launch an application in a few ways. Some programs launch from the Start screen, whereas others launch from the desktop. Some programs — namely File Explorer and Internet Explorer — can be launched from the Windows 8 desktop taskbar. Alternatively, you can open a file associated with that program in File Explorer. You can close a program when you finish working with it; you do not have to close Windows 8 apps.

Open and Close a Program

Launch a Program

1 From the desktop, double-click the shortcut icon for the program you want to open.

Ⓐ To launch a program from the Start screen, scroll to the program tile and click it.

B From File Explorer, navigate to and click the program you want to start.

The program you selected opens in a window on the desktop, and a button for the program appears in the taskbar.

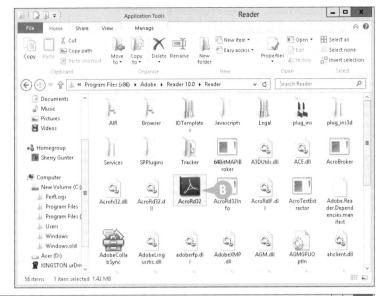

Close a Program

1 Click the program's **File** menu.

2 Click **Exit**.

Windows closes the program window.

Note: You do not have to close Windows 8 apps. Rather, Windows 8 suspends the app while you are not using it, and if the app remains unused, Windows eventually shuts it down.

TIPS

Can I pin a program to my Start screen?
In some cases, you can pin a program to the Start screen. Open File Explorer in the desktop to the folder containing the program file. Right-click the program filename and click **Pin to Start**, if available. If you do not see the command, you cannot pin the program to the Start screen.

Can I close a file without closing a program?
With some programs, like Microsoft Word or Excel, you can close the file you are working on and leave the program window open. Doing so closes only the file; if no other files are open in the same program, and empty work area appears on-screen. To close a file, click the **File** menu and click **Close**.

Explore a Program Window

Although not all program windows are the same, many share certain navigation elements in common. Taking time to familiarize yourself with these elements makes navigating program windows much easier. These elements include the Window Menu button, the Quick Access toolbar, the title bar, various buttons for resizing and closing the program window, scroll bars, a work area, and more. In addition, many programs now feature what Microsoft calls the *Ribbon*, which offers an intuitive way to locate and execute commands; other programs have retained traditional pull-down menus and toolbars.

A Title Bar

The program window's title bar displays the name of the program as well as the name of the file open in the program window.

B Window Menu Button

Clicking the Window Menu button reveals commands for restoring, moving, sizing, minimizing, maximizing, and closing the program window. (Note that the appearance of this button differs by program.)

C Program Window Controls

Use these buttons to minimize the program window, resize the window, or close the window.

D Work Area

The work area is where files you have opened in the program appear, and where you add and work with data in a program.

E Scroll Bars

If your file cannot be viewed in its entirety in the work area, drag the vertical and horizontal scroll bars to scroll through the data in the file.

F Status Bar

The status bar displays information about the file currently open in the program window.

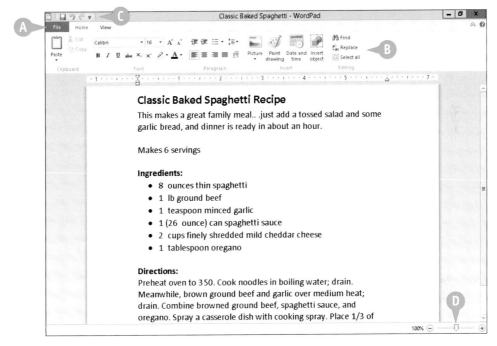

Ⓐ File Tab

Click the File tab to access options for creating a new file, opening an existing file, saving a file, printing a file, and more.

Ⓑ Ribbon

Some programs feature a Ribbon instead of traditional pull-down menus and toolbars. The Ribbon displays groups of related commands in tabs.

Ⓒ Quick Access Toolbar

You can use the buttons on this toolbar to launch the Save, Undo, or Redo command. Note that you can change which buttons appear here.

Ⓓ Zoom Controls

Use the Zoom In and Zoom Out buttons or the Zoom slider to zoom your view of the file open in the program window.

Resize and Move Program Windows

Often, you may need to move or resize a program window you have open on your Windows desktop. For example, you might need to make a program window smaller, move a program window in order to view other programs you have running on your laptop, or access an item on your desktop such as a shortcut icon. In addition to resizing and moving a program window, you can minimize it. When you minimize a program window, you remove it from the desktop; when you are ready to view it again, simply click its button on the taskbar.

Resize and Move Program Windows

Resize a Program Window

1 To reduce the size of a window that covers the entire screen, click **Restore Down** (🗗).

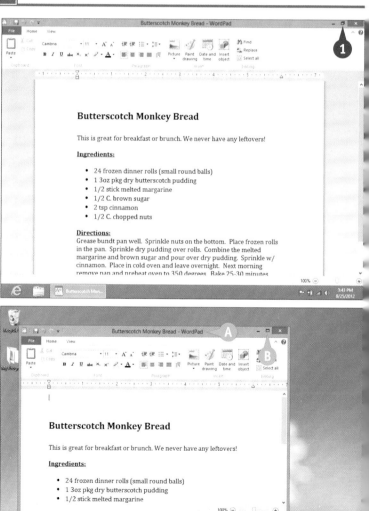

A The program window shrinks to a predefined size.

B The Restore Down button (🗗) changes to a Maximize button (🗖).

Note: To maximize the program window so it again covers the entire screen, click the **Maximize** button (🗖).

Move a Program Window

1 Click an empty section of the program window's title bar.

2 Drag the window in the direction you want it to move.

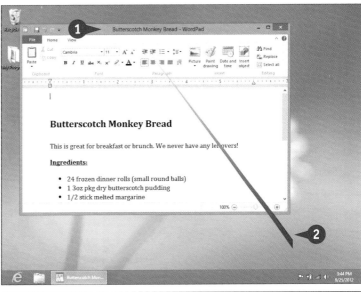

3 When the window is in the desired location, release the mouse button.

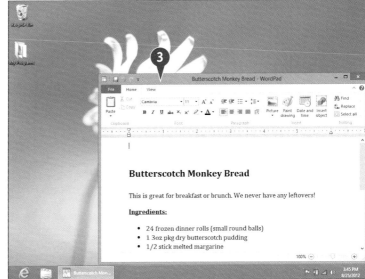

TIPS

Can you resize a window manually?

Yes. Resizing a window manually enables you to fine-tune its dimensions. Position your mouse pointer over the edge of the window border you want to move. When the pointer changes to a two-headed arrow, click and drag it inward or outward to resize the window, and then release the mouse button.

How do you minimize a window?

To minimize a window, click the **Minimize** button ([–]). The program window disappears, but its taskbar button remains in place. To restore the window to its original size and location, simply click its taskbar button. Alternatively, close a window by clicking its **Close** button ([x]). The program window and its taskbar button disappear.

Work with Multiple Program Windows

Many laptop users multitask, running more than one program at a time or launching multiple files in a single program. Multitasking, though certainly an efficient way to work, can make navigating your Windows desktop difficult. Fortunately, Windows includes several tools for switching among multiple open program windows, including taskbar buttons and keyboard commands. Also, using its Shake feature, Windows makes it easy to focus your attention on whatever program window is most important. And regardless of how many program windows you have open, you can access the desktop with a single click of a button.

Work with Multiple Program Windows

Switch Program Windows

1 Click the taskbar button for the program window to which you want to switch.

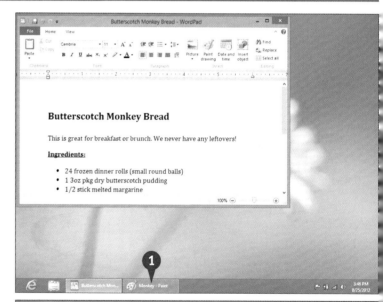

A Windows displays in the work area the program window whose button you clicked.

Note: Another way to switch program windows is to press Alt + Tab. Windows displays thumbnail images of each window currently open on your laptop; continue pressing Alt + Tab until the thumbnail for the window to which you want to switch is highlighted. Alternatively, press Alt + Esc to simply switch to the next window in the cycle.

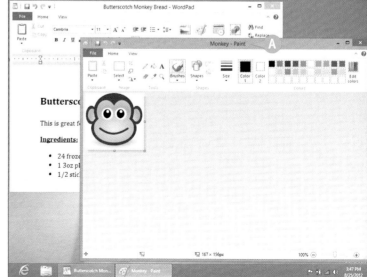

Shake to Minimize Extra Windows

1 Click the title bar of the window you want to remain visible and, holding down the mouse button, move the mouse pointer back and forth to shake it.

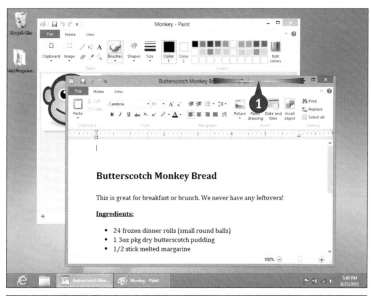

B Windows minimizes all the open windows except the one you shook.

Note: You can redisplay the minimized windows by shaking the visible window a second time.

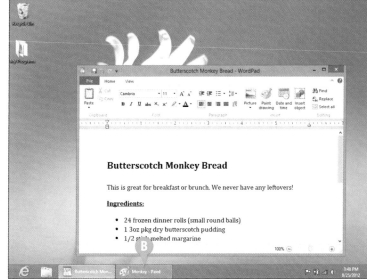

TIPS

How do you switch among multiple windows running the same program?

To switch to a different window running the same program, position your mouse pointer over the program's taskbar button and, in the list of open windows that appears, click the window to which you want to switch. Alternatively, press and hold **Ctrl** and click the program's taskbar button to cycle through the open windows.

Can you display two windows side by side?

Yes. Click the title bar of either window, drag it to the left edge of the screen, and release the mouse button. The window snaps into place, filling the left half of the work area. Repeat for the remaining window, dragging it to the right.

Using a Ribbon

Instead of the menus and toolbars found in many older programs, applications began featuring a Ribbon with the release of Windows 7. The Ribbon is commonly used in many programs today. It offers an intuitive way to locate and execute commands by grouping them into tabs, each containing sections of related commands. For example, WordPad's Home tab contains commands for changing the font, text alignment, and indents. Some tabs appear only when needed, such as when you are working with a table or picture. The Ribbon is maximized by default; you can minimize it to view more of your program window.

Explore the Ribbon

Use the Ribbon

1 Click a tab.

The tab organizes related tasks and commands into logical groups.

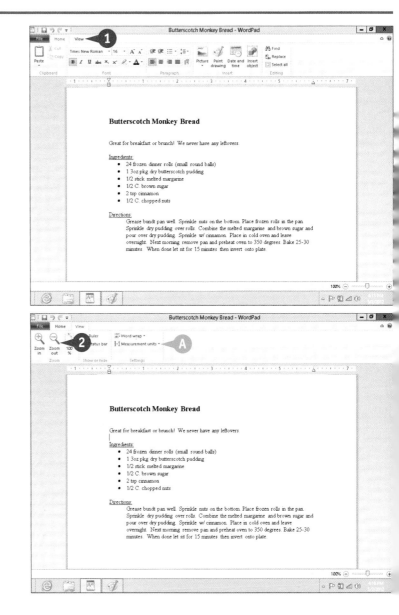

2 Click a button to activate a command or feature.

Ⓐ Buttons with arrows display additional commands.

Minimize the Ribbon

1 Double-click a tab name.

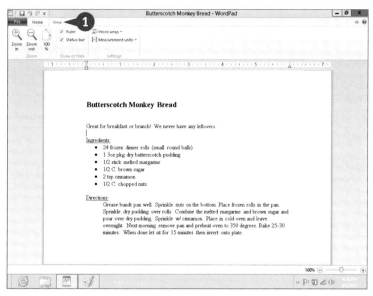

B The Ribbon is minimized.

2 Double-click the tab name again to maximize the Ribbon.

Note: To use a Ribbon while it is minimized, simply click the tab containing the tools that you want to access to reveal the Ribbon.

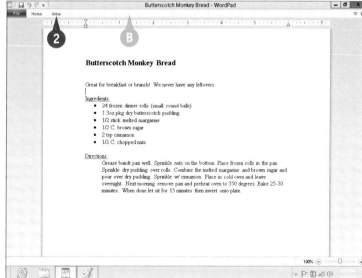

TIP

How do you use menu bars and toolbars?

Traditional pull-down menus and toolbars do still exist in certain programs. To use a pull-down menu, click the name of the menu you want to display, then click the command you want to run or the feature you want to enable or disable. You may need to click a submenu to access the desired command or feature. To use a toolbar, click the button that represents the command you want to run or the feature you want to enable or disable. (In some cases, clicking an item in a toolbar reveals a drop-down list with additional options; simply click the desired option in the list.)

Using Menus, Buttons, and Lists

Y ou can use menus, buttons, and lists to activate commands in your programs. Although most programs today utilize the new Ribbon style for presenting commands in organized tab groups, you can still encounter some programs that employ menu bars and toolbars across the top of the window to present commands. Regardless of the presentation, Ribbons, menus, and toolbars display the familiar drop-down menus, list boxes, and buttons for interacting with the software. Drop-down menus are easy to spot with their downward pointing arrow buttons; when clicked, a list of commands drops down. Buttons activate commands with a single click.

Using Menus, Buttons, and Lists

Use a Menu

1 To display a menu, click its drop-down arrow (▾).

2 Click a command.

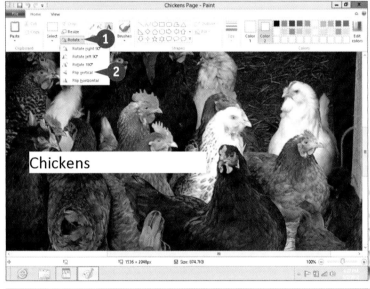

Use a Button

1 To activate a button, click the button.

The button appears highlighted when active.

Use a List Box

1 To select from a list of options, simply click an item in the list.

The item appears highlighted when it is active.

Use a Combo Button/Menu

1 To use a combo button/ menu, you can click the larger button to activate the default setting.

2 You can click the drop-down arrow connected to the button to activate more choices.

TIPS

How do I add buttons to the Quick Access Toolbar?

At the very top left corner of some programs sits a Quick Access Toolbar displaying common commands, such as Save and Undo. You can add or subtract buttons on this toolbar to customize it to the way you work. Click the drop-down arrow (⏷) at the end of the toolbar to display a menu of other shortcut buttons. You can toggle these on or off, as needed.

Can I still right-click in programs to access commands?

Yes. The right-click method still abounds in Windows 8. You can right-click areas of the program screen or work area to display a pop-up menu of context commands. For example, if you are working with text, right-clicking the text may display a menu with commands for cutting, copying, pasting, and formatting the text.

Work with Dialog Boxes

If a program needs you to supply additional information, it opens a dialog box. For example, when you save a document for the first time, a Save As dialog box appears; you can indicate the folder in which you want to save the file, the name you want to give the file, and so on. Dialog boxes feature various types of input controls to enable you to supply information, including drop-down lists, option buttons, spin boxes, check boxes, and text boxes. Many dialog boxes contain a Help button you can click to find out more about the settings.

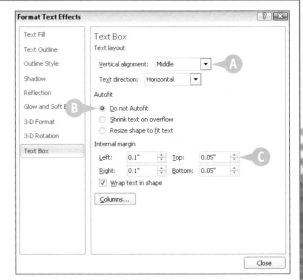

Ⓐ Drop-Down List Box

A drop-down list box looks somewhat like a text box, but with a down-arrow button (⏷) on the side. To change the setting, click the button and select a different option from the list that appears.

Ⓑ Option/Radio Button

You click an option button, also called a radio button, to enable (⦿) or disable (○) the feature associated with it. Only one option button in a group can be enabled at a time.

Ⓒ Spin Box

You can click the up and down arrows on a spin box (⏶⏷) to increase or decrease the value in the box, respectively. You can also simply type a value in the text box.

Ⓓ Text Box

You type text in a text box. For example, you might enter a page range to print in the Print dialog box or the name you want to apply to a file in the Save As dialog box.

Ⓔ List Box

A list box displays a list of options; you simply click the item you want to select. Scroll bars enable you to move through a longer list to see all available options.

Ⓕ Check Box

Clicking a check box enables (☐) or disables (☑) the feature associated with it. Unlike an option button, multiple check boxes in a group can be enabled at a time.

ⓖ Tab

Some dialog boxes have tabs along the top, each displaying a different set of controls. To switch tabs, simply click the desired tab.

ⓗ Slider Control

A slider control enables you to made incremental adjustments to a setting.

ⓘ Command Button

You click a command button to execute the command described on the button — for example, Cancel to close a dialog box without applying your changes.

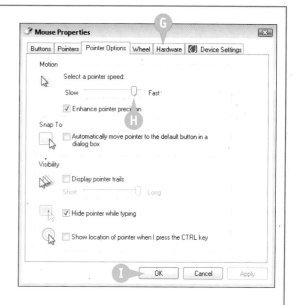

Keyboard Shortcuts for Navigating Dialog Boxes	
Keyboard Shortcut	**Associated Action**
Enter	Select the default command button (indicated by a highlight).
Esc	Close the dialog box without implementing your changes. (Pressing Esc is the same as clicking the Cancel command button.)
Tab	Move forward through the controls in the dialog box.
Shift + Tab	Move backward through the dialog box controls.
↑/↓	Move up or down within a group of option buttons.
Alt + ↓	Reveal the available options in the selected drop-down list box.

Create and Save a File

To work with data in a program, you must create a new file in which to store the data. If you want to be able to refer to the data in the file at some later time, you must save the file. You should also frequently save files you are working on in case of a power failure or computer crash. When you save a file, you can give it a unique filename, set the file type (also called a *file format*), and store it in any folder you choose. You can then open the saved file at a later time.

Create and Save a File

Create a File

1 Click the **File** tab.

2 Click **New**.

Note: Some programs require you to provide additional information when creating a new file. For example, if you are creating a new document in Microsoft Word, you are prompted to indicate what type of document you want to create.

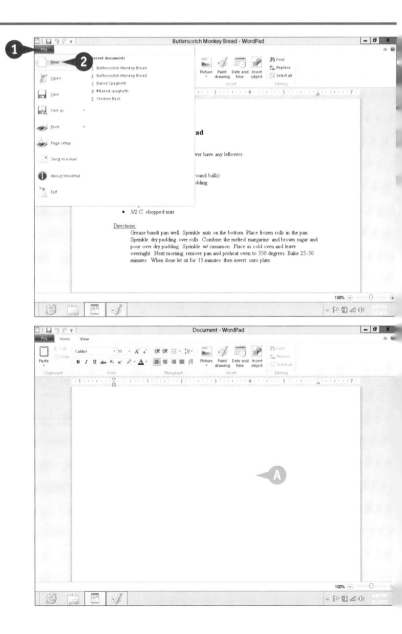

A The new file opens.

Note: An even faster way to create a new file is to press Ctrl + N.

Save a File

1 Click the **File** tab.

B For subsequent saves, you can click the **Save** button (🖫) on the Quick Access Toolbar to quickly save the file, or press Ctrl + S .

2 Click **Save**.

If prompted, click a file type.

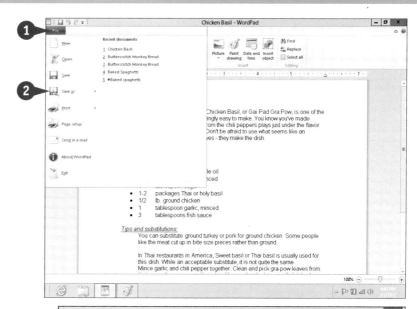

The Save As dialog box appears.

3 In the Navigation pane, click the library and/or subfolder in which you want to save the file.

4 Type a name for the file in the **File name** field.

5 Click **Save**.

The program saves the file and the new filename appears on the window's title bar.

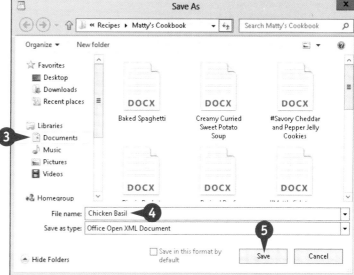

TIP

What if you want to save a new version of a file but leave the original version intact?
Suppose you are tweaking a form letter that you send out to clients but you want to keep a copy of the original for your records. To do so, launch the Save As dialog box and specify the library and folder in which you want to save the new version of the file, as described in this section. Then type a new name for the file in the File Name text box (so you do not overwrite the original file by accident) and click **Save**. Windows saves the file in the folder you chose, with the name you indicated.

Open a File

In addition to creating new files, you can open files that you have created and saved previously to continue adding data or to edit existing data. Regardless of whether you store a file in a folder on your computer's hard drive or on a CD, you can easily access files using the Open dialog box. If you are not sure where you saved a file, you can use the Open dialog box's Search function to locate it. When you are finished using a file, you should close it. Closing files and programs frees up processing power on your computer.

Open a File

1 Click the **File** tab.

A If the file you want to open is listed under Recent Documents, you can click it to open it.

2 Click **Open**.

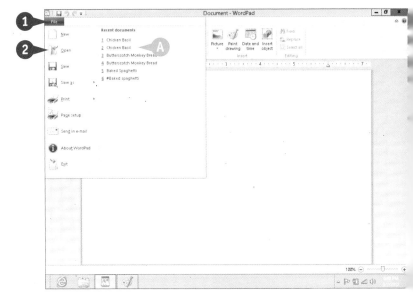

The Open dialog box appears.

Note: Another way to launch the Open dialog box is to press Ctrl+O.

3 In the Navigation pane, click the library in which the file you want to open has been saved.

4 In the file list, locate and click the file you want to open.

5 Click **Open**.

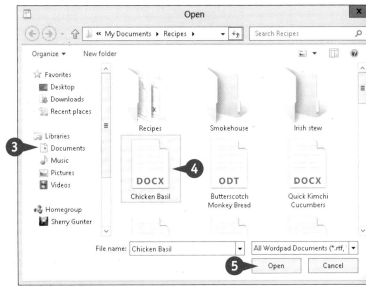

Print a File

CHAPTER 7

If you have connected a printer to your laptop — either via a cable or through a wireless network — you can create printouts of your files. For example, you might distribute printouts of a file as handouts in a meeting. When you print a file, you can send the file directly to the printer using the default settings, or you can open your program's Print dialog box to change these settings. For example, you might opt to print just a portion of a file, print multiple copies of a file, collate the printouts, and so on.

Print a File

1 Click the **File** tab.

2 Click **Print**.

Ⓐ To print the file using the default settings, click **Quick print**.

3 Click **Print**.

The Print dialog box appears.

Note: Another way to open the Print screen is to press Ctrl+P.

Ⓑ You can select a printer from the **Select Printer** list.

Ⓒ You can specify the number of copies to print using the **Number of copies** spin box.

Ⓓ You can select to print a selection from the file or specific pages using the available settings in the **Page Range** area.

4 Click **Print**.

The program sends the file to the printer for printing.

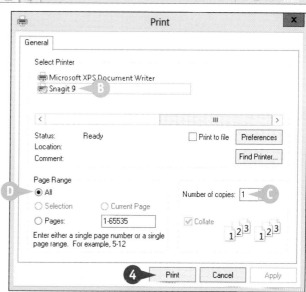

129

CHAPTER 8

Performing Popular Software Tasks

Software applications enable you to view images, listen to sounds, create text documents, crunch numbers, and much more. This chapter shows you how to use several of the preinstalled Windows 8 apps and Windows accessories available.

Schedule Dates with the Calendar App

You can use the new Windows 8 Calendar app to schedule and keep track of important dates, appointments, and other time-sensitive events. You can view your schedule by month, week, or day. You can set up recurring appointments, assign a reminder, and send out e-mail invites to others to attend an event. You can also sync your calendar with other calendar apps, like Google Calendar. Like the other Windows 8 apps, you can navigate the Calendar using touchscreen technologies or by swiping with the mouse or using the keyboard navigation keys.

Schedule Dates with the Calendar App

1 From the Windows 8 Start screen, click the **Calendar** app tile.

Windows opens the Calendar app.

2 Navigate to and click the date you want to set.

You can use the navigation arrows (‹ and ›) to move back and forth among months, weeks, or days.

The Details screen appears.

3 Type a title for the appointment.

A Optionally, click here to add a message.

4 Fill out the appointment details.

B Add a location here.

C Specify a start time, if applicable.

D Click here to set a recurring appointment.

5 Click **Save** (⊞).

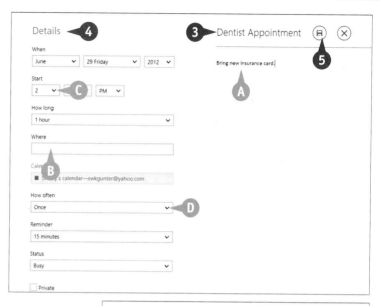

E Calendar adds the appointment to your schedule.

TIPS

How do I change the Calendar view to a weekly or daily view?

By default, Calendar starts you out in Month view. You can switch to Day or Week view to see your schedule in a daily or weekly format. To do so, swipe or move the mouse to the bottom of the screen, or press 🔲+🅩 to display the Calendar app bar. Click **Day** (🔲), **Week** (🔲), or **Month** (🔲) and Calendar immediately switches views.

How do I e-mail my event?

Click the event on the calendar to open the Details screen. In the **Who** field, type the e-mail addresses of everyone you want to invite to the event, separating each invitee with a semicolon. Click the **Send** button (🖅) to e-mail the details to everyone you specified.

Find a Location with the Maps App

You can use the Maps app to find a location on a map. Working with Microsoft's Bing website, the Maps app helps you find directions or locate a spot quickly and easily with an Internet connection. Using touch-base technology, you can swipe your way around the map using your finger, or if your laptop has a regular monitor, you can use the mouse or keyboard navigation tools. You can zoom in or out, as well as change the map presentation from Road View (which is the default) or Aerial View (satellite view).

Find a Location with the Maps App

1 From the Windows 8 Start
   screen, click the **Maps** app
   tile.

Windows opens the Maps
app.

2 Press ⊞+Q.

Ⓐ Windows displays the Search
   pane.

3 Type in the location you
   want to view on the map.

4 Press Enter or click 🔍.

The Maps app displays the destination on the map.

B Click the zoom tools (⊕ or ⊖) to zoom in or out, or with a touchscreen use your finger to pinch to zoom in and reverse pinch to zoom out.

Note: Keyboard users can press Ctrl+⊟ to zoom out and Ctrl+⊞ to zoom in.

5 Swipe up, right-click the mouse, or press ⊞+Z to display the Maps App bar.

C To view driving directions, click here or click the **Directions** button (⊕) on the Map App bar and enter a starting point and a destination.

D To clear the map, click the **Clear map** button (⊗).

E To further refine the location, click the **Refine** button (◉) and enter more details.

F To display traffic mode, click the **Show traffic** button (⊕).

G To change the view style, click **Map style** (◉) and choose an option.

H To return to your current location, click **My location** (◉).

TIPS

How do I find directions for a location?
You can click the **Directions** button (⊕) on the App bar to display options for looking up directions on the map. To display the App bar, swipe the bottom of the screen or right-click with the mouse. Type in a starting point and an ending point. Press Enter, and Maps routes out the directions, both on the map as well as driving directions listed above the map.

What is Bing Maps?
Bing is Microsoft's web search engine, and Bing Maps is a part of the site's many features. Previously, the search tool was known as Windows Live Search and MSN Search. Bing enables you to search the Internet using keywords. Offering expandable website descriptions, you can visit the Bing website using your web browser: www.bing.com.

Explore Windows Accessories

The Windows 8 operating system comes with several small applications, called Windows accessories, already installed and ready to go. Found in previous versions of Microsoft Windows, accessories are handy tools to have around for performing simple tasks, such as calculating with Calculator, or creating a word processing document with WordPad. You can view all the Windows accessories using the Apps screen. Grouped under the heading "Windows Accessories," you can find fourteen different programs to choose from, each with a special function. When you open a program from the Windows Accessories group, the program opens onto the desktop.

Calculator

You can use the Calculator tool to perform simple calculations — such as adding, subtracting, multiplying, and dividing — as well as statistical, programming, and scientific calculations. Resembling an actual calculator in appearance, the Calculator opens as a small window on the desktop. You can click or touch (with touchscreen-capable laptops) buttons on the calculator, or use the keyboard to enter data. You can switch modes with the View menu.

WordPad

You can use WordPad to create simple word processing documents on your laptop, such as letters, memos, or other word-based files. Included in just about every version of Microsoft Windows, WordPad now features the Ribbon interface introduced with Windows 7. Although WordPad does not offer the wide variety of features found in a full-blown word processing program, it does enable you to create professional, polished documents in several file formats.

Notepad

Notepad is a very basic text editor program, enabling you to create text-only files without graphics or special formatting. Unlike a word processing program which lets you save files in a variety of formats, Notepad is commonly used to view or edit text (TXT) files. Notepad is also handy for creating web pages, allowing users to enter HTML coding. Although Notepad normally saves files as TXT files, you can add the .htm extension yourself to create a web page document.

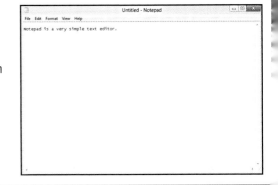

Paint

Paint is a drawing, or graphics, tool you can use to create all kinds of illustrations and save them to use in other programs. Paint is also handy for viewing and performing simple edits on photos and picture files. You can then save Paint files in other graphics formats, such as BMP, JPEG, PNG, or GIF. Like WordPad, Paint was introduced in early versions of the Windows operating system, and now sports the same Ribbon interface as the latest Microsoft apps.

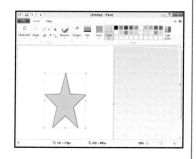

Sticky Notes

You can use the Sticky Notes tool to create digital sticky notes to place on your desktop screen. Much like the yellow adhesive notes you can stick around your desk or office, you can use Sticky Notes to post a reminder about a task, jot down a phone number, or create just about any kind of note you want to keep around. You can drag notes around the screen, and resize, delete, and recolor them to suit your needs.

Snipping Tool

You can use the Windows 8 Snipping tool to take a snapshot of your computer's screen. Introduced with Windows 7, the tool is known as a capture program. For example, you may want to take a snapshot of a news story or a recipe to save for later reading. The Snipping tool takes a picture of anything on your computer screen. You can snip a whole window, or just a specific section. You can then save the image to annotate it or e-mail it to a friend.

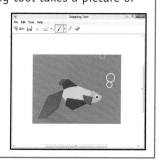

Windows Media Player

Windows Media Player is a player application you can use to play video and audio files, organize music and video libraries, and view images. You can use Windows Media Player to listen to music CDs, rip music from a CD to your personal library, stream music from the Internet, and more. You can learn more about using Windows Media Player in Chapter 14.

Enter and Edit Text in WordPad

WordPad is a word processing program included with Windows 8. When you launch WordPad or create a new WordPad file, a blank document appears in the WordPad window. In the top left corner of that blank document is a blinking cursor, or insertion point, waiting for you to start typing. Of course, the beauty of any word processing program is that it enables you to easily edit your text after you type it, and WordPad is no exception. With WordPad, you can add new text or delete existing text with the greatest of ease.

Enter and Edit Text in WordPad

Type Text

1 From the Windows 8 Start screen, type **wordpad**.

Ⓐ Windows opens the Apps search screen.

2 Click **WordPad**.

Note: You can also view the list of apps from the App bar and find WordPad listed among the Windows accessories on the Apps page. Press Ctrl + Z to view the App bar.

WordPad opens on the desktop.

3 Start typing your text; the cursor marks the current location where text will appear when you start typing.

Ⓑ WordPad automatically wraps the text to the next line for you.

Ⓒ Press Enter to start a new paragraph.

Ⓓ You can press Enter twice to add an extra space between paragraphs.

Ⓔ You can press Tab to quickly create an indent for a line of text.

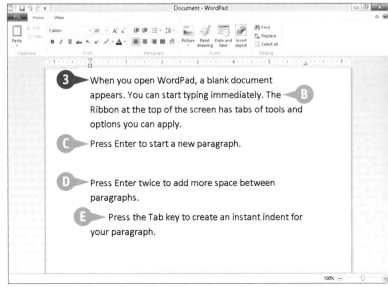

3 When you open WordPad, a blank document appears. You can start typing immediately. The Ⓑ Ribbon at the top of the screen has tabs of tools and options you can apply.

Ⓒ Press Enter to start a new paragraph.

Ⓓ Press Enter twice to add more space between paragraphs.

Ⓔ Press the Tab key to create an instant indent for your paragraph.

Edit Text

1 Click in the document where you want to fix a mistake and start typing.

2 Press `Backspace` to delete characters to the left of the cursor.

When you open WordPad, a blank document appears. You can start typing immediately. The Ribbon at the top of the screen has tabs of tools and options you can apply.

Press Enter to start a new paragraph.

Press Enter twice to add more space between paragraphs.

1

Press the Tab key to create an in|tant indent for your paragraph.

2

3 Press `Del` to delete characters to the right of the cursor.

You can also delete selected text.

When you open WordPad, a blank document appears. You can start typing immediately. The Ribbon at the top of the screen has tabs of tools and options you can apply.

Press Enter to start a new paragraph.

Press Enter twice to add more space between paragraphs.

3

Press the Tab key to create an inant indent for your paragraph.

TIPS

How do I select text in WordPad?
You can use your mouse or your keyboard to select a single character, a word, a sentence, a paragraph, or all the text in the document. You can click and double-click to select text with the mouse, or you can drag your mouse across the word or words you want to select. Selected text appears highlighted in the document.

How do I move or copy text?
You can use the Cut, Copy, and Paste commands to move or copy text elsewhere in the same WordPad document or in another WordPad document. When you cut text, it is removed from its original location; when you copy text, WordPad makes a duplicate of the selected data, leaving it in its original location.

Format Text in WordPad

You can change the text font, size, and color to alter the appearance of text in a document. For example, if you are creating an invitation, you might make the description of the event a different font and color to stand out from the other details. Likewise, if you are creating a report for work, you might make the title of the report larger than the body text, or even color-code certain data in the report. In addition, you can use WordPad's basic formatting commands — Bold, Italic, Underline, Strikethrough, Subscript, and Superscript — to quickly add formatting to your text.

Format Text in WordPad

Change the Font

1. Select the text you want to format.

2. Click the **Home** tab.

3. Click the **Font** ⌄.

4. Click a font.

   WordPad applies the font to the selected text.

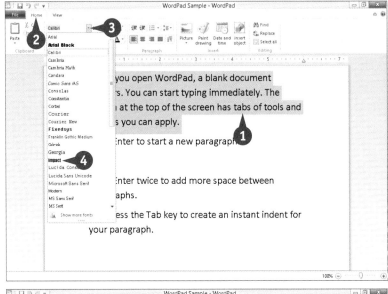

Change the Size

1. Select the text you want to format.

2. From the Ribbon's Home tab, click the **Font Size** ⌄.

3. Click a size.

   WordPad applies the font size to the text.

Note: Another way to change the font size is to click the **Grow Font** button (A˙) or the **Shrink Font** button (A˙) on the Home tab.

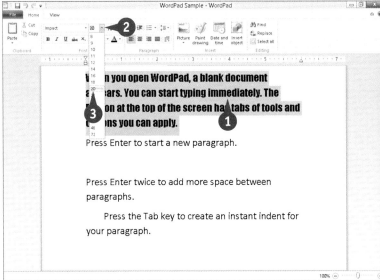

Change the Color

1. Select the text you want to format.

2. From the Home tab, click the ▾ next to the **Font Color** button ($\underline{\mathbf{A}}$).

3. Click a color.

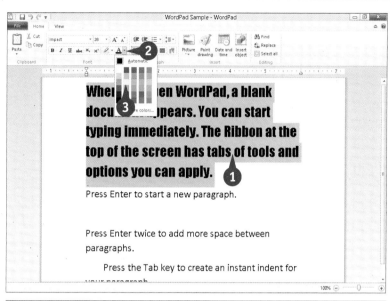

WordPad applies the color to the text.

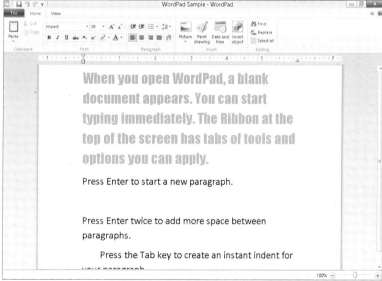

continued ▶

TIPS

How do you apply formatting to your text?

To apply formatting to your text, select the text you want to format, click the **Home** tab, and then click the **Bold** (B), **Italic** (*I*), **Underline** (U), **Strikethrough** (abc), **Subscript** (x₁), or **Superscript** (x²) button. WordPad applies the format you chose to the selected text.

How do you apply list formatting?

To format text as a numbered or bulleted list, select the text you want to change, then click the ▾ next to the **Start a List** button (≔) and select a bulleted or numbered list option from the list that appears. WordPad formats the selected text as a list.

Format Text in WordPad (continued)

You can use WordPad's alignment commands to change how text is positioned horizontally on a page, left-aligning text (the default), centering it, right-aligning it, or justifying it. Indents are another way of controlling the positioning of text in a document. For example, you might indent a paragraph such as a long quote to set it apart from the rest of the text on the page. Finally, you can adjust the amount of spacing that appears between lines of text in your paragraphs. For example, you might set double-spacing to allow for handwritten edits in your printed document.

Format Text in WordPad (continued)

Align Text

1. Select the text you want to align.

2. From the Ribbon's Home tab, click an alignment button.

   Click **Align Left** (≡) to left-align text.

   Click **Center** (≡) to center text.

   Click **Align Right** (≡) to right-align text.

   Click **Justify** (≡) to justify text between the left and right margins.

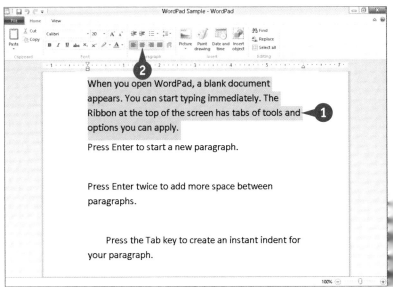

Indent Text

1. Select the paragraph(s) you want to indent.

2. From the Home tab, click an indent button.

   Click **Decrease Indent** (≕) to decrease the indentation.

   Click **Increase Indent** (≕) to increase the indentation.

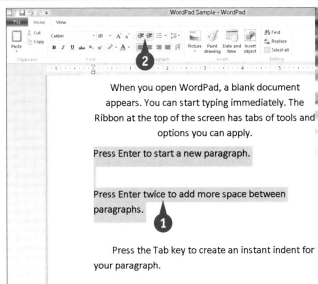

Set Line Spacing

1 Select the paragraph(s) whose spacing you want to change.

2 From the Home tab, click the **Line Spacing** button ($\equiv$).

3 Click a line spacing option.

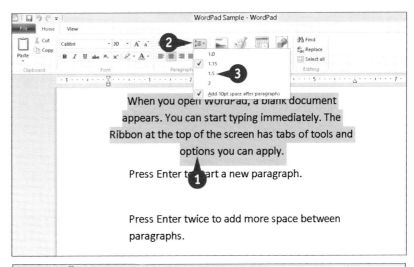

WordPad applies the new spacing.

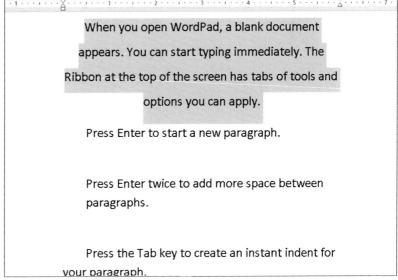

TIPS

Can you set a custom indent?
You can set a custom indent using the WordPad ruler. To do so, simply drag the indent marker ($\S$) on the ruler to the desired location. If the ruler is not shown in the WordPad window, click the **View** tab and select the **Ruler** check box ($\square$).

How do you undo your changes?
If you realize you have made a change to your document in error, you can undo it. Simply click the **Undo** button ($\circ$) in the Windows Quick Access Toolbar. If, after undoing a change, you realize you want to redo it, click the **Redo** button ($\circ$) on the Quick Access Toolbar.

Create Pictures with Windows Paint

P aint is a drawing program preinstalled with Windows 8. Part of a suite of Windows accessories, you can use Paint to create all kinds of graphics and illustrations. You can also import other graphics for editing, such as photos. Paint offers a variety of drawing tools to create different kinds of effects, such as a pencil for freehand drawings, or a library of predrawn shapes. You can apply an assortment of editing features, such as cropping, rotating, and resizing. You can add fill colors, change line thicknesses, and even change the style of your drawing tool to different brush effects.

Create Pictures with Windows Paint

Draw with the Pencil Tool

1 From the Windows 8 Start screen, type **paint**.

A Windows opens the Apps search screen.

2 Click **Paint**.

3 Click the **Home** tab.

4 Click the **Brushes** tool ( ).

5 Click a brush style.

B You can click a color to use from the palette.

6 Click and drag to draw.

Paint displays the paint brush stroke.

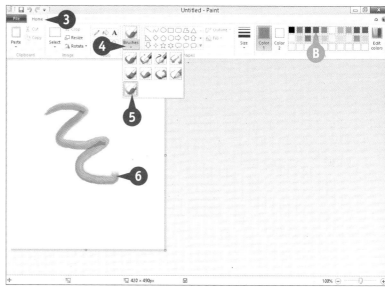

Draw a Shape

1 Click a shape from the **Shapes** list box.

2 Click here and click a color for the shape outline.

3 Click here and click a color for the shape fill.

4 Click and drag to draw the shape.

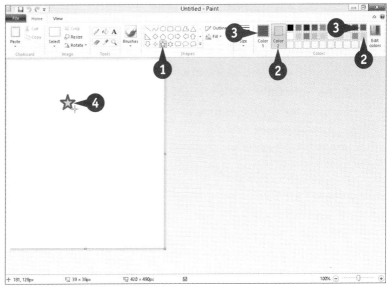

C Paint displays the shape.

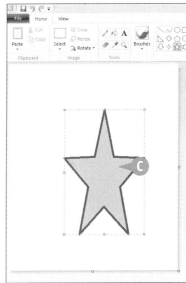

TIPS

How do I save a drawing?

To save a file, click the **File** tab on the Ribbon and click **Save**. Paint opens the Save As dialog box where you can choose a destination folder and type a name for the file. You can also specify a file format. You can choose between bitmap (BMP), GIF, JPEG, TIFF, and PNG graphic file formats.

Can I import other graphic files and photos?

Yes. To import another file into Paint, click the **File** tab on the Ribbon and click **Open**. Navigate to the folder containing the file and double-click its filename. Paint immediately opens the image. You can use the **Resize** tool ( ) to resize it, if necessary. You can apply any of the Paint tools to make changes or edits to the imported image.

Explore Microsoft Office

Microsoft Office is a suite of programs for accomplishing a variety of computer tasks and functions. Sharing a common look and feel, each program represents a major software type and function. Office includes Word (word processing), Excel (spreadsheet), PowerPoint (presentation), Access (database), Outlook (e-mail), Publisher (desktop publishing), and OneNote (information gathering). Although the apps and Windows accessories that come with Windows 8 are very useful, you may have need for full-blown programs that offer more features, tools, and options, such those offered in the Office bundle.

Word

Microsoft Word is the most popular word processing program on the market today. You can use Word to create all kinds of documents, from reports and letters to blogs and mailing labels. Offering powerful tools and features, you can create customizable templates, perform automatic spelling and grammar checks, add impact with picture-editing tools, collaborate with others, and design eye-catching tables and diagrams. Word is an asset to any office or home office environment.

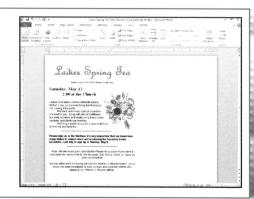

Excel

Microsoft Excel is a spreadsheet program — a category of apps for crunching numbers and storing, organizing, and manipulating data. Using a grid of intersecting columns and rows to create cells, you can build worksheets that hold numbers, text, or *formulas* — calculations involving data in other cells. You can use Excel to work with financial data, scientific data, graphing data, and more. Excel enables you to analyze data, collaborate with others, and create professional-looking charts and reports.

PowerPoint

Microsoft PowerPoint is a presentation program — an app designed specifically to help you give visual presentations, such as a sales pitch, a product overview, or even a book report. Information is presented on slides, rather like slide shows from decades past; you can progress through the presentation one slide at a time. Slides can hold all kinds of data, including text, graphics, pictures, video clips, audio clips, and more. You can also apply special effects to make the presentation more engaging. You can create presentations to run on their own, or manually in front of an audience.

Outlook

Microsoft Outlook is an e-mail and personal information manager program. You can use Outlook to send and receive e-mail messages, store contacts, manage a schedule, track tasks, and much more. Acting like a personal assistant, Outlook helps you organize e-mail, sort out spam and junk mail, add attachments, and sync with other mailboxes. You can use the Contacts tool to build a database of all the people you contact the most. The Calendar tool helps you to keep track of

appointments and meetings. The Tasks and Notes tools help you keep to-do lists and notes.

Access

Microsoft Access is a database program — an application designed especially for collecting and organizing large quantities of data. You can use Access to manage inventory lists, contacts and addresses, product catalogs, and other large collections of information. Using a format of records, forms, and tables, you can perform a variety of tasks on the database data, such as filter, sort, perform queries, make reports, extract, analyze, and more.

Publisher

Microsoft Publisher is a desktop publishing program — software that helps you create page layout projects and printed materials. Publisher offers more control over fonts, layout, and design than a word processing program. Using graphic design and prepress functions, you can quickly make professional publications such as flyers, brochures, newsletters, business cards, postcards, and more.

OneNote

Microsoft OneNote is a planner and note-taking app you can use to gather information on the go and keep it all in one spot to stay organized. You can use OneNote to collect research data, notes, pictures, freeform handwriting, audio and video clips, and more. Once you gather notes, you can collaborate with others, link information, and build a private knowledge base. You can find all kinds of

creative ways to use OneNote at work, school, or home.

Add a Game App

Gaming software is always a popular pursuit for many laptop users. A game app can help you while away the time waiting for an appointment or meeting. The new Windows Store offers a wide variety of game apps for all level of users. You can browse through the Store's Game category for spotlighted games, top games, and a broader listing of available game apps. Any apps you add from the Store appear as tiles on the Windows 8 Start screen.

Add a Game App

1 Click the **Store** tile on the Windows 8 Start screen.

Windows opens the Storefront and connects to the online marketplace.

2 Scroll through the listings to find the Games category.

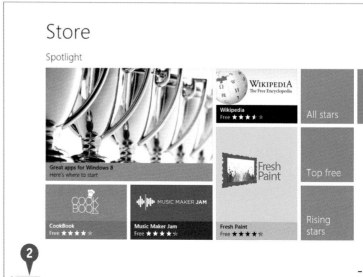

3 Click an app you want to know more about.

Details about the app appear.

Ⓐ Click **Install** to install the app.

Ⓑ Click **Details** to read release notes, system requirements, and other information.

Ⓒ Click **Reviews** to read what others have to say about the app.

Ⓓ Click here to return to the previous screen.

TIP

What is Xbox Live?

Xbox Live is the online service for Xbox systems and gaming. Xbox Live is integrated with Windows 8, and if you have an account, you can play games online using your laptop. When you click the **Xbox Live Games** app tile on the Windows 8 Start screen, you can sign in to your account and shop for games or play your laptop Xbox games online with others. If you do not have an Xbox Live account, you can create one following the on-screen prompts. The Pinball FX2 game, for example, prompts you to sign in to play. You can also choose to play "offline" as a single player.

CHAPTER 9

Managing Computer Files and Folders

Windows Explorer enables you to perform a variety of file management tasks, such as copying and moving files, renaming files, and deleting files.

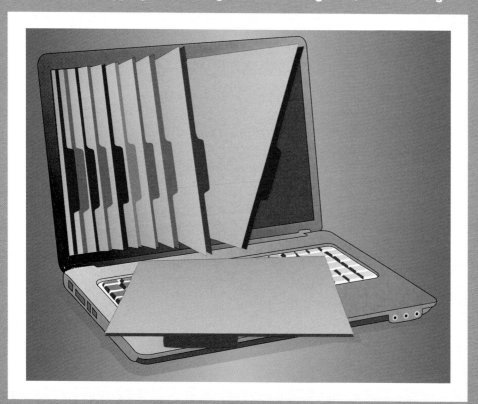

Understanding File Formats

You can create all kinds of different files on your computer; each type of software program you use creates different types of file formats. For example, a word processing application allows you to create document formats, whereas a graphics program creates graphic file formats. A *file format* is how information is encoded and saved to the file. The file format determines what sort of programs can read the file; for example, a photo app may not be able to read a document file format, but can read other types of digital image formats.

File Extensions

When you create files, you must give them distinct names; a default file format is also assigned. Some programs allow you to assign other, similar file formats. File formats appear as extensions added onto the filename preceded by a dot, such as Letter.doc. Usually, you cannot see a file extension unless you choose to view it. If you ever encounter a problem opening a file, it might help to view the extension to see what sort of format the file is.

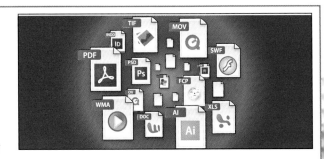

Program and System Files

You can recognize program files by their .exe extensions, which means *executable*. When viewing Windows system files, you quickly find a variety of file types pertaining to different parts of the operating system, such as DRV for device driver or DLL for dynamic link library. Other than recognizing these as important parts of Windows, there is no reason to try and open these file types other than the EXE format. If you open an EXE file, you are opening a program.

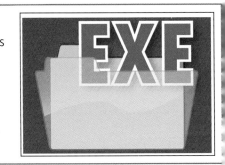

Document File Formats

You can create document files in word processing programs, such as Microsoft Word or WordPad (which installs with Windows 8), WordPerfect, and Corel Write, just to name a few. The DOC format is one of the most popular file formats for files you create with a word processor app. Other document formats include TXT, RTF, and ODT. Adobe's PDF format is another alternative to other document types, and can be read by a PDF reader that you can download free online.

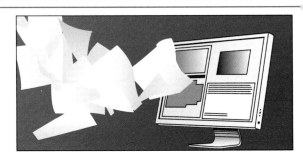

Graphics Formats

Graphics and drawing programs, such as Windows Paint, Adobe Illustrator, and Paint Shop Pro, are used to create, edit, and manage graphics files. Graphics can include clip art, web graphics, logos, backgrounds, illustrations, and other digital artwork.

Popular graphic file formats include GIF, JPEG, BMP, TIFF, and PNG. Each program may also utilize its own distinct format, such as AI for Adobe Illustrator. Assign a common format, such as PNG, if you want to share the file with non-Adobe Illustrator users.

Photo File Formats

If you have a digital camera, you can take pictures and store them on your laptop, sharing them with others through e-mail or social websites, or saving them to flash drives and other backup media devices. Photo file formats are the same as graphics file formats: GIF, TIFF, PNG, and JPEG. Digital

cameras also provide the RAW format, which produces images with smaller file sizes than the other formats.

Multimedia Formats

Music, movies and video files are easy to identify with their file extensions. Music files use formats such as MP3, WMA, or WAV. Music files can also utilize AIFF or AU formats. Video files include the AVI, MP4, MPEG, WMV, or MOV formats. Movies you create with

Flash, for example, can use the SWF format. When you open a multimedia file, Windows 8 automatically attempts to open the required app to play the file.

Other File Formats

As you view and create files on your computer, you are bound to encounter numerous other file formats. For example, Excel's XLS spreadsheet format or PowerPoint's PPT for presentations are common in the Microsoft Office suite of programs. If you are creating web pages, the HTML and XHTML

formats are used. Compressed files are often stored in the Zip file format. Just remember, the type of format often dictates what program is used to read the file.

View Files and Folders

You can use File Explorer much like a digital filing cabinet, with folders to store and organize your files and programs. Each folder contains tools for searching, navigating, and organizing the files and subfolders within it. File Explorer contains four main folders, called libraries, for storing files: Documents, Pictures, Music, and Videos. The Documents library is where word processor files, spreadsheets, and web pages are stored by default. The Pictures library acts as a central repository for digital image files. The Music library is where audio files that you download or rip are saved. The Videos library stores video files.

View Files and Folders

1 Open File Explorer. From the desktop, click the **File Explorer** icon (▭).

File Explorer opens with the main Libraries listed.

2 Click **Documents**, **Pictures**, **Music**, or **Videos**.

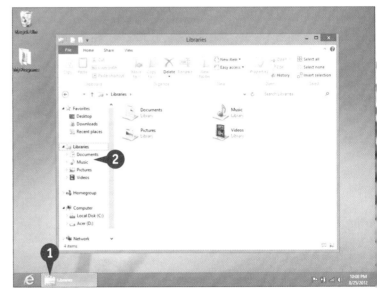

A File Explorer folder window opens, displaying the contents of the library you chose.

Ⓐ In this example, the Pictures folder displays a list of picture files displayed as large icons in the File list.

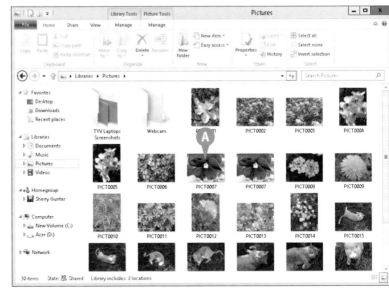

154

Navigate Folder Windows

Folder windows in File Explorer contain several panes to make it easier to find the files you need. Folder windows also offer several options when it comes to how files are displayed in the File list — for example, as icons of various sizes, in list form with details such as size and date created, and so on. In addition, each folder window contains a Ribbon with various tabs of toolbar buttons for organizing, sharing, and burning files; creating a new folder; changing how files in the folder window are displayed; and getting help. A Search field is also present.

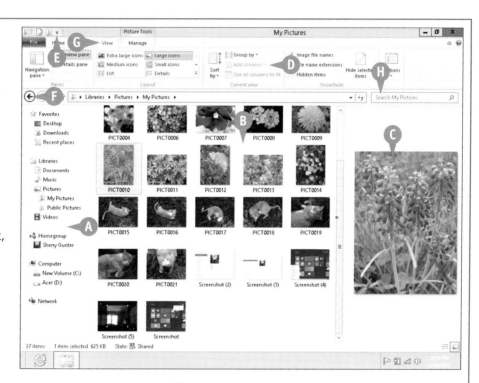

Ⓐ Navigation Pane

This pane contains clickable links to other folders on your Windows system.

Ⓑ File List

Files in the selected folder are listed in the File list.

Ⓒ Preview Pane

When you click, or select, a file in the File list, a preview of that file appears in the Preview pane. (You will learn more about selecting files later in this chapter.)

Ⓓ Folder Window Ribbon

Access folder and file options here. Note that specific options differ depending on what library is open.

Ⓔ Quick Access Toolbar

This toolbar at the top of the window displays common toolbar buttons; you can edit these to suit the way you work.

Ⓕ Navigation Arrows

Click the arrow buttons to move back and forth between opened folders.

Ⓖ Change Your View

Click the View tab to change the way in which you view items in your folder list and preview pane.

Ⓗ Search Box

Use the Search box to find files in the current folder. You will learn more about searching for files later in this chapter.

Open Files and Folders

You can open folders and files using the File Explorer window. When you open a file from within File Explorer, Windows 8 automatically launches the application associated with that file, and then opens the file in that application's window. For example, if the file you want to open is a rich text file, Windows 8 launches the WordPad application and then displays the contents of the file in the WordPad window. You can open the file in a different program if you choose, however.

Open Files and Folders

1 From File Explorer, double-click the folder that contains the file you want to open.

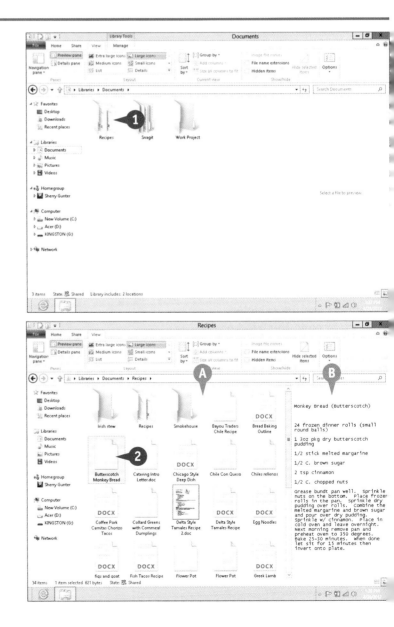

A The folder opens and its contents appear in the File list.

2 Double-click the file you want to open.

Windows opens the file in the default program.

B If the Preview pane is open, you can preview a selected file before fully opening the file.

3 Alternatively, to open the file in a different program, right-click the file.

4 Click **Open with**.

5 Click the program you want to use to view and/or edit the file.

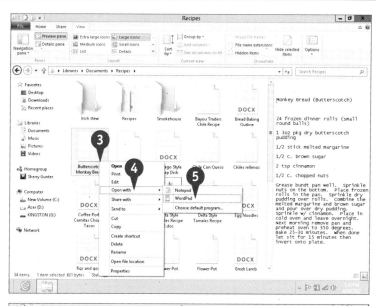

C Windows opens the file in the program you chose.

Note: To change the program that Windows uses to open a certain type of file by default, select **Choose default program** from the Open With menu, click the program you want to use in the Open With dialog box, select the **Always use the selected program to open this kind of file** check box, and click **OK**.

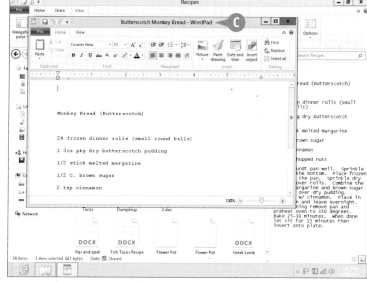

TIP

How do I open files on external media?
Insert your CD or DVD and follow these steps:

1 Open the File Explorer window.

2 Click **Computer**.

3 In the Computer directory, double-click a drive to view its contents.

4 Open the folder containing the file you want to view.

5 Open the file.

Create a New Folder

File Explorer contains several predefined folders, or libraries, such as Documents, Pictures, Music, and Videos. In addition to these, you can create your own unique folders. Creating folders makes it much easier to keep your files organized. For example, you might create folders for each project you are working on to store all the files associated with each project in one easy-to-find location; or you might create a folder to store all your photographs from a recent trip in a designated subfolder that helps you clearly identify its contents.

Create a New Folder

1 With the folder in which you want to create the new folder open in File Explorer, click the **New folder** button (▢).

Note: You can also right-click a blank area of the list and choose **New**, **Folder** from the pop-up menu that appears, or click the **New Folder** button (▢) found on the Ribbon's Home tab.

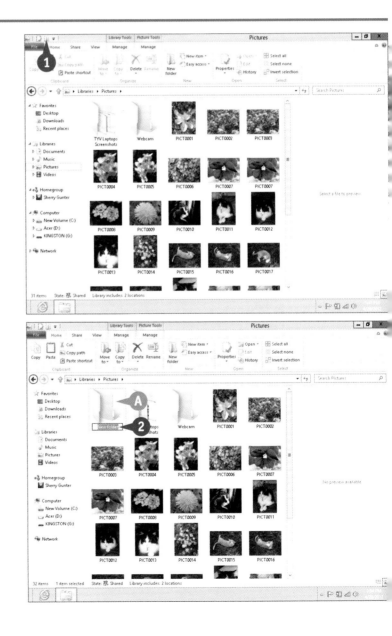

A Windows creates a new folder with the default name, New Folder, selected.

2 Type a descriptive name for the new folder and press Enter.

Select Files and Folders

You can use File Explorer to manage your files — for example, to copy, move, rename, delete, rate, and tag them. Before you can perform any of these actions on a file, you must select the file. That way, Windows knows exactly which file you want to work with. You can select files one at a time or select multiple files at once — useful, for example, if you want to move several files into a new folder.

Note that although the steps here cover selecting files, the technique for selecting folders is the same.

Select Files and Folders

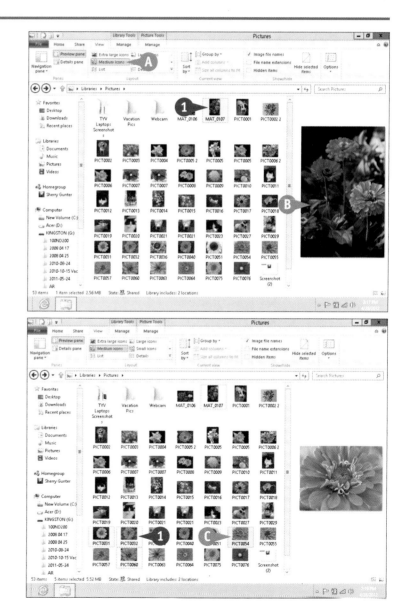

Select a Single File

1 Click a file.

The file is highlighted in the File list, indicating that it is selected.

A In this example, the File list displays files and folders as medium icons.

Note: You can click the Ribbon's **View** tab to change how files and folders are listed in the File list area.

B A preview of the selected file appears in the Preview pane.

Select Multiple Files

1 While pressing **Ctrl**, click each of the files you want to select.

C Each file you **Ctrl**+clicked is selected.

Note: To select multiple files that are grouped together, click the first file in the group and, while pressing **Shift**, click the last item in the group. The first file, the last file, and all the files in between will be selected.

Note: To deselect all selected files, click on empty area in the File list. If you have selected multiple files but need to deselect only one, press and hold **Ctrl** and click the file you want to deselect.

Move and Copy Files and Folders

Most likely, you will populate File Explorer with many files and folders over time. If you place a file in the wrong folder by accident, or simply create a new folder to store documents you have already created, you must move your files to the correct folder. In addition to moving files, you can copy them. Copying a file creates two versions of it — one in the original location and one in the new location.

Note that the steps for moving and copying files, covered here, are the same as the steps for moving and copying folders.

Move and Copy Files and Folders

Move a File

1. Select the file(s) you want to move.

2. Click the **Home** tab on the Ribbon.

3. Click **Cut** (✂).

Note: You can also click the Ribbon's **Move to** ( ) button and choose a location from the drop-down list.

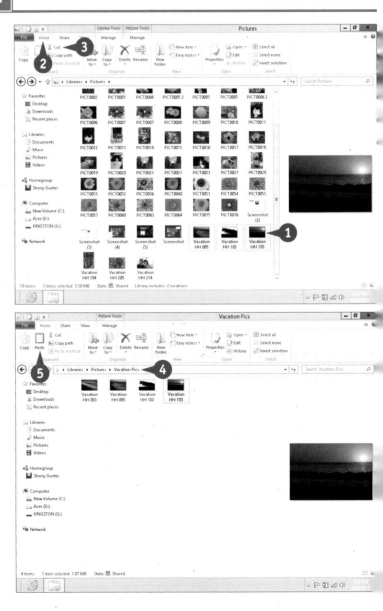

4. Open the folder into which you want to move the selected file(s).

5. Click **Paste** ( ).

   The selected file(s) is moved from the old location to the new one.

Copy a File

1 Select the file(s) you want to copy.

2 Click the **Home** tab on the Ribbon.

3 Click **Copy** ( ).

Note: You can also click the Ribbon's **Copy to** ( ) button and choose a location from the drop-down list.

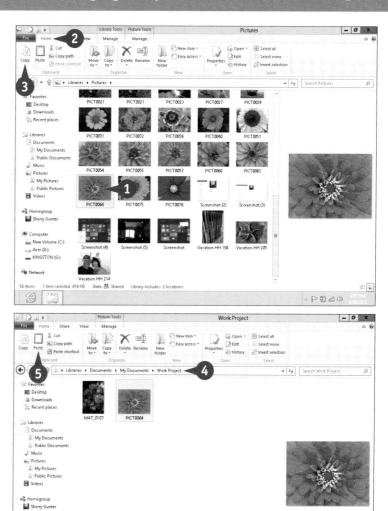

4 Open the folder into which you want to copy the selected file(s).

5 Click **Paste**.

A copy of the selected file(s) is placed in the new location.

TIP

How do I copy a file to a CD or DVD?

If your computer has a recordable CD or DVD drive, you can copy files and folders to a recordable disc. Select the file(s) you want to copy, or burn, to disc. Click the Share tab on the Ribbon bar, then click the **Burn to disk** option. When prompted, insert a blank disc into the drive. Windows displays the Burn a Disc dialog box; type a title for your disc. Click **Like a USB Flash Drive** to create a data CD or DVD (as opposed to a music CD or video DVD). Click **Next**. Windows formats the disc, and then copies the files.

Rename a File or Folder

Giving your files and folders descriptive names makes it easier to keep things organized. If a file or folder's current name is not adequately descriptive, you can rename it. File and folder names can be as long as 255 characters, although the following characters cannot be used:

< > , ? : \ *

You should only rename files and folders that you have created yourself or have been given to you by others. Never rename Windows system files or folders, or files or folders associated with installed programs. Otherwise, your computer could behave erratically or crash.

Rename a File or Folder

1 Click the file or folder you want to rename to select it.

2 Right-click the selected file or folder.

3 Click **Rename** from the menu that appears.

Note: If the Home tab is displayed on the Ribbon, you can click the **Rename** button ( ).

Windows selects the current filename or folder name.

4 Type a new name for the file or folder and press **Enter**.

Windows renames the file or folder.

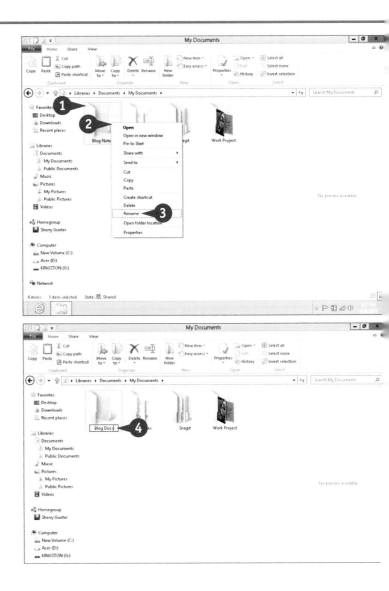

Compress a File or Folder

File Explorer enables you to compress, or *zip*, files and folders to save space. When you compress files and folders, you reduce the number of bytes they contain. Compressing files and folders is especially useful if, for example, you need to share several files or folders with others via e-mail. Uploading and downloading very large files is time consuming at best and impossible at worst. You might also compress files and folders to squeeze them onto a recordable CD or DVD. When a compressed file or folder is uncompressed, it is identical to the original, uncompressed file or folder.

Compress a File or Folder

1 Select the file(s) or folder(s) you want to compress.

2 Right-click a selected file or folder.

3 Click **Send to**.

4 Click **Compressed (zipped) folder**.

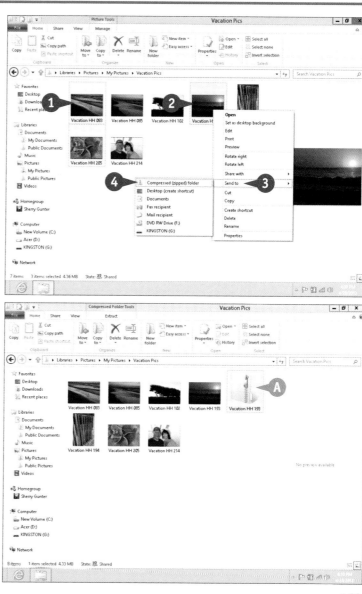

A Windows copies the selected files and/or folders, compresses the copies, and places them in a special compression folder (also called a Zip folder).

Note: You can rename a Zip folder just like you would any other type of folder or file.

Extract Compressed Files

Suppose you receive a compressed or Zip folder via e-mail or you have copied a Zip folder to a CD, and you need to access the files or folders it contains. To do so, you must *extract* the compressed files or folders from the Zip folder. The extracted items will be identical to the original versions, before they were compressed. When you extract items, you can specify the folder in which the extracted items should be saved. You can also instruct File Explorer to open the folder you choose in its own window after the extraction is complete.

Extract Compressed Files

1 Select the Zip folder containing the files you want to extract.

2 Right-click the Zip folder.

3 Click **Extract All** from the menu that appears.

Note: You can also click the Ribbon's Extract tab when a zipped file is selected and use the tools to work with zipped files.

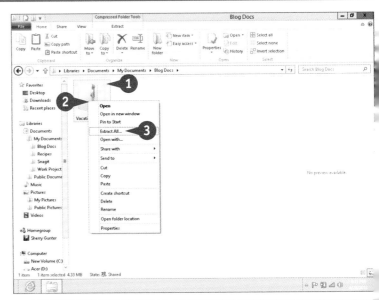

The Extract Compressed (Zipped) Folders window appears.

A You can click the **Browse** button to extract the files to a location other than the default.

4 Click **Extract**.

Windows extracts the files and/or folders into the folder you specified.

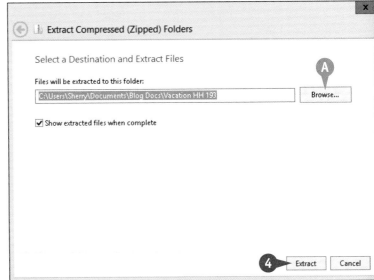

Search for Files and Folders

As you work with more and more files and folders on your computer, finding the one you need can become difficult. Fortunately, File Explorer offers a robust search function. If you have a general idea where the file or folder you are looking for is located — say, somewhere in your Documents folder — you can use the Search box found in the folder window to search for the file or folder. You can search using various criteria including name, file type, author, date, even words or phrases that appear within the file (assuming you are searching for a text file).

Search for Files and Folders

1 Click in the **Search** box.

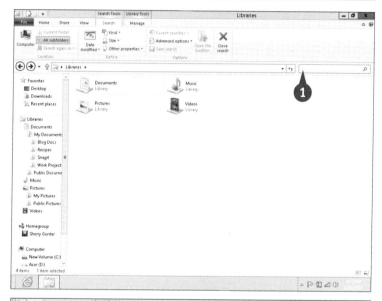

2 Type part or all of the file's name, type, author, or other criteria.

A As you type, Windows displays files and folders within the current folder that match your criteria.

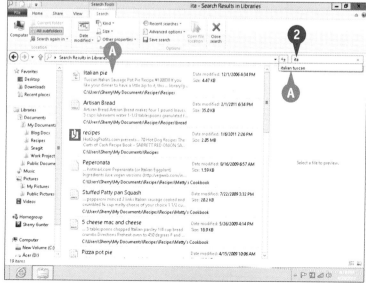

Sort and Filter Files

If you have lots of files in a folder, you can sort them based on various file properties. By default, files are sorted by name, but you can sort by any other property, including Date Modified, Author, Type, and so on. You can also filter files so that only those files with a particular property value are shown in the folder window. For example, you might opt to display those files of the TIFF file type. To sort and filter files, the folder window must be in Details view. To switch to Details view, click the View tab on the folder ribbon and choose Details from the list box.

Sort and Filter Files

Sort Files

1 Open the folder you want to sort.

2 Click the **View** tab on the Ribbon.

3 Click **Details** view.

4 Click the column header that contains the property by which you want to sort — for example, the Date Modified header.

Note: You might need to hide the Preview pane to view all available columns. To do so, click the **Preview Pane** button ( ). Click the button a second time when you are again ready to reveal the pane.

A File Explorer sorts the files by the property you clicked.

Note: To switch the sort order (from ascending to descending or vice versa), simply click the column header again.

Note: You can also click the **Sort by** button ( ) on the Ribbon to sort a folder.

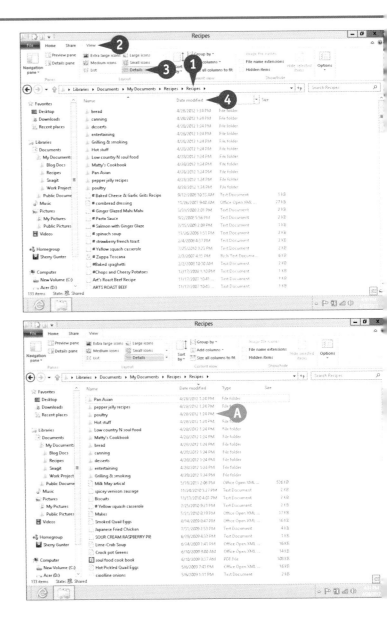

Filter Files

1 In Details view, position your mouse pointer over the column header for the property you want to filter (here, Type).

A down arrow appears on the right side of the column header.

2 Click the ⏷ to see a list of values associated with the column's property.

3 Click the check box with the property value by which you want to filter.

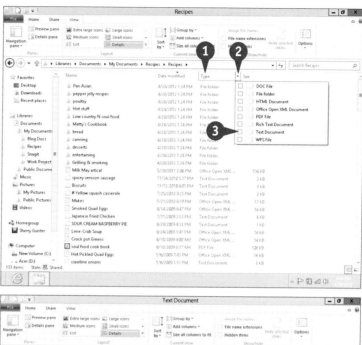

B Windows displays only the files with the property value you chose.

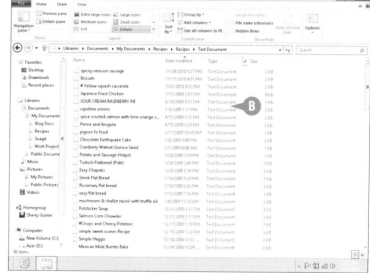

TIP

How do I sort by a different property?

If the column header for the property by which you want to sort or filter your files does not appear in File Explorer, you can add it. With the folder that contains the files you want to sort or filter open in Details view, right-click one of the existing column headings. Select the property by which you want to sort or filter from the list that appears. Alternatively, click **More** to open the Choose Details dialog box; then, click the check box next to a property to select it, and click **OK**. Windows adds a column for the property you chose.

Tag Files

Windows applies certain properties to files, such as Name, Date Modified, Author, File Type, and so on. You can use these properties as criteria when searching for files. In addition, you can apply tags — brief descriptions embedded in the files' metadata — to certain types of files, which you can also use as sort, filter, and search criteria. These tags could be anything you choose — the name of the person featured in a digital photo, the project with which a document is associated, keywords, and so on. The easiest way to apply a tag is to use Explorer's Details pane.

Tag Files

1. Click the **View** tab on the Ribbon.

2. Click **Details pane**.

3. Select the file you want to tag.

Ⓐ Information about the file appears in the Details pane.

4. Click **Add a tag**.

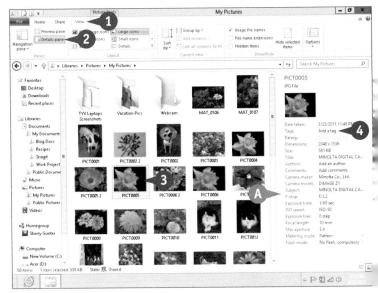

A blinking cursor appears in the Add a Tag field.

5. Type a tag.

Ⓑ Windows adds a semicolon (;) after the tag so you can add additional tags. Tags must be separated by a semicolon.

6 Type another tag.

C If the tag you type has already been applied to other files, a menu appears listing the tag alongside a check box.

7 Click the check box to select it or keep typing to create a new tag.

8 Click **Save**.

Windows saves your tag(s).

TIP

How do you rate files?

To rate a file, follow these steps:

1 Select the file you want to rate.

2 In the Details pane, next to the **Rating** entry, click the star that represents the rating you want to apply. For example, to give the file a two-star rating, click the second star.

3 Click **Save**.

Delete a File or Folder

If you no longer need a file or folder, you can delete it. Deleting unwanted files and folders can help you avoid cluttering your computer. You should delete only files and folders that you create yourself or that others have given to you to avoid removing important system files. New to Windows 8, you can choose to permanently delete a file or folder from the Folders window, or you can remove it to the Recycle Bin, where it remains until the bin is emptied or until Windows removes the item to make room for other deleted items.

Delete a File or Folder

Delete a File or Folder

1. Select the file(s) or folder(s) you want to delete.

2. Click the Ribbon's **Home** tab.

3. Click the **Delete** drop-down arrow.

4. Click an option:

   Choose **Recycle** to move the file or folder directly to the Recycle Bin.

   Choose **Permanently delete** to completely remove the file from your computer.

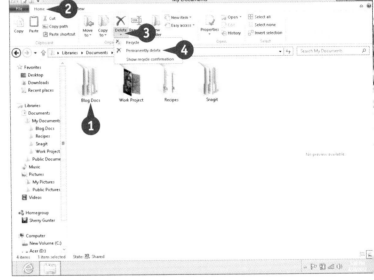

If you selected a permanent deletion, Windows prompts you to confirm the deletion.

5. Click **Yes**.

   The file is deleted from the folder window.

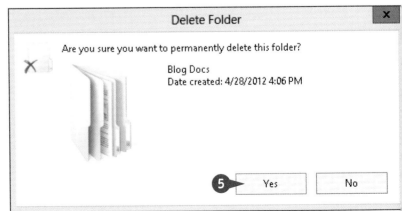

Empty the Recycle Bin

1 Right-click the **Recycle Bin** icon (🗑) on your desktop.

Note: If you cannot see the desktop because you have program and/or folder windows open, click the **Show Desktop** button on the rightmost edge of the taskbar.

2 Click **Empty Recycle Bin**.

Windows prompts you to confirm that you want to permanently delete the files in the Recycle Bin.

3 Click **Yes**.

Windows empties the Recycling Bin.

TIP

How do you restore a deleted item from the Recycle Bin?

You can restore items you deleted through the Recycle Bin by following these steps:

1 Double-click the **Recycle Bin** shortcut icon (🗑) on the desktop.

2 The Recycle Bin window appears. Select the item you want to restore.

3 Click the **Restore the selected items** button in the window's toolbar.

CHAPTER 10

Connecting to a Network

You can connect multiple computers to a network to share files and equipment. Wireless networks are commonplace at home or in the office, as well as out and about when you travel. Wireless networks offer laptop users the most mobility. Using your laptop with a wireless network is the focus of this chapter.

Understanding Computer Networks and Devices

A network consists of two or more connected computers. A network connection can be set up through cables or by using a wireless connection. Networks enable collaboration through sharing of files, equipment (such as printers), and Internet connections. The Internet is an example of a worldwide computer network.

Local and Wide Area Networks

A local area network, called a LAN for short, is useful for computers in close proximity, such as in a home or small office. LAN networks are the most common. A wide area network, or WAN, is a collection of LANs that may be more geographically remote, often connecting through fiber-optic network connections or satellite links. The Internet is an example of a WAN.

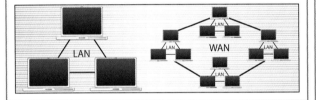

Types of Network Connections

There are several types of networks. Ethernet networks use cables to transmit information; HomePNA networks relay data via existing telephone wires; and powerline networks use existing electrical wires to transmit information. The easiest type of network to set up is a wireless network. It transfers data via radio waves rather than wires or cables.

Network Models

The most common network model in larger organizations is the client/server model. One centralized *server* — a computer that provides services to other computers — handles most of the networking tasks on behalf of the *clients* — other computers plugged into the network. In the peer-to-peer model, each computer on the network handles networking tasks, such as file storage and resource sharing. Most Windows-based computers have built-in peer-to-peer networking functionality.

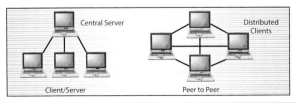

Benefits of Networking

If you have two or more computers and a single printer, scanner, or fax, everybody on the network can share that piece of equipment. You can also share hard drive space, as well as CD and DVD drives, among networked computers. If one computer on a network is connected to the Internet, other users on the network can access that connection. Users can easily exchange files on a network.

Types of Network Devices

You need certain pieces of hardware to set up a network of two or more computers. Some hardware, such as a network interface card, is likely to be included with your computer. You may have to purchase other hardware, such as cables or a router, to create a network. For

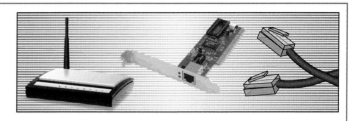

example, with a wired connection, you can use cables to connect computers, or you can use a wireless router to create a wireless broadcast.

Network Interface Card

Just about every laptop has a built-in wireless network interface card — also called a NIC, network adapter, or network card. Most network interface cards take the form of a circuit board installed inside your laptop, but you can also find PC cards that plug into a port

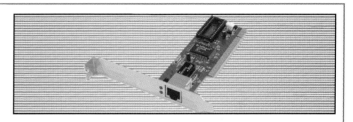

on your laptop that provide NIC functionality. Whether your network card is internal or external, you need the card to connect your laptop to a network.

Routers

A router is an external box that acts as a traffic cop, directing data "traffic" between the connected devices. By connecting a router to a DSL or cable modem, you can allow multiple computers to share one connection to the Internet. A wireless router converts the

Internet connection into a wireless broadcast, and any computers in your house with wireless capabilities can access the Internet.

Administer a Network

In a larger network, you have to spend time administering the network; the more computers connected to it, the more administrative tasks you have, such as overseeing user accounts and passwords, software installations, security, and more. Most

small home networks require little administration and offer considerable convenience. However, even with a single laptop, you are still an administrator of your own network connection and have administrative privileges for controlling how your computer connects.

Understanding Wireless Computing

Most laptops you purchase today have built-in wireless capabilities that allow them to connect through radio waves, just like cell phones and televisions use. Wireless networks abound, and you can connect to the Internet from a variety of places. In many cases, you only have to turn on your computer and let it find the nearest wireless network. Still, it can be helpful to understand just how a wireless network works.

Wireless Technologies

One of the most popular wireless technologies is Wireless Fidelity, or Wi-Fi. Wi-Fi is a high-speed Internet connection without the use of wires and cables. Wi-Fi comes in several versions built on 802.11 standards established by the Institute of Electrical and Electronics Engineers (IEEE). Wi-Fi technology typically operates at a frequency of 2.4 GHz. Wi-Fi certified electronics are guaranteed to work with each other, regardless of brand.

Radio Signals and Transceivers

Wireless technology uses radio signals and a receiver, which in most cases can both transmit and receive radio signals. For example, a computer's wireless adapter translates data into a radio signal and transmits it with an antenna, or receives data and decodes it. A wireless keyboard, on the other hand, is an example of a device that does not have to receive data, so it contains a transmitter for sending a signal to a receiver that you attach to your laptop.

Access Points

A wireless network includes two or more computers connected through radio signals. To go online, these computers connect through an *access point* that establishes the Internet connection. You can set up an access point, known as WAP (wireless access point), using a piece of equipment called a *router* to allow your computers to share an Internet connection.

Wireless Hotspots

A wireless hotspot, such as those you find in cafes, hotels, and airports, allows you to connect your laptop to the Internet as you roam across the country. Typically available in public establishments, hotspots let you connect through a fee-based portal or using an open public network for free. Some require you to authenticate yourself before using the services, whereas others offer security options.

Wireless Ranges

Wireless devices have certain range limitation. Once you move them out of range of a wireless network, access point, or hotspot, they lose their connection. If you attach wireless peripherals, such as a mouse, you can use them only within a couple feet of your computer. In a wireless home network, you may have a range of between 75 and 150 feet, depending on the technology used by the router and your laptop.

Wireless Speeds

Transmission speeds for wireless networks are measured in megabits per second (Mbps). Using more sophisticated wireless technology such as 802.11g or 802.11n provides much faster connection speeds (as much as 300 Mbps with 802.11n), which is useful when downloading data or communicating online.

Wireless Pros and Cons

Wireless networks can offer you freedom from cords and cables. If you buy a new laptop and set up a home wireless network, the laptop is likely to recognize and connect to the network automatically. However, wireless networks can also cause your laptop to disconnect if you move too far away from them, or if there is interference from other electrical devices.

Wireless on Windows 8

Microsoft has significantly optimized the way in which users connect to wireless devices and networks in Windows 8. Broad support for many types of wireless devices and connectivity is built into the new operating system. Microsoft's Homegroup technology makes it easier than ever to share files and devices across multiple computers in a network at home or in the office. Using a Windows Live account, you can synchronize settings and data among computers.

Review a Home-based Network Setup in Windows 8

reating a network on Windows 8 is easy, but you must understand what components you need to make sure you have everything before starting. Thanks to vast improvements in technology and the Windows 8 operating system, establishing a home-based network, particularly a wireless one, is pretty straightforward and easy to accomplish without a lot of headaches. In fact, Windows 8 does a lot of the work for you, recognizing when your wireless router is up and running and ready to connect you to your Internet account.

Determine a Network Setup in Windows 8

The first step for setting up a network at home is determining whether you want a wireless or wired scenario. Although wired can sometimes be more reliable, all the equipment must be in a fixed location when cables are involved. With a wireless scenario, you are not tethered to one place and there is no need to hook up cables and wires. For most users these days, a wireless network makes more sense, particularly for the home or small office.

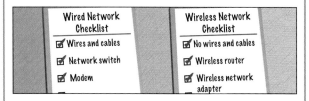

Wired Network Checklist	Wireless Network Checklist
☑ Wires and cables	☑ No wires and cables
☑ Network switch	☑ Wireless router
☑ Modem	☑ Wireless network adapter

Check for Necessary Hardware

A router is key to the network, and a wireless router makes it easy for every computer in the household to connect with each other. Every computer that is part of the Windows 8 network needs a network adapter card to receive and transmit data.

Establish an Internet Account

If you want all the computers on your home-based network to connect to the Internet, you need an account with an Internet Service Provider (ISP). Internet accounts come in different formats and packages, such as DSL, cable, or wireless. Some ISPs even provide the essential connection equipment you need, such as a broadband modem. If you do not yet have an Internet account, you will need one for online access; without one, you can still create a network and share files between computers.

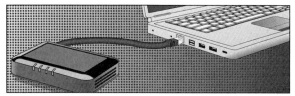

Set Up the Router

Using Windows Connect Now (WCN) technology, Windows 8 can configure your router and laptop to establish a network for you. All you have to do is plug the router in. Lots of WCN-compatible devices are available in the marketplace, including routers and printers. If your router is not WCN-compatible, it probably comes with instructions and a setup CD to help you connect the device.

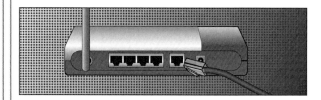

Connect the Router to the Internet

When the time comes to actually connect your network to the Internet, you must follow any special instructions from your ISP to make the proper connection, including using passwords, security keys, and other special settings. If you do not have the information, you may need to contact the provider for help. Depending on your setup, connecting your router to the Internet may be as simple as plugging an Ethernet cable into the router and into the broadband modem.

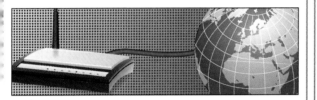

Connect Other Computers and Devices to the Network

The next phase in a home network setup is to connect all the computers and devices to the network. If all your devices, such as a printer, are compatible with Windows, all you have to do is connect them and Windows does the rest. Windows-compatible hardware typically features the Windows logo to the phrase "Compatible with Windows." If a device is not Windows-ready, you can follow the setup instructions that come with the device.

Create a Homegroup and Share Files

A Homegroup is an amazingly simple way to share files on a home-based network. To utilize the technology, all the networked computers need to be running Windows 8 or Windows 7. One computer takes the lead and creates the Homegroup, and others join in using a password. You can decide which data to share. If you are networking with computers using older versions of Windows, you can still share files using the Public folders. Anything in a Public folder is viewable on the network.

New to Windows 8

You can use a Microsoft account, which is your Windows Live ID or your Live e-mail address, to create an account in your Windows 8 network. Doing so allows you to synchronize user settings and data among networked computers. If you do not want to participate with a Live account, you can use a standard local account — a conventional logon account for your computer.

Connect to a Wireless Network

After you set up your wireless network, you can connect to it with your laptop — assuming your laptop has a wireless card installed. If your wireless network is connected to the Internet, you can then access the Internet from your laptop. You may also be able to access files other computers are sharing on the wireless network. In addition to connecting to your own wireless network, you can connect to public wireless networks, often found in airports, hotels, cafes, libraries, and other public places.

Connect to a Wireless Network

1 From the Start screen, swipe from the right edge of the screen or move the mouse pointer to the lower right corner.

Windows displays the Charms bar.

Note: You can also press ⊞+C to display the Charms bar.

2 Click **Settings** (⚙).

3 Click the **Network** icon (📶).

A A list of wireless networks in your area appears.

4 Click the wireless network you want to use to connect.

A Connect button appears.

5 Click **Connect**.

B You can click here to always connect automatically to this network.

If prompted, enter the network password or network security key.

If this is the first time you have connected to this wireless network, Windows prompts you to specify sharing status; make your selection by clicking a response.

C Windows 8 verifies your connection.

TIPS

How do you disconnect from a network?
Redisplay the Networks list as shown in this section and select the network you want to disconnect from; a Disconnect button appears. Just click **Disconnect** to terminate the connection.

How do you connect to a public wireless network?
You connect to a public network the same way as a private one, but you may have to create an account with the public network provider to log on. To find out, launch your web browser after connecting to the network; if an account is required, you are directed to a special web page where you can create one.

Share Files and Folders via Public Folders

Windows 8 offers special folders, called Public folders, which you can use to share files with other users. There are four Public folders: Public Documents, Public Music, Public Pictures, and Public Videos. These folders are subfolders of the main Documents, Music, Pictures, and Videos folders, respectively. When you place an item in a Public folder, any other person with a user account on that same computer can view it by default. In addition, you can make these folders accessible to other users whose computers are connected to your network. To do so, you must enable sharing.

Share Files and Folders via Public Folders

① From the Windows 8 desktop, right-click the **Wireless Networks** icon (▦) in the taskbar's notification area.

Note: You can press ⊞ + D to quickly access the desktop at any time.

② Click **Open Network and Sharing Center**.

The Network and Sharing Center window opens.

③ Click **Change advanced sharing settings** on the left side of the Network and Sharing Center window.

The Advanced Sharing
Settings window opens.

 **4** If necessary, click the ⊗ to
the right of your current
profile to expand it.

5 Click **Turn on file and
printer sharing**.

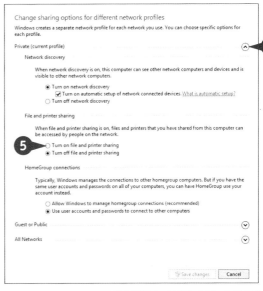

6 Click **Save changes**.

File and printer sharing is
now activated.

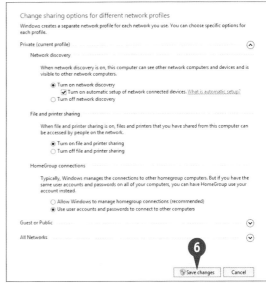

![TIPS]

How do you share a file or folder?
To share a file or folder, simply move
or copy it to the relevant Public folder
to make it accessible to others. When
you do, others can open and work
with the file or folder as if it were
stored on their own PC.

How do you limit what other users can do with shared items?
To limit what others can do with items you share, you can apply
permissions. Permissions are like rules that specify the level of
access a user has. For example, you can limit others to simply
opening files you share, or you can allow them to modify them, or
even create new files in your shared folders. For details, see the
Windows help information.

Set Up a Homegroup

You can share files and folders by creating a Homegroup, which other computers running Windows 8 or Windows 7 on your network can join. When you create or join a group, you specify which of your items you want to share and which should remain private. A Homegroup is a great way to share files in a home-based network or a small office network. To create a Homegroup, your network must be a home network, as opposed to a work or public network.

Set Up a Homegroup

1 From the Windows 8 desktop, right-click the **Wireless Networks** icon ( ) in the taskbar's notification area.

Note: You can press + to quickly access the desktop at any time.

2 Click **Open Network and Sharing Center**.

The Network and Sharing Center window opens.

3 In the Network and Sharing Center window, click **HomeGroup**.

4 Click **Create a homegroup**.

The Create a Homegroup Wizard starts.

Note: You may already have a default Homegroup ready to go. You can always add new ones as needed.

5 Click **Next**.

6 Click the drop-down arrow (▾) next to each library or folder you want to share with the Homegroup and choose **Shared**.

Note: You can also share a printer with your Homegroup.

7 Click **Next**.

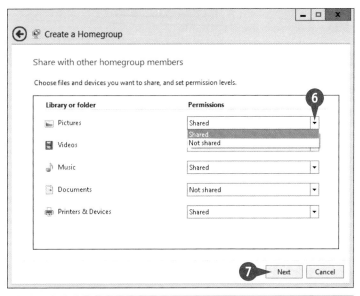

The Create a Homegroup Wizard generates a password.

8 Write down the password.

Note: You need this password to add other PCs to the Homegroup.

9 Click **Finish**.

Windows 7 creates the Homegroup.

Note: To add another Windows PC to the Homegroup, open the PC's Control Panel and click **Choose Homegroup and Sharing Options** under Network and Internet. Click **Join Now** in the screen that appears and follow the on-screen prompts.

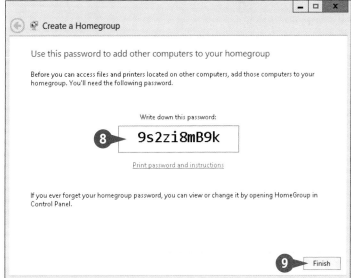

TIP

How do you set up a workgroup?

Only computers running Windows 8 and Windows 7 can join a Homegroup. If computers on your network are running a different version of Windows, you must use a workgroup instead. Windows creates a workgroup and gives it a name when you set up a network; the problem is, the name of the workgroup may be different depending on what version of Windows you are running. To share files and folders among the various computers on the network, you must ensure that the workgroup name listed for each computer is the same. To find out how, view each computer's help information.

Share Within Your Homegroup

When you set up a Homegroup, you specify what top-level folders should be shared. You can also opt to share individual files and subfolders with others. These resources can be shared with Read permissions, enabling others to simply open and view your files. Alternatively, you can share with Read/ Write permissions, enabling others to both view and modify your files. You can share with everyone in your Homegroup or with specific individuals. Shared resources appear under Homegroup in the File Explorer Navigation pane. Of course, if you change your mind, you can always unshare a resource.

Share Within Your Homegroup

1 Open the File Explorer window.

Press ⊞+E to open the Explorer window or launch the File Explorer app from the Start screen.

2 Navigate to the resource you want to share.

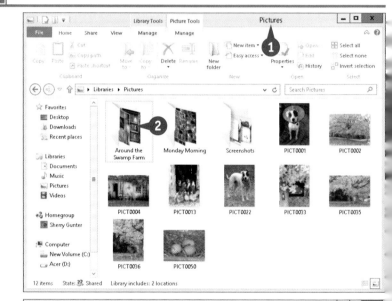

3 Right-click the resource.

4 Click **Share with**.

5 Choose a sharing option.

Ⓐ Click **Homegroup (view)** to share the resource with Read permissions with everyone in your Homegroup.

Ⓑ Click **Homegroup (view and edit)** to share the resource with Read and Write permissions with everyone in your Homegroup.

Ⓒ Click **Specific people** to share the resource with specific people in the Homegroup, as shown here.

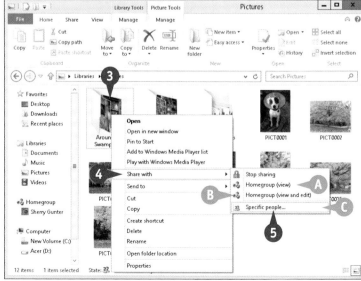

Windows launches the File Sharing Wizard.

6 Type the username of the person with whom you want to share the resource.

7 Click **Add**.

Note: If you are not sure what the person's username is, click the ⊡ to the left of the **Add** button and select the user from the list.

Ⓓ Windows adds the selected user to the list of users with access to the resource.

8 To set the permission level, click the ⊡ next to the current permission and select **Read** or **Read/Write**.

9 Click **Share**.

The resource you selected is shared.

Note: To stop sharing a resource, right-click the resource you want to keep private, click **Share with**, and select **Stop Sharing**.

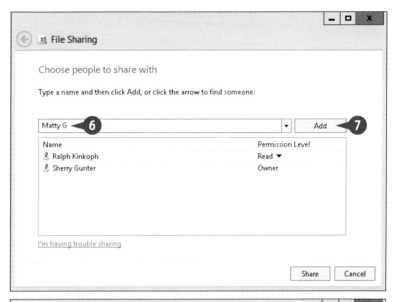

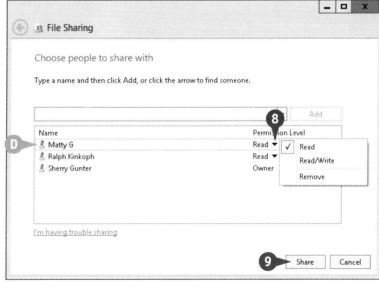

Can you share a printer with a Homegroup?
Yes. You can share a printer with other members of your Homegroup, who then access the printer through the Print dialog box. To do so, connect the printer to any computer in the Homegroup. Then, in that computer's main Control Panel window, click **Choose Homegroup and Sharing Options** under **Network and Internet**. The HomeGroup screen appears; under Libraries and Devices, select **Change what you're sharing**. Change the Printers & Devices setting to **Shared**. Next, set up each computer on the Homegroup to print by opening its Control Panel window, clicking **Choose Homegroup and Sharing Options**, clicking **Install Printer**, and clicking **Install Driver** if prompted.

CHAPTER 11

Exploring the Internet

The Internet and the World Wide Web revolutionized how we communicate, conduct business, socialize, get information, and learn. You can make use of all they have to offer with a few simple-to-learn skills, as demonstrated in this chapter.

The Internet is a massive network of interconnected computers that spans the globe. The enormous amount of information that resides on this network of interconnected computers is the World Wide Web. This linked collection of data, composed of text, images, and other files, is stored on special computers called web servers and is presented in the form of websites. Websites are composed of web pages, which users can access using a special program called a web browser. Each web page on the World Wide Web has its own distinct address, also called a uniform resource locator, or URL.

Web Page

Information on the web is organized into web pages. A web page may include text, images, sounds, and even videos. There are literally billions of web pages on the World Wide Web, centered on almost every imaginable topic. These web pages are created by individuals, businesses, governments, and other organizations.

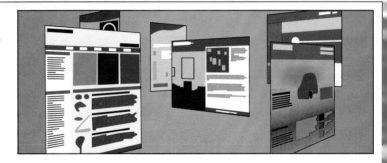

Website

A collection of web pages offered by an individual, business, government, or other organization is called a website. The many types of websites include community sites, corporate sites, e-commerce sites, forums, news sites, personal sites, social-networking sites, web portals, wiki sites, and more. You might visit a website for a variety of reasons, such as to find information about a topic, to socialize, to buy or sell products, to play online games, or to attend a distance-learning class.

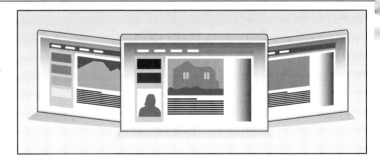

Web Server

Websites are stored on web servers. A web server is simply a computer running special software. Web servers serve web pages to web browsers, enabling users to browse the pages' contents. More powerful web servers can be set up to handle heavy traffic, such as thousands of visitors, at any point in time.

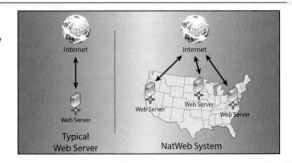

Web Browser

A web browser is a type of software program that you use to find, display, and interact with web pages on the World Wide Web. Examples of web browsers include Apple Safari, Google Chrome, Mozilla Firefox, Opera, and Internet Explorer. (Because Internet Explorer is included with Windows 8, it will be the web browser discussed in this chapter.)

Web Address

Each web page on the World Wide Web has its own unique web address, also called a uniform resource locator, or *URL*. Your web browser uses a web page's web address to locate the page. You can type a web address into the Address bar of your web browser to display the corresponding web page. Many web addresses are fairly intuitive; for example, many company websites include the company's name.

URLs in Detail

A URL usually consists of four parts. The first is the protocol, such as http for Hypertext Transfer Protocol or ftp for File Transfer Protocol. The second part is the host name of the computer where the page is located, such as www, for World Wide Web. The third part of the URL is the domain name, such as Amazon. The fourth part is the top-level domain, such as .com for business, .edu for school, or .gov for government.

Internet Explorer 10

The new Internet Explorer (version 10) comes in two user interfaces: a traditional desktop version and a streamlined, touch-friendly IE app. The IE app does not support browser plug-ins. If you prefer browsing the Internet in the traditional way, with toolbars and Address bar, use the desktop IE. If you are using Windows 8 on a touch-screen laptop or tablet, the IE app may be more to your liking. You can switch back and forth between the two.

Launch the Internet Explorer App Tile

ou can launch the touch-friendly Internet Explorer browser window from the Start screen. The
IE app is a streamlined version of the traditional desktop version found in previous versions of
Windows. The IE app version does not support browser plug-ins and add-ons, but you have more room
on-screen to view web pages without the interference of tools and menu bars. You can navigate pages
using the buttons at the bottom of the window to move back and forth between pages.

Launch the Internet Explorer App Tile

1 From the Start screen, click the
Internet Explorer app tile.

Internet Explorer opens and
displays a default web page.

A Click a link to open another page,
section of a page, window, or
another site.

B Click the navigation buttons (
and) back and forth among
viewed pages.

C Click the **Refresh** button () to
reload a page.

D Click the **Pin** button () to pin
a page to the Start screen.

E Type a URL for a page you want
to visit in the Address bar.

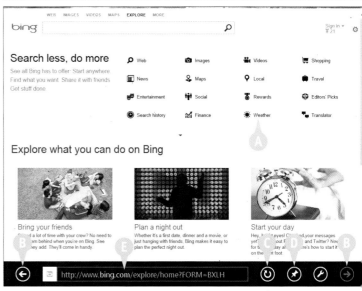

You can launch the traditional Internet Explorer browser window from the Windows 8 desktop. The traditional version features the familiar toolbars, menu bar, and navigation buttons utilized in previous versions of the browser. The desktop IE also fully supports browser plug-ins and add-ons.

Launch the Desktop Internet Explorer Browser

1 From the desktop screen, click the **Internet Explorer** icon ( ).

Internet Explorer opens and displays a default web page.

A Click a link to open another page, section of a page, window, or another site.

B Click the navigation buttons (and) back and forth among viewed pages.

C Click the **Refresh** button ( ) to reload a page.

D Type a URL for a page you want to visit in the Address bar.

E Click the **Home** button ( ) to return to the default home page.

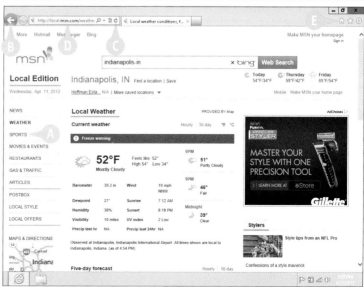

Open a Web Page

Y ou can open a web page in Internet Explorer using a variety of techniques. For example, you can click a link on a web page to open a new page. Or, if you have recently visited the web page, you may be able to access it by right-clicking the Internet Explorer button on the taskbar and choosing the page from the list that appears. Otherwise, if you know the page's web address, you can simply enter it in the Address bar.

Open a Web Page

1 In the Address bar, type the URL of the web page you want to visit.

2 Press **Enter** or click the **Go** button.

Note: As you type a web page's address in the Address bar in the desktop IE, a list of URLs to choose from appears. If the URL for the page you want to visit appears, you can click it in the list.

Note: As you type a web page's address in the Address bar in the IE app, a page listing possible matches appears. If the URL for the page you want to visit appears, you can click it in the list.

Internet Explorer displays the web page whose address you entered.

Search the Web

You will often want to perform searches to locate web pages of interest. You can direct your web browser to a search engine website, such as Google or Yahoo!, or simply use the Search box on the default Bing site that appears when you launch Internet Explorer. When searching, using more specific keywords or phrases yields more targeted results. For example, instead of simply using the keyword *motorcycle*, try *Ducati Monster 1100 S*. To search for a specific phrase, surround it with quotation marks.

Search the Web

1 Type a keyword or phrase in the window's Search box.

A As you type, Internet Explorer displays a list of suggestions of topics that match your text. If the topic you are searching for appears in the list, click it.

2 Press **Enter** or click the **Web Search** button.

B A results page appears with possible matches.

3 Click a link in the search results list.

Keep Track of Your Favorite Pages

oasting billions of web pages, the Internet is without question an incredible resource for information. Its sheer scope, however, can make finding the information you need a chore. When you do find a page that you know you will want to revisit, you can use Internet Explorer to mark it as a favorite, creating a bookmark that takes you back to the page again at a later time. When you mark a page as a favorite, IE saves it in a special list, called the Favorites list. To revisit the page, simply click the page's entry in the list.

Keep Track of Your Favorite Pages

Save a Page as a Favorite

1 Open the page you want to save as a favorite in the desktop Internet Explorer browser window.

2 Click the **Favorites** button (☆).

The Favorites Center opens.

3 Click **Add to favorites**.

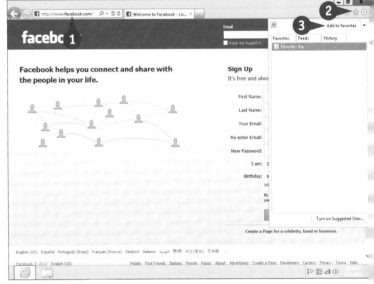

The Add a Favorite dialog box opens.

4 Type a name for the favorite.

Optionally, click ▾ and select the folder in which you want to save the favorite.

5 Click **Add**.

The page is added to your favorites.

Open a Favorite

1 Click the **Favorites** button (⭐).

2 If necessary, click the **Favorites** tab.

If the page you want to visit has been saved in a folder, click the folder.

3 Click the page you want to visit.

The page opens and the Favorites Center closes.

Note: To keep the Favorites Center open, click the **Pin the Favorites Center** button (Favorites) before you click the site you want to visit.

Note: To delete a favorite, right-click it in the Favorites list and click **Delete** in the menu that appears. Internet Explorer prompts you to confirm the deletion; click **Yes**.

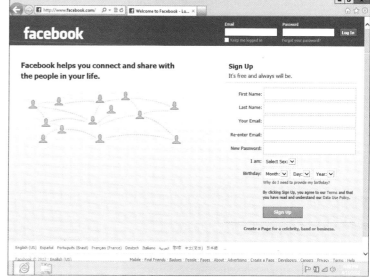

TIP

How do you pin a favorite page?

If the page you want to save as a favorite is one you access on a daily basis, you might prefer to pin it to the Start screen. Start by navigating to the page using the Internet Explorer app on the Start screen (press 🪟 to display the Start screen). Click the **Pin** button (🔘) to pin the web page as a tile on the Start screen. The next time you want to visit the page, simply click its tile.

Change Your Home Page

If you frequently visit a particular web page, such as a news site, you can direct Internet Explorer to open that page by default anytime you launch the program or click the browser's Home button. This saves you the trouble of typing the site's URL in the Address bar or selecting the site from your Favorites list. You can change the default home page through the Windows 8 Control Panel.

Change Your Home Page

1 From the desktop Internet Explorer window, click the **Tools** button ( ).

2 Click **Internet options**.

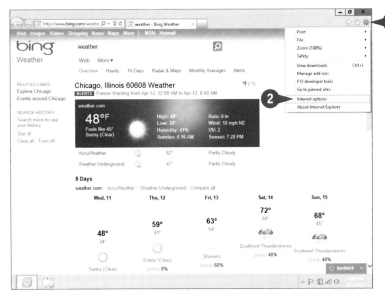

The Internet Options dialog box appears.

3 Type the address (URL) of the page you want to use as your home page.

4 Click **OK**.

The Internet Options dialog box closes.

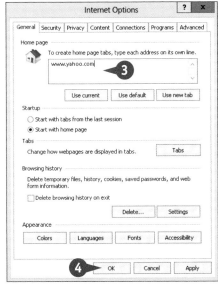

5 Click the **Home** button (⌂).

Internet Explorer displays the new home page.

TIP

What is the History list?

The History list keeps track of sites you have visited. One way to view your History list is to click the Favorites button (☆) and click the History tab in the Favorites Center box. A list of pages you have visited, sorted by date, appears. Simply click a page in the list to open it in the browser window.

CHAPTER 12

Communicating Online

With all the various ways to communicate online — e-mail, messaging, video chat, social networking sites — keeping in touch is a prevailing reason for purchasing a laptop. You can find an array of e-mail services and programs, including Windows Live Mail and the new Windows 8 Mail app. This chapter looks at ways you can use your laptop to communicate with others.

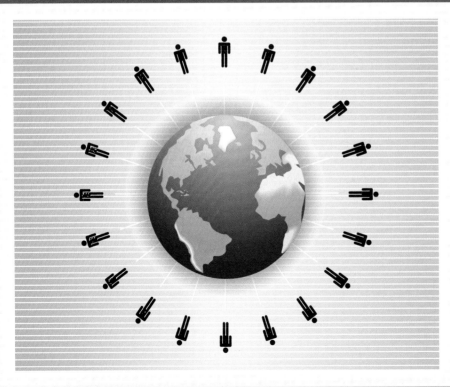

Understanding E-Mail

E-mail, short for *electronic mail*, has revolutionized the way that people communicate today. E-mail delivers messages and files almost instantly around the world. Anybody who can access the Internet can use e-mail. You can send e-mail anytime, whereas regular mail, commonly referred to as "snail mail" these days, can only be sent and delivered at certain times. In addition, e-mail is virtually free. Before you jump into e-mailing tasks with Windows 8, take a few moments and familiarize yourself with how e-mail works and what you need to send and receive messages using your laptop.

How E-Mail Works

E-mail messages do not go directly from one computer to another; rather, they pass through a series of e-mail *servers* — computer programs that provide services to other computers. Many e-mail providers utilize dedicated computers to act solely as servers. An e-mail message is sent through your Internet connection using your service provider's outgoing mail server. The message is then routed and received by the recipient's incoming mail server. When the recipient logs on to check messages, the e-mail is delivered.

E-Mail Providers

You can sign up for e-mail in several different ways. Many e-mail service providers offer free e-mail; others provide e-mail and other features for a fee. Web-based services allow you to access e-mail using a web browser. POP e-mail services store your messages on a remote server which you can connect to using an e-mail program. IMAP services offer greater control over how messages are handled and synchronized. Gmail, Hotmail, and Yahoo! Mail are examples of e-mail service providers.

Windows Live E-Mail

Windows Live is a collection of services and software from Microsoft. Windows Live includes Mail, Messenger, and SkyDrive, just to name a few of the applications. With a free Windows Live account, you can send and receive e-mail messages on your laptop. You can also set up multiple e-mail accounts. To access the website, use Internet Explorer to visit www.windowslive.com. Sign up for a new Windows Live ID to access Hotmail, Messenger, and Xbox Live, among other features.

E-Mail Programs

E-mail programs, also called e-mail *clients* or *readers*, are standalone programs you can install on your laptop to help you access and manage messages. Unlike web-based e-mail services which you access using a browser, e-mail programs open as applications on your computer. Popular e-mail programs include Microsoft Outlook, Pegasus Mail, Mozilla's Thunderbird, and IBM Lotus Notes. The new Windows 8 Mail app is also an example of an e-mail program; learn more about it later in this chapter.

E-Mail Features

E-mail programs typically include address books for storing contact information, such as names and e-mail addresses. E-mail programs also typically offer some design features for formatting outgoing messages, such as adding electronic signatures, HTML coding, and more. Just about every e-mail program offers a folder system for organizing and retrieving received e-mail messages. In addition, many programs provide filters to flag junk mail messages, prevent spam, and create rules for controlling how messages are treated.

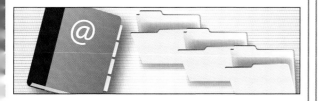

Organizing E-Mail

Just about every e-mail program uses a main Inbox for receiving incoming messages. The Inbox folder is just one of several folders you can use to keep your messages organized. You can create additional folders and move messages around as needed. By default, most programs also have a Sent folder where every message you send is saved, a Draft folder where you can store drafts, and a Delete folder for deleted e-mail.

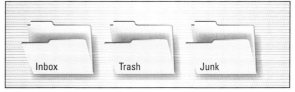

E-Mail Storage

Your e-mail service provider allocates a certain amount of storage on its server for e-mail messages. You may need to pay an additional fee for more storage space. Some free e-mail services, such as Google Mail, offer as much as 10GB of storage with your account. If you clean out old e-mail on a regular basis, you are not likely to run out of storage.

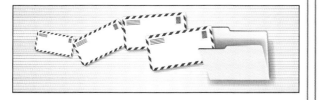

E-Mail Safety

When you use e-mail, you need to be aware of certain security issues, most of which rely on your own behavior to maintain your safety. *Spam* is e-mail sent out to thousands of accounts, and some spam may contain computer viruses. Look out for *phishing* e-mails, which are financial scams that may encourage you to give out credit card or bank account numbers, which are then used to steal from you. Learn more about safety issues in Chapter 17.

Using the Mail App

New to Windows 8, you can use the Mail app to access your e-mail accounts. You can view and respond to messages, compose and send new messages, forward messages, and delete messages you no longer want clogging up your Inbox. Like the other apps on the Windows 8 Start screen, you can launch Mail with a click of its tile. You can use Mail to connect to multiple e-mail accounts at home or at work. Mail is powered by Windows Live Mail, an online e-mail service you can sign up and use for free.

Using the Mail App

① From the Start screen, click the **Mail** app tile.

The Mail app launches.

Note: If this is your first time using the app, you may be prompted to enter your e-mail address or set up an account so Mail can connect you.

② Click the **Inbox**.

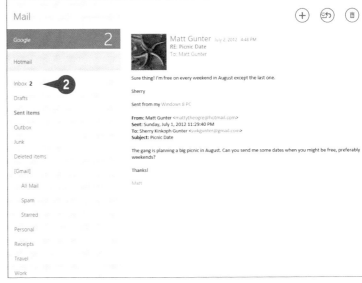

A Mail lists your messages.

3 Click a message to view it.

B Swipe the bottom of the screen, or press ⊞+Z to display the App bar for Mail.

C To check for new messages, click the **Sync** button (⟳).

D Click the **New** button (⊞) to compose a new message.

E Click the **Respond** button (↩) to reply to the message.

F Click the **Delete** button (🗑) to delete the message.

<h1>TIPS</h1>

How do I find an e-mail service?

You can find lots of free e-mail services on the web, including Windows Live Mail, Hotmail, and Google. To use Windows 8 Mail, you must sign up with an Internet service provider (ISP) and set up an e-mail address either with that provider or with some other source. You must also set up your account within Mail using the username and password you established with your e-mail provider. You can use your own e-mail address to create a Windows Live ID to use in Mail.

Do I have to use the Mail app as my e-mail program?

No. If you use a special software program for your e-mail reader, you can install it in Windows 8 (if it is compatible) and use it to connect to your e-mail server. If you use a web-based e-mail service, you can use the Internet Explorer web browser to navigate to the site and check your messages. Learn more about using Internet Explorer in Chapter 11.

Add an Account to the Mail App

You can add multiple e-mail accounts to the Mail app. For example, you might have accounts with Microsoft Exchange and Google, as well as Hotmail. You can use the Mail app to check messages from all three. Windows 8 Mail enables you to combine accounts and access them all at the same time from one convenient spot. All you need to do is point Windows 8 to the servers you use, via your e-mail addresses and account passwords, and Mail handles the synchronizing, sending, and receiving.

Add an Account to the Mail App

1 With the Mail app open, swipe the right side of the screen or point the mouse in the lower right corner to display the Charms bar.

Note: You can also press 🪟+🇨 to display the Charms bar.

2 Click the **Settings** charm (⚙).

3 Click **Accounts**.

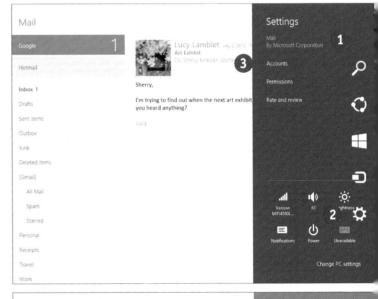

The Accounts screen opens.

4 Click **Add an account**.

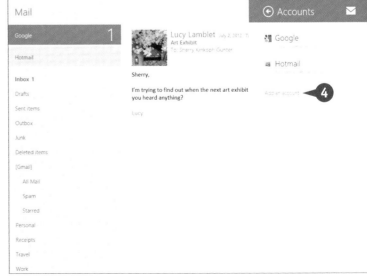

5 Click the type of account you want to add.

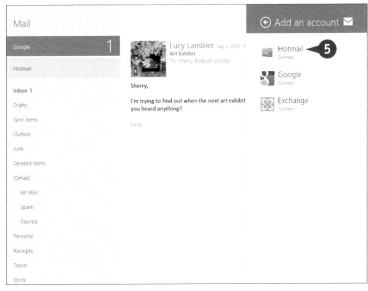

6 Type the e-mail address for the account.

7 Type the password for the account.

8 Click **Connect**.

Mail makes the connection and displays a message box declaring its success.

Note: If Mail cannot connect to your account, you can try again later, or you may need to check with your e-mail service for more details.

TIPS

What sort of features does the Mail app offer?
You can use the Mail app just like any other e-mail reader program. You can perform the typical e-mailing tasks (composing, sending, forwarding, carbon copies, and so on), plus you can find formatting tools on the App bar you can use to make your messages look good. You can also use the **Share** charm (◉) on the Charms bar to share photos, documents, and videos from other Windows 8 apps via e-mail.

How can I turn on the Mail app's notifications to make a "live" tile?
Live tile technology displays app notifications on the app's tile out on the Start screen. In the case of Mail, the Mail tile shows you how many unread e-mails await you, as well as your most recent message. This information also appears on the Lock screen, much like on the Windows Phone counterpart. To turn on the Mail app tile, open the PC settings options, click the **Notifications** category, and turn on the notifications for Mail.

Send an E-Mail with the Mail App

You can use the Mail app to compose and send a new e-mail message. When composing a message, you must enter the e-mail address of the recipient. Using the left pane of the message window, you can address a message to a single person, or to multiple recipients. You can also use the carbon copy field (Cc) to send a copy to a third-party recipient. The right pane is where you type a subject heading and message text. You can use the formatting tools that appear on the App bar to add formatting or a priority status.

Send an E-Mail with the Mail App

1 Display the Inbox for the account you want to use.

2 Click the **New** button (⊕).

Mail opens an empty message window.

3 Click in the **To** field and type the recipient's e-mail address.

Optionally, repeat Step **3** to add more recipients to the To field, separating each with a semicolon.

A To copy the message to another person, click in the Cc field and type the recipient's e-mail address.

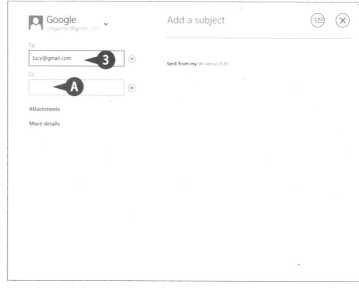

④ Click in the **Subject** field and type a subject for your message.

⑤ Click below the subject area and type your message.

Ⓑ Optionally, you can use the formatting tools on the App bar to add formatting to your message text.

Note: You can press ⊞+Z to quickly display the App bar.

Ⓒ You can click **More Details** to view a pop-up menu for setting a priority level for the message or adding a blind carbon copy to another recipient.

⑥ Click **Send** (🖂).

Mail sends the message and places a copy in the Sent Items folder.

q

TIPS

Can I use Windows Live Mail rather than the Mail App?
Yes. If you sign up for an account with Windows Live Mail, you can use Internet Explorer and the Windows Live website to send and receive e-mail and instant messages. The Mail app works alongside Windows Live Mail to help you manage your e-mailing tasks.

Is etiquette a concern with e-mail?
Yes. Practicing good etiquette when communicating online is always a good idea. Remember, humor and sarcasm do not always translate digitally; if people cannot see your facial expressions, they may not know you are joking. Also, it is good practice to keep things short. Your subject line and the body of your message should be clear, concise, and to the point.

Reply to a Message

It is not unusual to receive a message for which you want to send a reply. With the Mail app, you can quickly and easily reply to any message you receive. You can use the same message window to compose a reply, accessing the App bar for formatting tools. Sometimes, you will receive messages that were also sent to others. If the message to which you are replying was sent to multiple people, you can reply to the sender only; alternatively, you can choose to reply to the sender as well as to all the other recipients.

Reply to a Message

1 View the message to which you want to reply.

2 To reply to the sender only, click **Respond** (🖂).

3 Click **Reply**.

Ⓐ Alternatively, to reply to the sender and to all other recipients of the original message, click **Reply all**.

A new message window opens with the original message text.

Ⓑ The original subject is preceded with RE: which stands for reply.

Ⓒ The e-mail address of the original sender (and, if you clicked **Reply all**, the e-mail addresses of the other recipients of the original message) appears here.

4 Type your reply.

5 Click **Send** (🖂).

Mail sends your reply.

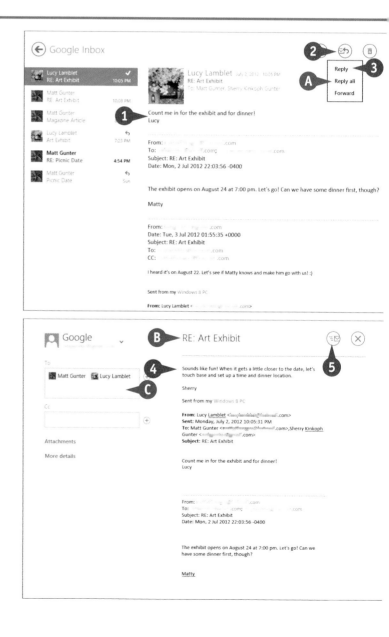

Forward a Message

Often, you will receive e-mail messages that you want to forward to others. For example, you might receive a positive e-mail message from your supervisor that you feel should be shared with other members of your team. Or you might receive an amusing e-mail message from a friend that you want to forward to a mutual acquaintance. Windows Mail makes it easy to forward e-mail messages. You can also add your own text to the forwarded message if desired.

Forward a Message

1 Open the message you want to forward.

2 To reply to the sender only, click **Respond** (⟲).

3 Click **Forward**.

A new message window opens with the original message text.

Ⓐ The original subject is preceded with FW.

4 Click in the **To** field and type the recipient's e-mail address.

5 Type any text you want to add to the forwarded message.

6 Click **Send** (⟳).

Mail forwards the message.

Work with File Attachments

There may be times when you want to send attachments in your e-mail messages — that is, files you have saved on your computer's hard drive. For example, you might want to e-mail a document containing your resume to apply for a job, or you might want to e-mail a PowerPoint presentation to a co-worker for his or her review. When the recipient receives your message containing the attachment, that person can open and view the attached file on his or her computer (with the necessary software installed to read the file). File attachments are noted with a paper clip icon.

Work with File Attachments

Add a File Attachment

1. In a new message window, address and compose your message.

2. Click the **Attachments** button (🔘) on the App bar.

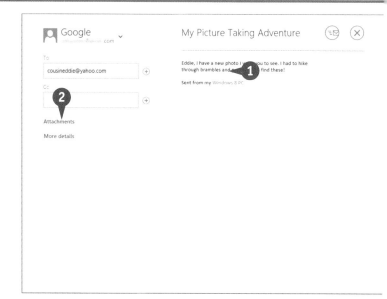

3. Navigate to the file you want to attach and select it.

4. Click **Attach**.

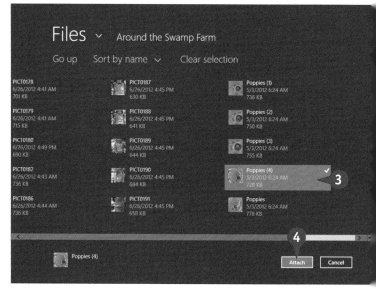

Ⓐ Mail attaches the file to the message.

5 Click **Send** (⊞).

Mail sends the message and file attachment.

Open a File Attachment

1 Open the message containing the attachment file.

2 Click the attachment.

Windows opens the necessary software required to read the file.

Note: You can save a file attachment to a designated folder. Right-click the attachment and specify a folder.

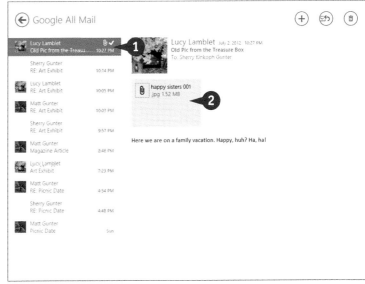

TIP

What do I do if my file attachment is really large?
You can compress a file to make it easier to send and receive over the Internet. Windows 8 has a preinstalled compression, or zipping, program you can use. Using File Explorer, navigate to the file, right-click it, then choose **Send to** and **Compressed (zipped) folder**. You can learn more about using File Explorer and compressing files in Chapter 9.

Save a Message as a Draft

Suppose you are writing an important e-mail message — for example, a lengthy e-mail about a legal matter or perhaps a personal e-mail sharing the details of a recent vacation with friends — but you do not have time to finish it during the current session. If so, you can save the message as a draft. Messages saved in this manner are stored in the Drafts folder, one of several predefined folders in the Mail app. When you are ready to work on the e-mail again, you can access it from the Drafts folder.

Save a Message as a Draft

1 In a new message window, click **Delete** (🗑).

2 Click **Save draft**.

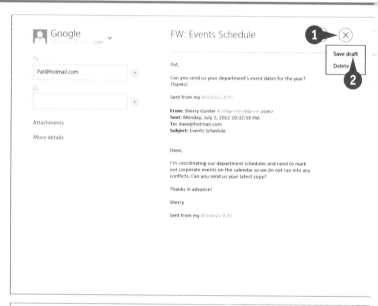

A When you are ready to work on the message again, open the **Drafts** folder.

3 Click the message in the Drafts folder to open it and work on it again.

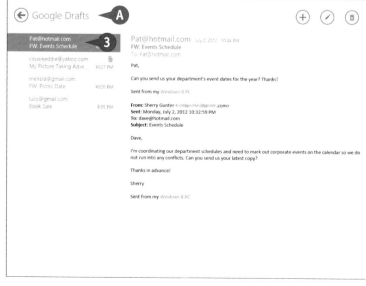

Move a Message to a Folder

You can move messages in Mail to folders to help you keep them organized. For example, suppose you frequently receive e-mail messages from a friend. You can put them in the Personal folder for safekeeping. Or perhaps you receive a large number of messages regarding a project you are working on. If so, you can store those messages in the Word folder. To display your account's Folders list, open the App bar to find the Folders button.

Move a Message to a Folder

1 From the Inbox, click the message you want to move.

2 Swipe the bottom of the screen or press ⊞+Z to display the App bar.

3 Click the **Move** button (🖳).

4 Click a folder from the list.

Mail moves the message.

Using the People App

You can use the People app to build a contacts list of people you know or work with the most. Considered a contacts management app, the People app places all your contacts from various sources into one convenient place. You can automatically add people from other online sources, such as Twitter, Facebook, or LinkedIn. You can also add dynamic information, such as photos, latest status postings, tweets, and more. The People app offers three unique view modes to assess information. You can choose to view the latest updates, your own postings, or a list of everyone.

Using the People App

Launch People

1 From the Start screen, click the **People** app tile.

The People app launches.

A The All view is the primary view; you can scroll through to view an alphabetized list of contacts.

B You can connect to a variety of account types to gather contact information; click an account to get started.

C To view individual contact data, click a contact.

D Click **What's new** to view the latest postings from your contacts.

E Click **Me** to view your own postings.

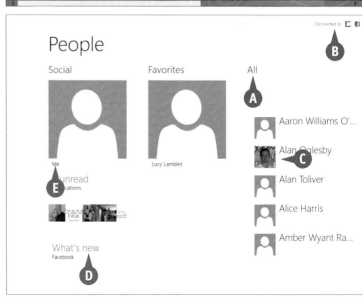

Add a Contact

1 Swipe the bottom of the screen, or press 🪟+Z to display the App bar.

2 Click **New** (⊕).

People opens a New Contact form.

3 Fill out the contact information, as needed.

4 Click **Save** (💾).

The contact is added to your list.

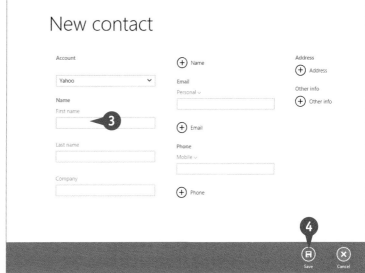

TIP

How do I edit existing contacts?
You can easily edit an existing contact, whether it is a contact from another source or one you have added manually. From the All view mode, click the contact you want to edit. Swipe the bottom of the screen or press 🪟+Z to display the App bar. Click the **Edit** button (✏️) and the contact form opens. You can make changes to the various fields as needed.

Using the Messaging App

You can use instant messaging as another form of online communication with your laptop. Using text-based messages, called IMs for short, you can send and receive real-time messages over the Internet through the new Messaging app. Online conversations are displayed as a scrolling dialog, called a *thread*. Messaging requires you to be logged on at the same time as the person you are messaging. The Messaging app connects you to online messaging sources on Facebook and Windows Live Messenger, so you can carry on live chats with your friends, family, and co-workers.

Using the Messaging App

1 From the Start screen, click the **Messaging** app tile.

The Messaging app launches.

Ⓐ Message threads appear in the left panel.

Ⓑ Dialog appears as conversational balloons.

Ⓒ Type new message text here and press Enter.

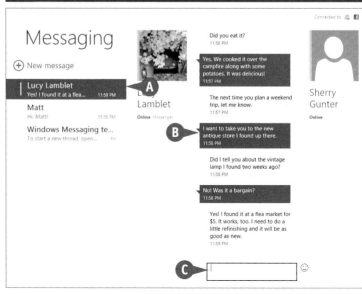

2 To start a thread, click New message.

D To invite someone to message, display the App bar and click Invite.

Note: Swipe the bottom of the screen, or press [⊞]+[Z] to display the App bar for Messaging.

3 Click a person.

4 Click **Choose**.

Messenger now displays the message thread.

TIP

How do I use visual tools in my messages?
Windows Live Messenger includes several visual tools for expressing yourself during your IM sessions. For example, you can include *emoticons* in your messages — small icons that convey a facial expression or other idea. This can help ensure that the true meaning of your message is conveyed.

Explore Video Conferencing

If your laptop has a built-in web camera, or if you add one as an external device, you can participate in video conferencing. Along with a microphone and speakers, video conferencing is much like a phone call, but audio and video picture are involved. Using Voice Over Internet Protocol, or VOIP, you can make video phone calls through the Internet to connect people anywhere on the planet. Also called *video chat* or *video calling*, there are numerous tools available to help you connect via video feed, including the popular Skype software.

Video Connection Benefits

Video conferencing started out as a business-oriented venture, helping to connect colleagues and departments across great distances. Online meetings offer a great deal of collaboration without all the travel costs. With improvements in broadband performance, it did not take long for the technology to find its way into other areas, such as college classrooms online, video surveillance, video chatting, and person-to-person video connections, such as grandparents calling grandchildren.

What is VOIP?

VOIP, or Voice Over Internet Protocol, is a technology that allows you to make calls across the Internet through electronic packets of data that contain your digitized voice. Depending on the quality of the connection, the images may lag in broadcast time, but the transmission occurs in real time. You can also use VOIP services and a web camera (webcam) to exchange video images with someone during a call. Also called *Internet telephony*, services that transport video signals are becoming very popular.

Services and Providers

You can find a variety of services and providers offering video calls on the Internet, many for free. Internet phone calls, for example, bypass the traditional phone company and utilize the Internet technology to make the connection. VOIP providers like Vonage have been around for awhile now. You can find many others with a quick search on the web. You can use your own Internet service provider to utilize video-calling tools found with Windows Live Messenger and Skype.

Video Call Programs

Lots of software is available for video calls and conferencing, some with a business focus, others geared more toward personal use. Some even offer the services for free. For example, Windows Live Messenger offers a webcam feature through its online messaging tool. Skype is another popular software program for making video calls, offering both a free and a premium service. Mac users can take advantage of iChat or FaceTime. Other examples include ooVoo, Google Talk, GoToMeeting, SightSpeed, and Tokbox.

Equipment Requirements

To participate in video chat or video calls, you need a web camera, a microphone, speakers, and an Internet connection. Most laptops sold today have built-in web cameras. You can also add on web cameras as peripheral devices. Built-in microphones and speakers are also standard features in laptops. The only missing puzzle is choosing an Internet connection. You need to set up video calling first before making an attempt. Setup usually involves turning on some video conferencing tools.

Calling Features

In addition to helping you establish video call connections, video conferencing software can also offer additional features you may find attractive. For example, ooVoo offers a variety of features including video call recording, desktop sharing, text chat, and high-definition video streaming. With Skype, you can add on file transfer and up to 12-way video calls. Many applications offer the basics for free and additional features for a price upgrade. Do your research before choosing one particular program over another.

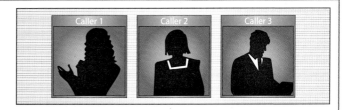

Video Calls with Windows Live Messenger

Windows Live Messenger is one of several tools included in Windows Live Essentials — free programs that offer integrated e-mailing, instant messaging, photo sharing, online storage, and blogging. Within the instant messaging feature is a tool you can use for video chat. Following the setup instructions on the Windows Live Messenger web page, you can set up your webcam and microphone and start chatting immediately.

Video Calls with Skype

Skype, now owned by Microsoft, offers a free video calling service that allows computer users to chat face-to-face. You can talk to anyone in the world who also uses a Skype connection. For example, you can use Skype to video chat with a family member in another country. You can also use Skype in the office to collaborate on projects even if the participants are miles apart. You can download Skype on your laptop from the Skype website: http://www.skype.com. Skype also offers mobile and landline calling, for a fee.

CHAPTER 13

Working with Digital Images

Windows 8 offers you several ways to work with digital images, including the Pictures folder, Windows Photo Viewer, and Paint. You can also download and install Windows Live Photo Gallery, a free program available from the Windows Live Web site. While the other methods are great for viewing photos, Windows Live Photo Gallery offers additional editing features.

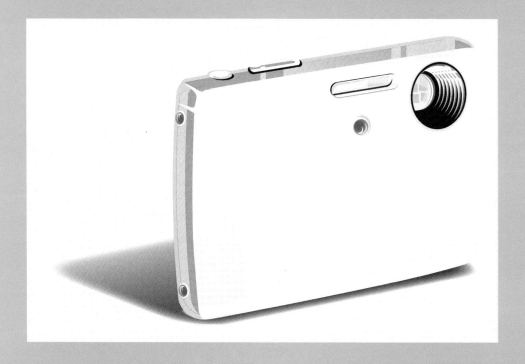

View Photos with the Photos App

You can use the Photos app on the Start screen to view digital image files on your laptop. Whether you call them photos, images, or pictures, if they utilize a common digital image format, you can view them in the Photos app. You can use the app to view photos stored in your Pictures library, or you can view online content from your SkyDrive folders, Facebook, or Flickr. The Photos app displays images much like a slide show, allowing you to peruse from one to the next using navigation buttons.

View Photos with the Photos App

1 From the Start screen, click the **Photo** app tile.

Note: To learn more about uploading photos from a camera, see the section "Import Pictures from a Camera" later in this chapter.

Windows opens the app.

2 Click the location containing the files you want to view.

Note: The first time you use the app, you may need to establish connections to online data, such as Facebook and Flickr photos, and photos stored on SkyDrive.

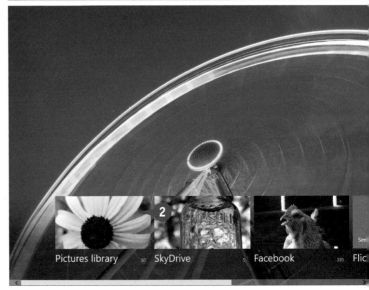

The Photos app displays the contents.

If more than one photo appears, you can scroll through the photos using the scroll bar.

3 To view a single photo, click the photo.

The photo opens in a full window.

Ⓐ Click the navigation arrows to view other photos in the folder.

Ⓑ Click here to return to the main Photos app screen.

TIP

Why does the Photos app open when I double-click a photo in File Explorer?
Windows 8 assigns the Photos app as the default viewer for image files. Any time you double-click an image file, the default viewer opens automatically so you can see the image. You can choose another viewer as your default if you prefer. For example, you may want to use Windows Live Photo Gallery or another image-based program you have installed. To change the default viewer, open File Explorer and follow these steps:

1 Right-click an image file.

2 Click **Open with**.

3 Click **Choose default program**.

4 Select a program from the list.

View Photos in the Pictures Library

Windows 8 makes it easy to store and view photos in the Pictures library. The Pictures library is one of four default library folders available to help you organize and manage files on your laptop; you can view the library using File Explorer. You can quickly browse your photos as thumbnails — small images — or larger images in the Preview pane. When you select an image in File Explorer, the Ribbon's Manage tab offers tools for rotating photos, viewing folder contents as a slide show, or turning a photo into a desktop background.

View Photos in the Pictures Library

1 Open File Explorer. From the Start screen, click the **File Explorer** app. From the desktop, click the **File Explorer** icon ( ).

File Explorer opens with the main libraries listed.

2 Click **Pictures**.

Note: To learn more about using File Explorer, see Chapter 9.

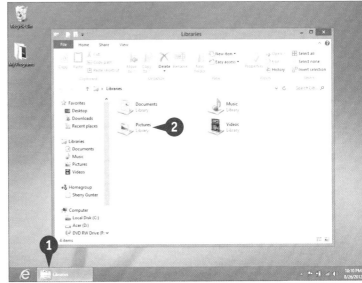

A File Explorer folder window opens, displaying the contents of the Pictures library.

3 Click the file you want to view.

Ⓐ Make sure the Preview pane is selected in the View tab.

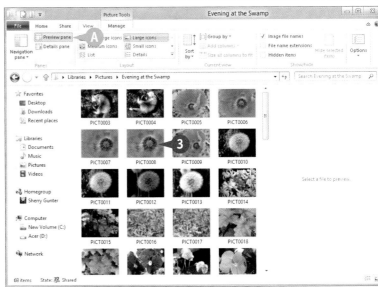

B The Preview pane displays the photo.

C Click the **Manage** tab to view tools for working with the selected photo.

D To rotate the photo, click a rotation button (or).

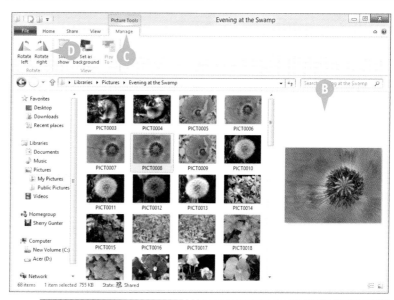

E To view the entire folder as a slide show, click the **Slide show** button ( ).

F To turn the selected photo into your desktop background, click the **Set as background** button ( ).

G To open the selected file with another viewer app, right-click the photo and choose **Open with**, then select a viewer.

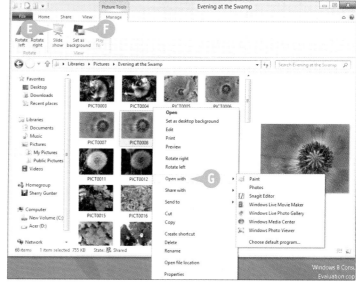

TIPS

How do I organize photos in the Pictures library?

You can manage and organize photos into subfolders in the Pictures library. For example, you might place all your vacation pictures in a folder and view them all as a slide show. Or you might create a folder for pictures you want to print. See Chapter 9 to learn more about adding folders.

How do I turn a photo into a desktop background?

If you select a photo and click the **Set as background** button ( ) on the Ribbon's Manage tab, Windows immediately replaces the current desktop background with the new photo. If you want to return to the previous background, right-click an empty area of the desktop and click **Personalize**. Choose another background from the Desktop Background options.

View Photos with Windows Photo Viewer

Viewer apps are designed especially for viewing specific types of data, such as Windows Media Player for video and sound files. You can use the Windows Photo Viewer app to view digital image files. Windows Photo Viewer is a built-in app, part of the Windows 8 desktop. You can access the app through File Explorer. Unlike the Explorer window, Photo Viewer lets you view much larger photo sizes, including full size. In addition, the viewer's menus offer tools for ordering prints, e-mailing pictures, and burning images to a disc.

View Photos with Windows Photo Viewer

1 From File Explorer, right-click the photo you want to view.

2 Click **Open with**.

3 Click **Windows Photo Viewer**.

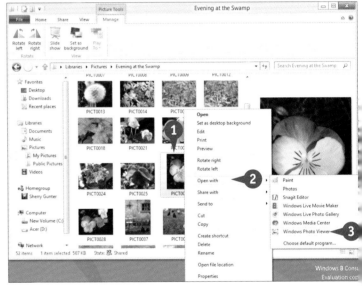

Windows opens the app.

A You can find printing, e-mailing, and disc-burning options on the menu bar.

B Click the navigation buttons (⏮ and ⏭) to view the previous or next photo in the folder.

C Click the **Play Slide Show** button (🖼) to view the folder's contents as a full-screen slide show.

D Click the **Magnifier** button (🔎) to zoom in and out.

E To rotate a sideways photo, click the Rotate Left (↺) or Rotate Right (↻) buttons.

F Click the **Actual Size** button (⊕) to view the photo at its actual size.

G Click the **Fit to Window** button (⊞) to change the size back again.

H To delete a photo from the library, click the **Delete** button (✕).

4 Click the **Close** button (✕) to exit the viewer window and return to File Explorer.

TIPS

How do I e-mail a photo?

To e-mail the displayed photo in Windows Photo Viewer, just click the **E-mail** command on the menu bar and choose a picture size. Click the **Attach** button and your default e-mail program opens, where you can add an e-mail address, compose a message, and send the photo as a file attachment.

How do I order prints online?

Windows Photo Viewer includes a feature to help you order prints of your photos. Click the **Print** command on the menu bar and then click **Order Prints**. This opens the Order Prints dialog box, which connects to the Internet and displays links to printing services. Click a link to visit the corresponding site presenting instructions for ordering prints.

Play a Slide Show Using Windows Photo Viewer

Y ou can use Windows Photo Viewer to play a slide show of all the photos in a specified folder. A slide show displays your photos as full-size pictures filling up the entire screen. Windows Photo Viewer automatically advances from one slide to the next, or you can use your keypad's navigation buttons to move back and forth between slides. You can right-click a slide to display playback controls, such as Pause or Loop. You can also adjust the slide show speed. To stop the show at any time, press the Esc key.

Play a Slide Show Using Windows Photo Viewer

1 In File Explorer, open the folder containing the photos you want to view.

2 Click the **Manage** tab on the Ribbon.

3 Click the **Slide show** button ( ).

Windows Photo Viewer displays the first slide.

Ⓐ The slide show advances automatically; however, you can click on-screen to move to the next slide manually.

Ⓑ To view playback options, right-click a slide.

4 To stop a slide show, press Esc.

230

Explore Windows Live Photo Gallery

You can use Windows Live Photo Gallery to view and edit photos. Part of the Windows Live suite of programs, Photo Gallery is a photo management app you can download and install for free. Use your browser to search for the Windows Live website and download the app. When you install it, Windows adds a tile to the Start screen; when you open Photo Gallery the first time, you may be prompted to sign in to the Windows Live site. Though similar in appearance to the Pictures folder window, Photo Gallery offers far more features and tools.

Ⓐ Navigation Pane

Use the Navigation pane to specify what photos should be shown.

Ⓑ File List

Photos in the selected folder, taken on the specified date, or containing the people tags or descriptive tags you select, appear here.

Ⓒ Ribbon

The Windows Live Photo Gallery Ribbon offers access to tools for fixing your photos, organizing them, publishing them, e-mailing them, and more.

Ⓓ Find Tab

To locate a photo with a certain tag or name or of a specific type, enter your criteria in the Search tab.

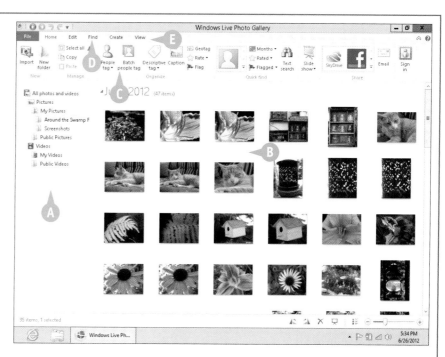

Ⓔ View Tab

Access view options here, including options for rotating photos and zooming.

Import Pictures from a Camera

To view and edit your digital photos on your laptop, you must first import them from the digital camera you used to capture them. One way to make the images stored on your camera's memory card accessible to your laptop for import is to use a cable to connect the camera directly to your computer. Another method is to remove the memory card from the camera, insert it into a memory-card reader, and then plug the memory-card reader into your PC's USB port. Alternatively, if your laptop boasts a built-in memory-card reader, simply insert the memory card into it.

Import Pictures from a Camera

1 Insert your memory card or connect your camera to your laptop.

Note: Windows may recognize your memory card as soon as you plug it in and display the prompt box shown in step **6**. Skip these initial steps to import your photos.

2 In Windows Live Photo Gallery, click **File**.

3 Click **Import photos and videos**.

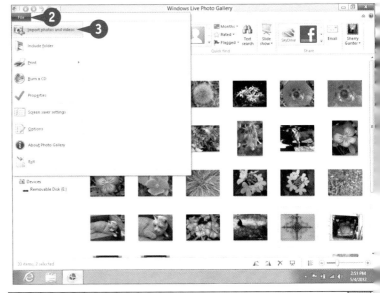

The Import Photos and Videos Wizard starts.

4 Click the icon for your camera or memory card.

5 Click **Import**.

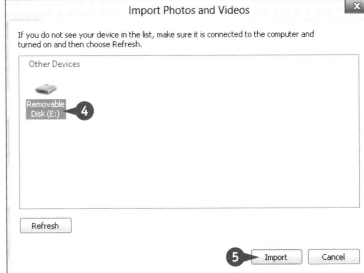

The Import Photos and Videos Wizard detects any image or video files on your camera or memory card.

6 Click the **Review, organize, and group items to import** option button (⊙).

7 Click **Next**.

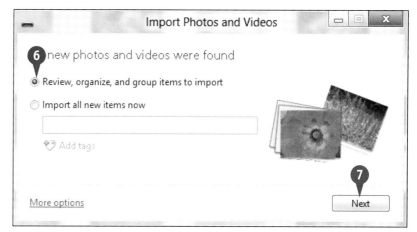

8 Make sure the check box next to each group you want to import is checked (☑).

9 Click **Import**.

Windows Live Photo Gallery imports the images from your camera or memory card to your laptop.

TIP

How do you scan photos?
Many people have albums or shoeboxes stuffed with photos taken with a traditional film-based camera — holdovers from before they went digital. If you are one of these people, you can use a scanner to convert these photo prints to digital images. To do so, connect your scanner to your PC; Windows 8 should detect it and install the necessary drivers. Then place a photo print in the scanner as outlined in the scanner's manual. Finally, in Windows Live Photo Gallery, click **File**, click **Import from a camera or scanner**, click the scanner in the list of devices that appears, and click **Import**.

Batch-Rename Photo Files

In the past, people painstakingly organized their favorite photos in albums, haphazardly stashing the rest in shoeboxes. Today, digital photos can be stored and viewed on your computer with the click of a button. An important part of organizing your photos in Windows Live Photo Gallery is giving them descriptive names. This makes it easier to locate the photos you want to view and edit. To expedite this, Windows Live Photo Gallery enables you to rename files in batches, replacing the filenames your camera creates (think "DC000591.jpg") with more meaningful names (for example, "FranceTrip2010.jpg") for several image files at once.

Batch-Rename Photo Files

① In Windows Live Photo Gallery, select the pictures you want to batch-rename.

Note: To select multiple pictures, press **Ctrl** as you click each picture.

② Right-click a selected picture.

③ Click **Rename**.

Ⓐ The Info pane opens with the contents of the Filename field selected.

④ Type a name for the files and press **Enter**.

Windows Live Photo Gallery applies the name to each selected picture along with a sequential number to differentiate the files.

Tag Photo Files

You can apply tags using Windows Live Photo Gallery. Tags are brief descriptions embedded in the files' metadata that you can use as sort, filter, and search criteria. In addition to applying descriptive tags in Windows Live Photo Gallery, you can apply special people tags — that is, tags that identify the people in your photos. This makes it easier to sort and locate photos of your friends and family. If you link Photo Gallery to your Facebook account, you can choose from your Facebook contacts for people tags. You can apply tags using the Photo Gallery's Info pane.

Tag Photo Files

1 In the Windows Live Photo Gallery, click the **View** tab.

2 Click **Tag and caption pane**.

3 Click the picture or pictures you want to tag.

4 Click the person you want to tag.

5 Click their name from the list, or type a new name.

To tag yourself, select **That's Me!**

6 Press Enter.

Note: If adding multiple tags, separate them with a comma.

Auto-Adjust a Photo

If an image lacks in contrast, seems slightly off color-wise, or is a bit skewed, you can use Windows Live Photo Gallery's Auto Adjust tool to fix these problems. The Auto Adjust tool automatically applies the Adjust Exposure, Adjust Color, and Straight Photo fixes at once. (Note that you can, if you prefer, apply these fixes manually on an individual basis.) Before you edit an image, you should make a copy of it and preserve the original. That way, if you are unhappy with the edits, the photo is not permanently damaged.

Auto-Adjust a Photo

1 Open the image you want to auto-adjust.

Note: You can double-click a thumbnail image to open a larger image for editing.

Ⓐ Photo Gallery automatically displays the Edit tab.

2 Click the **Auto adjust** button (▨).

Ⓑ Windows Live Photo Gallery assesses your image, applies the necessary exposure and color settings, and straightens the image as needed.

Ⓒ If clicking Auto Adjust does not yield the desired results, click the **Fine tune** button (▨) and use the sliders to adjust the settings manually.

Note: You can double-click the image to return to Thumbnail view.

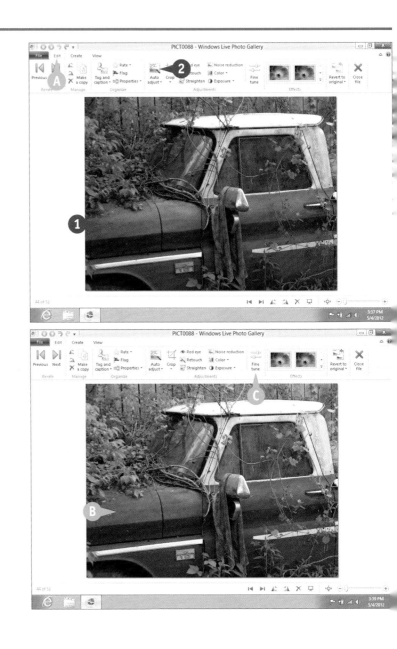

Crop a Photo

A key aspect of image composition is ensuring that only what should appear in the image does appear in the image. If you discover that your image contains some unwanted elements — for example, a telephone pole that appears to be growing out of your subject's head — you can crop those elements out. You might also crop an image simply to improve its composition. When cropping an image, you can select from several preset proportions. Alternatively, you can create your own custom crop. As always, you should make a copy of your image and preserve the original before applying your edits.

Crop a Photo

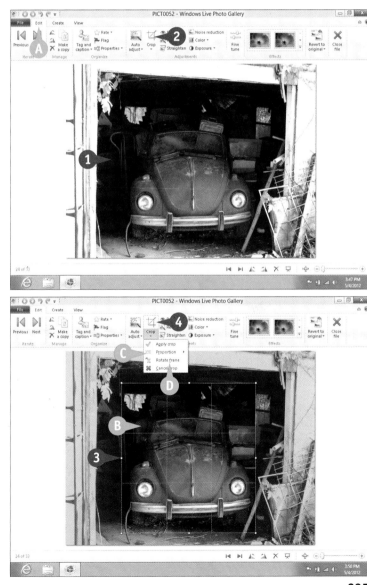

1 Open the image you want to crop.

Note: You can double-click a thumbnail image to open a larger image for editing.

A Photo Gallery automatically displays the Edit tab.

2 Click the **Crop** button ( ).

B A cropping frame appears in the image.

3 Click and drag the side or corner of the crop frame to the desired spot on the photograph.

C To change the proportion of the cropping frame, click the **Crop** drop-down arrow (▼) and click **Proportion** to select a preset.

D To rotate the crop frame, click the **Crop** (▼) and click **Rotate frame**.

4 When the cropping is to your liking, click ( ) again.

Note: You can double-click the image to return to Thumbnail view.

Windows Live Photo Gallery crops the photo.

Create and Publish an Online Photo Album

great way to share your digital photos with others is to publish them in an online album. Windows Live Photo Gallery lets you share albums online through SkyDrive, Facebook, Flickr, YouTube, and Windows Live Groups. After you publish the album, you can e-mail a link to that album to others, who can then view and even comment on your photos. As an added benefit, publishing your photos online protects you by giving you access to copies of all your precious photos in the event of a hard drive failure. You may need to sign in to Windows Live in order to publish an album.

Create and Publish an Online Photo Album

1 In the Windows Live Photo Gallery window, select the pictures you want to include in the album.

2 Click the **Create** tab.

3 From the Publish list box, click the online service you want to publish to.

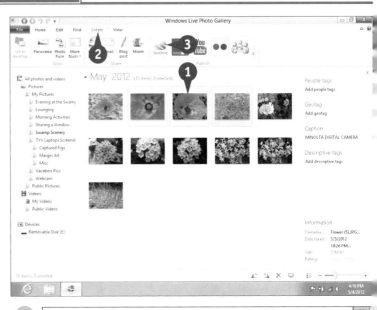

A A dialog box opens with instructions for publishing. Depending on the service you select, the options may vary.

4 Click **Publish**.

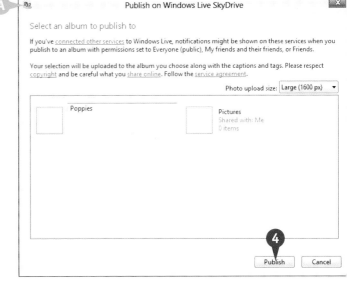

B Windows Live Photo Gallery uploads the selected images to the specified website.

C Windows Live Photo Gallery notifies you when the upload operation is complete.

5 Click **View online** to view the album online.

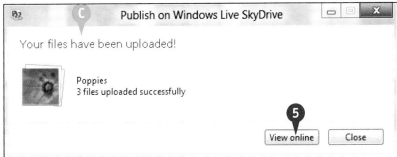

TIPS

What does the blogging feature do?

You can use the Windows Live Writer app to compose a blog, then use Windows Live Photo Gallery to add photos to your blog. Windows Live Writer is just one of several apps available in the Windows Live suite. If you have not installed the Writer app yet, click the **Blog post** button (/) on the Create tab and follow the prompts for downloading and installing the app.

How do I add photos to my SkyDrive account?

SkyDrive is Microsoft's file hosting service that you can use to upload and sync your image files and then access them from any browser and Internet connection. Using your web browser, visit the SkyDrive site (skydrive.live.com) and set up an account. If you already have a Windows Live account, SkyDrive features are ready to go.

CHAPTER 14

Working with Audio and Video

You can work with media files in a variety of ways in Windows 8. Using the new Music and Video apps, you can purchase music and videos online. You can use Windows Media Player, bundled with Windows 8, to organize your media collection, rip music from CDs in your personal library, create playlists of your favorite songs, and more.

Use the Music and Video Apps

You can use the Music and Video apps on the Start screen to play music and videos on your laptop. Both apps offer access to online content you can purchase through the Marketplace. You can peruse through recommendations or search through genres to find music or videos. You can choose whether to download files or stream them, or use them on your Xbox if you are linking your laptop to a gaming device. You can also use the apps to play music or videos from your own libraries.

Use the Music and Video Apps

1 From the Start screen, click the **Music** or **Video** app tile.

Windows opens the Music or Video app, in this example, the Music app.

2 Scroll though the featured artists, your own library, or the Marketplace.

Note: Mouse users can use a scroll bar located at the bottom of the screen to move left and right.

3 Click an item to open it.

242

A If you click an item from your own library, the app plays the file on its own screen.

B Use the playback controls that appear to control how the clip plays.

C Click outside of the item display to return to the app's main screen.

D In this example, a video plays in the Video app in its own screen with its own set of playback controls.

E Use the playback controls to control how the clip plays.

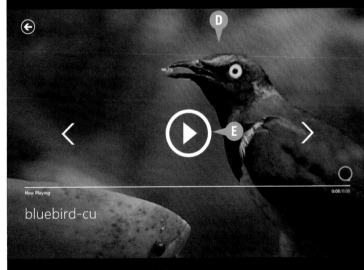

TIPS

How do I buy music or videos?
When you find a video or album you want to purchase, click the name of the item and click **Buy Album**. The first time you attempt to purchase music or video online, the app asks you to set up an account by creating an Xbox LIVE membership, which is free to set up. You can buy Microsoft Points to purchase music and videos.

How do I change the app's settings?
If you swipe the right side of the screen while using the Music or Video app (or move the mouse pointer to the bottom right corner) and click **Settings** (⚙), a list of settings relating to the app appear. You can use these settings to change accounts, edit permissions, or rate and review the app.

Open Windows Media Player

You can use Windows Media Player to organize your media collection, including music and sound files, videos, and pictures. You can listen to CDs, watch DVDs, rip music from CDs in your personal library, create playlists of your favorite songs, sync your audio and video files to a portable media player, and more. You can find Windows Media Player listed among your computer's apps, or you can type its name to access it more quickly, as shown in this section. Windows Media Player is one of several accessories built into the Windows 8 operating system.

Open Windows Media Player

1 From the Start screen, type **Windows Media Player**.

The Apps screen opens and displays a list of possible matches.

2 Click **Windows Media Player**.

Note: You can also open the Apps screen and scroll to Windows Accessories to find the Windows Media Player.

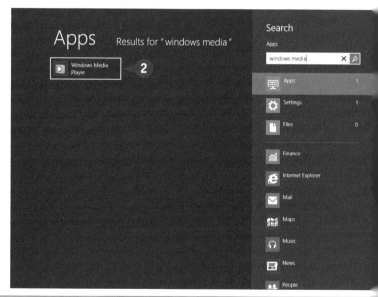

Windows Media Player opens on the desktop.

A Media folders are listed in the left pane.

B You can click here to expand a folder and view subfolders.

3 Click a media folder to view its contents.

Note: You can also use Windows Media Player to organize image files.

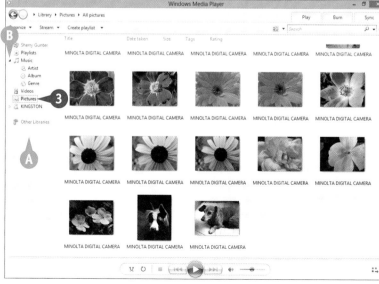

Ⓒ If you select a music folder, tracks are listed here.

Ⓓ You can use these tabs to create playlists, burn tracks to a CD or DVD, or sync with a portable player device.

Ⓔ You can use this area to create a playlist.

4 Click **Close** (✕) to exit Windows Media Player.

How do I find Windows Media Player through the Apps screen?
Press ⊞+Z to display the Apps bar, then click the **All Apps** icon (▣). This opens the Apps screen listing all the apps on your laptop. You can scroll through the list to find Windows Media Player listed under the Windows Accessories category.

Where can I shop for more music?
You can shop for more media content on Microsoft's web portal. Visit www.windowsmedia.com for music, movies, and Internet radio selections.

Build Your Media Library

Audio and video files in your Windows 8 Music and Video folders appear in the Windows Media Player library by default. To further build your media library, you can use Windows Media Player to *rip*, or copy, tracks from CDs in your collection (assuming your laptop has a CD drive) or to obtain content online. If your laptop is connected to the Internet, you can also use Windows Media Player to shop for music online, listen to Internet radio broadcasts, and access video content such as movie previews.

Build Your Media Library

Rip Tracks from a CD

1 With Windows Media Player open, insert the CD that contains the tracks you want to rip in your computer's CD drive.

2 Select the drive.

A Windows Media Player displays a list of the tracks on the CD.

B By default, all tracks on the CD are selected. To deselect a track, click its check box (☑).

3 Click **Rip CD** ( ).

Note: You may need to maximize the Windows Media Player window to view all the toolbar buttons on the Ribbon.

C Windows Media Player rips, or copies, the selected tracks to your music library.

Note: Although Windows Media Player makes it easy to rip, burn, store, and organize your digital media, it is up to you to avoid copying or otherwise using copyrighted material without authorization. Unauthorized use of such materials may subject you to criminal and/or civil penalties.

Access Online Content

1 Using Internet Explorer, navigate to the Windows Media Guide: http://www.windowsmedia.com

2 Click the content you want to listen to.

3 Click the link you want to play.

A Media Player opens the Now Playing window, a much abbreviated player window with playback controls.

B Click here to return to the full-size Windows Media Player window.

TIPS

Can I pin the Windows Media Player to my Start screen?
Yes. To do so, display the Start screen (press 🪟) and type **Windows Media Player**. The Apps search screen opens and displays a list of matches. Right-click the **Windows Media Player** app name from the list to display the Apps bar at the bottom of the screen. Click the **Pin to Start** button (📌) to add the Windows Media Player as an app tile on the Start screen.

How do you import content from a video camera?
You can import video content from a digital video camera, but not with Windows Media Player. Instead, you use Windows Live Photo Gallery. To import items, follow the steps in Chapter 13. After you import your video, it appears in Windows Media Player by default.

Listen to Music

You can use Windows Media Player to listen to music on your laptop in a few different ways. One approach is to play back audio files stored on your laptop's hard drive. Alternatively, if your laptop has a CD drive, you can insert a CD into the CD drive and use Windows Media Player to listen to tracks on that CD. You use the same controls when playing a music CD as you do when playing back music files on your hard drive. You can also use Windows Media Player's Media Guide feature to access Internet radio stations.

Listen to Music

Listen to Music on Your Hard Drive

1 From Windows Media Player, click the **Music** folder.

2 Double-click the song or album you want to hear.

Windows Media Player plays back the song or album.

A The **Play** button ( ) changes to a **Pause** button ( ).

B Drag the **Volume** slider to adjust the volume.

C To mute the volume, click the **Mute** button ( ). The Mute button changes to a **No Sound** button ( ); click it to unmute the volume.

Note: To listen to music while performing other tasks on your laptop, click the **Switch to Now Playing** button ( ). To switch back, click the **Switch to Library** button ( ).

D To shuffle the order in which songs are played back, click the **Shuffle** button (🔀).

E To play back a song or playlist more than once, click the **Repeat** button (🔁).

F To stop playback, click the **Stop** button (◼).

G To return to the previous song, click the **Back** button (◀◀).

H To skip to the next song click the **Next** button (▶▶).

Play a CD

1 With Windows Media Player open, insert into your computer's CD drive the CD that contains the tracks you want to hear.

2 Click the drive.

Windows Media Player displays a list of the tracks on the CD.

3 Click the track you want to play or double-click the album name.

4 Click ▶ .

Windows Media Player automatically plays back the selected songs on the CD.

TIP

Where can I find more commands for using Windows Media Player?
You can right click the window's navigation bar (directly below the title bar) and display a pop-up menu of commands. To view the commands as a menu bar across the top of the window. click **View, Show menu bar**.

Watch Video Content

As with audio, you can watch videos in a few different ways in Windows Media Player: by playing back the video files stored on your computer's hard drive, or by playing a DVD inserted into your computer's DVD drive. You can also use Windows Media Player's Media Guide feature to access video content online. When you play a video, Windows Media Player automatically switches to Now Playing mode; to view the player controls, simply position your mouse pointer over the Now Playing window. You use the same controls to play back videos as you do to play back music.

Watch Video Content

Watch Videos on Your Hard Drive

1. From Windows Media Player, click the **Videos** folder.

2. Double-click the video you want to watch.

Windows Media Player plays back the video in Now Playing mode.

Note: You use the same controls when playing a video file as you do when playing back music files.

Play a DVD

1 With Windows Media Player open, insert into your computer's DVD drive the DVD you want to watch.

2 Click ⊙.

If the DVD menu does not appear automatically, right-click the DVD in the folder list and click **Play**.

Ⓐ To play a single file on the DVD, select it and then click ⊙.

Note: To play commercial DVDs on your laptop, you may need third party software for decoding the movie. You can find plug-in decoders you can download.

Ⓑ Windows Media Player displays the DVD in Now Playing mode.

If applicable, select the desired option from the DVD menu that appears.

Ⓒ To view the DVD in full-screen mode, click the **View Full Screen** button (⊡).

TIP

Can I change the screen size to play my video?
The Now Playing mode displays your video in a special window which you can size to full-screen to take advantage of your monitor size. You can also drag a corner or edge of the video window to resize the viewing area.

Create and Save Playlists

If you want to listen to more than just a single song or a single album or watch multiple videos in a row, you can stack up files in a playlist. Windows Media Player then plays the songs or videos in your playlist in the order you specify. If you develop a playlist you particularly like, you can save it. When you save a playlist, you can then open it in a later session to listen to the set of songs or view the videos it contains. You can also burn saved playlists to CD or DVD.

Create and Save Playlists

1 From the Windows Media Player window, click the **Play** tab to display it.

A If the Play tab already contains other items, click **Clear list** to remove them.

2 Click an audio or video file you want to include in your playlist.

3 Drag the selected file to the Play tab.

B Windows Media Player adds the item to the playlist.

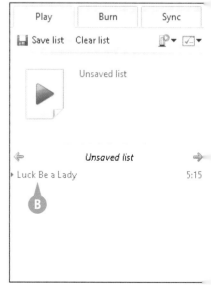

④ Add more files to the playlist.

ⓒ To sort the playlist, click the **List Options** button (▣), click **Sort list by**, and select a sort parameter (for example, Title).

Note: To move a file in the playlist, click it and drag it to the desired location in the list.

Note: To remove a file from the playlist, right-click it and select **Remove from list** from the menu that appears.

⑤ Click **Save list**.

⑥ Type a name for the playlist and press `Enter`.

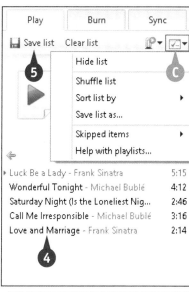

How do you play back a playlist?
To play a saved playlist, click the **Playlists** entry in the folder pane, select the playlist you want to play, and click the **Play** button. When you play back files in a playlist, you use the same controls as when you play back a video, song, or album.

How do you delete a playlist?
To delete a playlist, click the **Playlists** entry in the folder pane, right-click the playlist you want to delete, and select **Delete** from the menu that appears. Specify whether the playlist should be deleted from your library only or from your library and your computer; then click **OK.**

Burn CDs and DVDs

If your laptop has a CD/DVD drive capable of recording to disc, you can use Windows Media Player to create an audio CD that can be played back on any standard CD player. In addition, you can burn music as data files to a disc; this enables you to fit many more songs on a single disc. You can also burn video files in this way. When you burn audio or video files to disc as data files, they can be played back only on a computer or other device that supports the data format used.

Burn CDs and DVDs

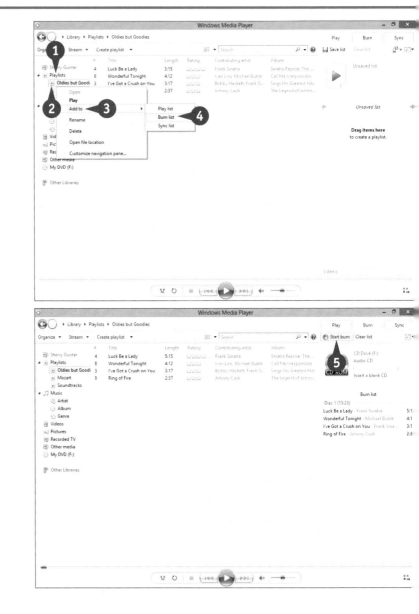

1 Click the **Playlists** folder.

2 Right-click the playlist you want to burn to a disc.

3 Click **Add to**.

4 Select **Burn list**.

Note: Another way to specify what files to burn is to click the **Burn** tab to open it and then simply drag items from your Windows Media Player library into it.

Windows Media Player opens the Burn tab, with the contents of the playlist shown.

5 Click **Start burn**.

Ⓐ Windows Media Player prompts you to insert a blank disc.

⑥ Insert a blank recordable disc into your laptop's CD/DVD drive.

Insert Media ☒

Ⓐ

Please insert a blank disc in CD Drive (F:). Once Windows Media Player detects the new disc, it will automatically start burning.

Cancel

Windows Media Player burns the contents of the Burn tab onto the blank disc. (Note that this may take several minutes.)

Ⓑ Windows Media Player tracks the progress of the burn operation.

Note: If the contents of the Burn tab will not fit on a single disc, Windows Media Player gives you the option of burning the remaining items on a second blank disc.

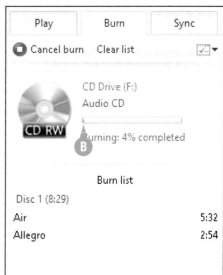

| Play | Burn | Sync |

⏹ Cancel burn   Clear list   ☑▾

CD Drive (F:)
Audio CD

CD RW

Burning: 4% completed

Ⓑ

Burn list

Disc 1 (8:29)

Air   5:32

Allegro   2:54

Can I sync music to my mobile device?

Some mobile phones and portable media players can be synced with Windows Media Player. To find out if your device is compatible, connect it to your laptop. Some devices may sync automatically, whereas others may require a manual sync. You can use the Sync tab in the Windows Media Player window to add your playlists, albums, and other media to your device.

How do you burn data files to a CD or DVD?

To burn song or video files to disc as data files, repeat steps **1** to **4** in this section. Then click the **Burn options** button in the Burn tab and select **Data CD or DVD** from the menu that appears. Next, click **Start burn** and insert a blank disc when prompted; Windows Media Player burns the files to disc.

Connect and Test a Microphone

If you plan to record sound files, such as narrations for PowerPoint presentations, you need a microphone. You can also use a microphone to take advantage of the Speech Recognition features in Windows 8. Finally, you need a microphone if you intend to use your laptop to communicate with others using VoIP services such as Skype or MSN. Many laptops come with built-in mics, others do not. You can always add a microphone, especially if you need to capture sounds that a built-in mic cannot. You can use the Microphone Setup Wizard to help you connect and test a microphone.

Connect and Test a Microphone

1 After plugging in your microphone, type **microphone** at the Start screen.

Windows displays a Search box and a list of items that match what you typed.

2 Click **Settings**.

3 Click **Set up a microphone**.

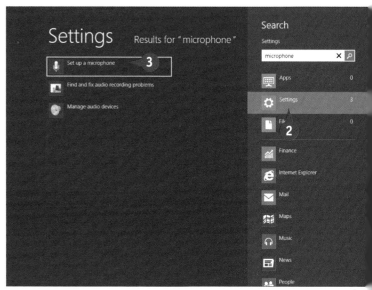

The first screen of the Microphone Setup Wizard opens.

4 Click the radio button (●) next to the type of microphone you want to set up (here, **Desktop Microphone**).

5 Click **Next**.

6 Click **Next** again to skip the next screen, an informational screen offering details about the type of chosen microphone.

7 With the microphone situated near your mouth, read the sample sentence.

8 Click **Next**.

Windows sets up your microphone.

9 Click **Finish**.

Note: If the wizard informs you that it could not hear your speech, click the **Back** navigation button (⊙) in the upper left corner and try again. Check the connection of your microphone to your laptop and ensure that the microphone's Mute button has not been engaged. Then read the sentence again.

TIPS

How do you set up headphones?

Headphones come in several types, from clip-on, earbud, and ear-canal headphones to earpad-style headphones that fit over your ear to full-size headphones that cover your ears completely. Setting up headphones is a simple matter of plugging them into your laptop's headphone jack. (For help identifying a headphone jack, refer to Chapter 1.)

How can I check to see if I have a built-in mic?

Open the Control Panel window; right-click the lower left corner of the screen and choose **Control Panel** from the pop-up menu. Click **Hardware and Sound**, then click **Sound**. This opens the Sound dialog box; click the **Recording** tab to see a list of any installed mics and whether they are turned on or off.

CHAPTER 15

Managing Laptop Power

Laptops are ideal for people who use their computers on the go. However, laptop batteries do not stay charged forever, so you need to learn how to manage your power efficiently to get the most out of your battery. Various settings in Windows allow you to control power usage and know whether your power is running low.

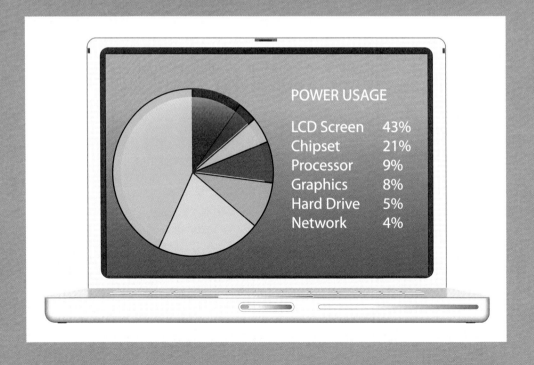

POWER USAGE

LCD Screen	43%
Chipset	21%
Processor	9%
Graphics	8%
Hard Drive	5%
Network	4%

Understanding Power Management

Power management means understanding how your laptop uses power and how you can get the most out of your battery. On average, a laptop battery significantly decreases in life after a year or so; if your battery had four hours of life when it was new, it decreases by 50%, for example. Effective power management can help you improve the performance and life of your battery.

Battery Life

When you are on the road with your laptop, away from a power supply, you rely on your battery to keep your laptop working. Laptop battery life can range anywhere from one to six hours or more. By using your computer in certain ways and modifying settings, you can maximize your battery life.

What Drains Batteries Most

Obviously, leaving your computer on, or having a computer that takes longer to power down or power up, can drain your battery. An average of 30 percent of your laptop's battery power goes to running your LCD screen. A larger monitor with higher resolution or one used at a higher brightness setting can increase that number. Add-on devices, such as flash drives and PC cards, can also drain a battery, as well as items like Ethernet adapters.

Using Adapters

When you do have access to electricity, take advantage of it and use your adapter to power your laptop from a wall outlet. Keep in mind that your laptop is likely to function only with the adapter designed for your model. If you travel a great deal, invest in an auto adapter for your car that allows you to plug into your car's cigarette lighter. It may also be a good investment to purchase a second adapter cord, such as a universal power adapter.

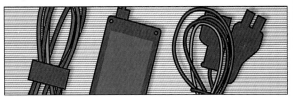

Monitoring the Health of Your Battery

Batteries last only so long. At some point you may notice signs that you need to get a new battery. Such signs can include a battery that never fully charges, a battery that does not hold a charge as long as it used to, or a laptop that gets too hot after running on a battery for an hour or so. You can contact your manufacturer to purchase a new battery for your model or shop around online.

Windows 8 Power Improvements

Running a laptop is more energy efficient than ever before in the new Windows 8 operating system. Even with significant feature changes, Windows 8 is designed to maintain the same energy use as the previous version. When redesigning the software, Microsoft applied

smartphone power models to allow users to switch in and out of low-power mode with ease, improved the device power management framework, and improved how software influences power consumption.

Sleep Mode

One thing you can do to help stretch your battery life is to put your laptop into sleep (or standby) mode when you are not using it. Sleep mode turns off the screen and internal fan, and generally uses less energy. This mode also preserves the state of your system in RAM,

meaning that when your laptop comes out of sleep mode, whatever you were doing when the laptop went into sleep mode is still open for you to return to work.

Hibernate Mode

Hibernate mode is another power-saving option you can apply. Primarily designed for laptops, hibernate mode saves the computer's current state to the hard drive and turns off the computer's power completely. This mode is ideal if you do not plan on using your laptop

for an extended period of time, such as during a long meeting or lunch break. It takes longer to wake up a laptop from hibernate mode than from sleep mode.

Windows Power Plans

Windows offers three power plans: Power Saver, High Performance, and Balanced. Use Power Saver when the laptop is running on battery. It shuts down various components after the system has been idle for a short period of time to conserve power. Use High Performance when

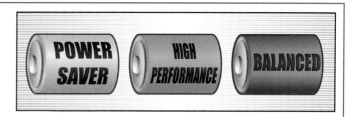

the laptop is plugged in; this plan waits longer to shut down components. Use Balanced, the default, if you do not want to bother changing plans when your power supply changes.

Create a Power Plan

You can set a power plan in Windows 8 to help you manage your laptop's power and battery life. The Power Saver plan is ideal when the laptop is running on battery alone; it shuts down various components after the system has been idle for a short period of time. If you are using your laptop while it is plugged in, the High Performance plan is a better option because it waits longer to shut down components when the system is idle. If you do not want to bother changing plans when your power supply changes, use the Balanced plan.

Create a Power Plan

1 From the Start screen or desktop, right-click the bottom left corner.

2 Click **Power Options**.

The Power Options window opens on the desktop.

3 Click **Create a power plan**.

Note: You can also set a power plan from the Windows Mobility Center. From the desktop taskbar, right-click the battery meter icon (🔋) and choose **Windows Mobility Setting**.

The Create a Power Plan screen appears.

④ Click a power plan
(○ becomes ◉).

Ⓐ Optionally, you can name the plan.

⑤ Click **Next**.

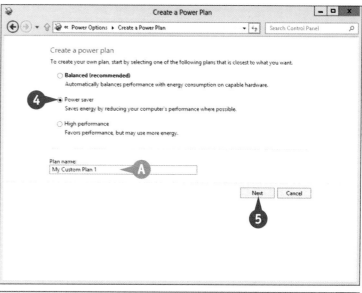

⑥ Choose the sleep and display settings you want to apply.

Ⓑ Choose display and sleep settings when on battery power here.

Ⓒ Choose display and sleep settings when on AC power here.

⑦ Click **Create**.

TIP

How do you customize a power plan?

You can customize an existing power plan from the desktop, including turning on hibernate mode for maximum power saving. Right-click the battery meter icon (🔋) on the taskbar and click **Power Options**. Click the **Change plan settings** link next to the power plan you want to customize and make your changes. To find more advanced options, such as battery alarm settings and hibernate mode, click the **Change advanced power settings** link. This opens the Power Options dialog box; click the **Sleep** ⊞ to find the hibernate option.

Adjust Screen Brightness

You can change your laptop's screen brightness level to improve your battery life. Your laptop screen consumes more battery power than any of the other elements of your laptop. Studies show that LCD screens drain as much as 43 percent of your battery's power. Larger screens can increase the drain even more. By adjusting the brightness level, you can help conserve battery power.

Adjust Screen Brightness

1 Swipe the right edge of the screen and click **Settings** (⚙).

2 Click **Screen Brightness** (🔆)

Note: You can also use the keyboard (**Fn**) key along with the designated brightness keys (◄ and ►) to adjust brightness.

3 Drag the slider up or down to adjust the brightness level.

4 Press **Esc** or click anywhere to deselect the option.

Note: You can also adjust screen brightness from the Windows Mobility Center. From the desktop taskbar, right-click the battery meter icon (🔋) and choose **Windows Mobility Setting**.

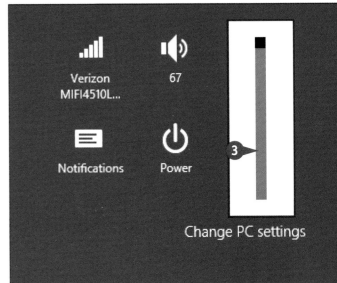

You can quickly check your laptop battery's charge level from the Windows desktop. The taskbar displays an icon indicating power charge. You can click the icon to view more details about the assigned power plan and links for adjusting screen brightness or adjusting power options. You can also view your charge level at a glance from the Windows 8 Lock screen when your laptop is in sleep mode.

Check Battery Charge

1 Display the desktop (click the Desktop app on the Start screen or press ⊞+D).

2 Click the battery meter icon.

Windows displays information about the charge level, power plan in use, and links to other power options.

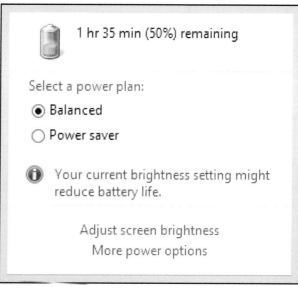

1 hr 35 min (50%) remaining

Select a power plan:

◉ Balanced

○ Power saver

ⓘ Your current brightness setting might reduce battery life.

Adjust screen brightness

More power options

Using Your Battery Efficiently

Your battery is like your computer's lifeblood when you take your laptop on the road. Knowing how to use the battery and take care of it is vital to keeping it charged and functioning properly. You can do several things physically as well as in the operating system to keep your battery at its optimum level.

Battery Life Expectancy

Batteries are one area of computing that lag a bit behind in terms of advancements in technology. Different types of batteries offer different durations for both battery charge and life expectancy. Just because the manufacturer says your

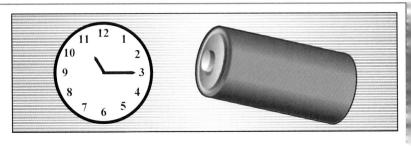

battery is good for 6 hours does not necessarily mean so, especially if you use power-hungry apps and hardware devices. In other words, your own usage may vary.

Develop Good Charging Habits

One of the best tips for battery efficiency is remembering to keep it charged. Getting in the habit of keeping your battery charged can help you avoid situations on the road where the battery life is

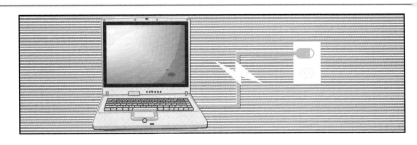

suddenly at a minimum and you still have lots of work to do. If feasible, a backup battery is a good investment, and you can carry it along with you in the laptop case for emergencies.

Tweak Your Power Plan Settings

A good power plan setting is another great tool in your arsenal for prolonging battery life. As described in the section "Choose a Power Plan" earlier in this chapter, you can choose a power option

that works best for your situation to power down your laptop when not in use. The Balanced or Power Saver plans work best for maximizing battery life, but you can also tweak each plan to make adjustments to when the screen dims or goes to sleep, or how bright the screen remains during idle time.

Optimize Your Hardware for Power Consumption

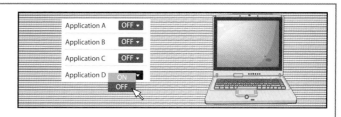

If your laptop has hardware you are not using, such as Bluetooth cards or USB devices that are always turned on when plugged in, disabling them can save a little battery power. For example, if you are out and about without a wireless hotspot, disable your Wi-Fi setting. If your computer seems to run constantly, whirring away with every task, you may not have enough RAM. Upgrading RAM can help with battery life, or consider running few applications at the same time.

Turn Off Background Processes and Services

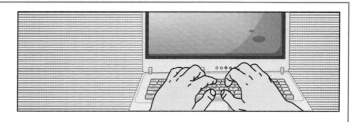

Software and services, such as scheduled tasks and updates, can run constantly in the background without your knowing it, consuming battery power. Be sure to close any unnecessary background applications you have running whenever you are operating on just battery power. For example, consider removing items hiding in your taskbar's system tray that you do not need or Windows gadgets that you no longer use.

Use Hibernate Mode

Sleep mode, hibernate mode, or a hybrid of both, helps your laptop power down or use minimal power while idle. Just because your power plan has put the computer to sleep, however, does not mean it will not wake up again to perform a scheduled background task, or even accidentally when you touch the keypad. Consider assigning hibernate mode rather than sleep mode to power down the computer completely when not in use.

Avoid Heat

Nothing saps a battery more than excessive heat or a dirty fan. If your laptop is constantly overheating, or you leave it in an overly hot environment (like the confines of a car on a hot, sunny day), your battery's life capacity is sure to dwindle. Consider buying a laptop cooling pad. Cooling pads are designed specifically to help your laptop circulate air under the chassis. Also clean your laptop's fan occasionally.

Control Power Button Function

The laptop power button turns on your computer, but when the computer is already on, you can use the button to put it to sleep, hibernate, or shut down. You can control exactly what action you want the power button to perform when pressed. For example, if you want to manually force the computer into sleep mode, you can assign the sleep mode function to the power button. Or if you want the computer to fully hibernate and power down to just minimal power, you can assign hibernate mode to the button.

Control Power Button Function

1 From the desktop, right-click the battery meter icon (🔋).

2 Click **Power Options**.

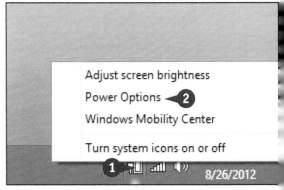

Windows opens the Control Panel to the Power Options.

3 Click the **Choose what the power buttons do** option.

The Define Power Buttons and Turn On Password Protection screen appears.

④ Click the **When I press the power button** ▾.

⑤ Click a function to assign.

Note: You can assign the power button function to operate on battery or AC power.

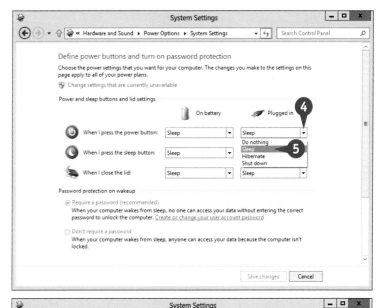

⑥ Click **Save changes**.

Windows applies the new setting.

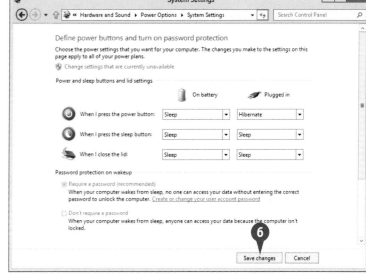

TIP

How do I control what happens when I close the laptop lid?
Depending on your laptop, it may power down completely when you shut the lid or just go into sleep mode. You can use the Windows 8 power options to assign a specific function to the lid, such as hibernating or shutting down. Look for the power settings for your laptop lid in the same window as the settings for controlling the power button function described in this section. Right-click the battery meter icon (🔋) and click **Power Options**. Click the **Choose what closing the lid does** link, then specify an action for the lid function.

CHAPTER 16

Maintaining Your Laptop

To keep your laptop in good condition, you can follow some basic hardware and software maintenance procedures. You can utilize maintenance tools to optimize your laptop's performance and keep your operating system up to date. Periodically performing a bit of housecleaning goes a long way toward keeping your laptop running smoothly.

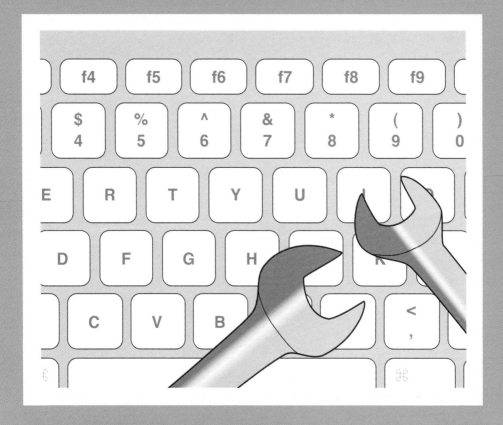

View PC Settings

From the Start screen, you can use the PC Settings panel to view and make changes to basic laptop settings, such as notifications, personalization options, Windows updates, user accounts, and more. You can access PC Settings through the Charms bar on the far right side of the Start screen. Take time to familiarize yourself with the various options available. For more detailed settings, such as hardware and sound or system and security settings, use the classic Control Panel, as described in the next section.

View PC Settings

1 From the Start screen, swipe from the right edge of the screen or move the mouse pointer to the upper or lower right corner.

Windows displays the Charms bar.

Note: You can also press ⊞+C to display the Charms bar.

2 Click **Settings** (⚙).

3 Click **Change PC settings**.

The PC Settings window opens.

Ⓐ You can scroll up and down the left pane to view all the main setting categories.

④ Click a setting category.

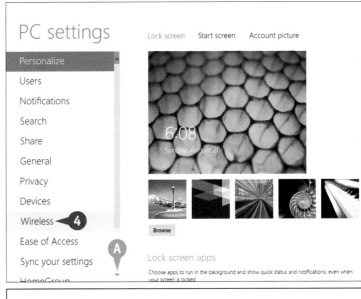

Ⓑ The PC Settings screen displays the associated settings.

TIPS

What happened to the traditional Control Panel?
If you are familiar with working with the Control Panel from previous versions of Windows, the panel is still an essential part of Windows 8. You can access it over on the Desktop, as demonstrated in the next section. Both the PC Settings and the Control Panel offer access to system settings; however, PC Settings offers a limited selection of options.

What basic system settings can I change using PC Settings?
The PC Settings window has thirteen sections ranging from user account settings and background personalizing options to system updates and app notifications. Many of the settings toggle on or off. In addition, you can also access several common settings when you display the Charms bar and click **Settings** (⚙), such as volume, notifications, and power settings.

Explore the Control Panel

The Windows 8 Control Panel acts like a master console of sorts. It serves as a launching point for performing many system-maintenance tasks, such as backing up your files, freeing disk space, defragmenting your hard drive, and more. The main Control Panel window features several links. You click a link to access related tools or wizards. If you know the name of the tool you need to access but are not sure which series of links to click to access it, you can use the Control Panel window's Search box to find it.

Explore the Control Panel

1 Right-click the bottom left corner of the screen.

Note: You can right-click the bottom left corner from the Start screen or from the Desktop screen to view the same pop-up menu.

2 Click **Control Panel**.

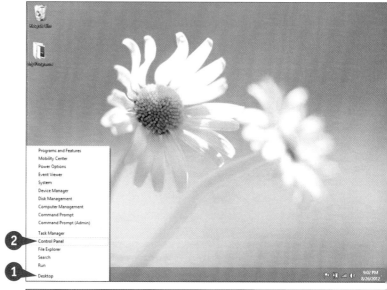

The Control Panel window appears.

3 To view maintenance tools, click **System and Security**.

The Control Panel displays a further list of settings.

4️⃣ Click **Administrative Tools**.

The Administrative Tools window opens with access to tools for freeing disk space, defragmenting your hard drive, and scheduling system tasks.

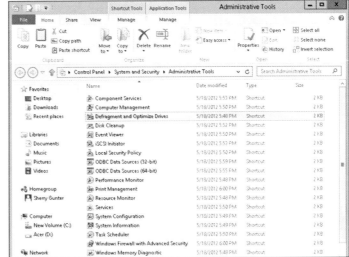

TIPS

How do you find a specific tool in Control Panel?

If you are not sure what link to click to access a particular tool, you can use the Control Panel window's Search box to find it. Simply type the name of the tool you want to find in the Search box; a list of tools that match what you typed appears.

How do I find information about my laptop?

You can open the System window to display information about your laptop, such as make and model, RAM, product ID, and more. Right-click the bottom left corner and click **System** to open the Control Panel to the System information. To view additional information, such as the type of disk drive, monitor, or adapters installed, click **Device Manager** in the System window to open the Device Manager window.

Update Your Operating System

Microsoft regularly releases updates for Windows 8 — that is, changes to the operating system designed to prevent or fix problems or to enhance security or performance. Windows 8 automatically checks for updates and installs those it deems essential. But there are additional, optional updates that Windows 8 does not automatically install; you should regularly view these updates and install them as needed. You can also perform a manual update if Microsoft has released a new update but your system has not yet run its automatic-update operation. To download an update, your laptop must be connected to the Internet.

Update Your Operating System

① From the Start screen, swipe from the right edge of the screen or move the mouse pointer to the upper or lower right corner.

Windows displays the Charms bar.

Note: You can also press ⊞+C to display the Charms bar.

② Click **Settings** (⚙).

③ Click **Change PC settings**.

④ Click **Windows Update**.

⑤ Click **Check for updates now**.

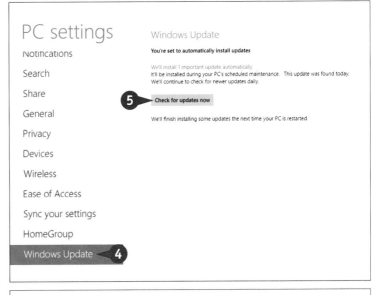

PC settings

Notifications
Search
Share
General
Privacy
Devices
Wireless
Ease of Access
Sync your settings
HomeGroup
Windows Update ◄ ④

Windows Update

You're set to automatically install updates

We'll install 1 important update automatically.
It'll be installed during your PC's scheduled maintenance.   This update was found today.
We'll continue to check for newer updates daily.

⑤ — Check for updates now

We'll finish installing some updates the next time your PC is restarted.

Windows checks for any updates. The process may take a few moments or a few minutes.

If updates are found, Windows downloads and installs any updates and informs you when the operation is complete.

Note: You may be prompted to restart your computer for the updates to take effect.

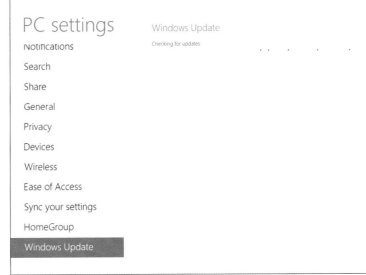

PC settings

Notifications
Search
Share
General
Privacy
Devices
Wireless
Ease of Access
Sync your settings
HomeGroup
Windows Update

Windows Update

Checking for updates

TIPS

How do I check for software updates?
With some programs, you can update your software just like you can update your operating system. Depending on the program, it may even prompt you to update whenever you open the app. Many programs include a "Check for Upgrade" or "Check for Update" feature on the program's Help menu. Check with your software manufacturer to learn more.

How do I know if Windows updates are installed?
You can check your update history to see which updates are installed and when. From the Control Panel's System and Security options, click **Windows Update** and then click the **View update history** link. This opens a detailed listing of your laptop's updates, including when the update installed, its level of importance, and its current status.

Back Up Data with File History

You can use Window's File History feature to back up files in your libraries. If a disaster such as theft, loss, breakage, or virus attack were to befall your computer, certain files, such as digital pictures, would be impossible to replace. Others, such as files used for work, would be at best extremely difficult to reconstruct. For this reason, you should back up your files — that is, copy them to an external hard drive, a Flash drive, a CD, or a DVD. Wherever you save your backup, you should keep it in a safe location.

Back Up Data with File History

① Connect the drive on which you want to save your backup to your laptop, or insert the necessary media.

② Right-click the bottom left corner of the screen.

Note: You can right-click the bottom left corner from the Start screen or from the Desktop screen to view the same pop-up menu.

③ Click **Control Panel**.

④ Under System and Security, click **Save backup copies of your files with File History**.

5 Click **Turn on**.

If you have a Homegroup set up on your laptop, Windows prompts you to recommend the same drive to other members; click **Yes** to continue.

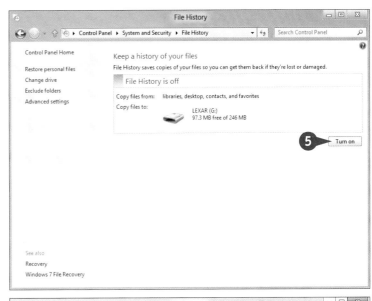

A The File History setting now appears as on and Windows 8 begins saving your data files.

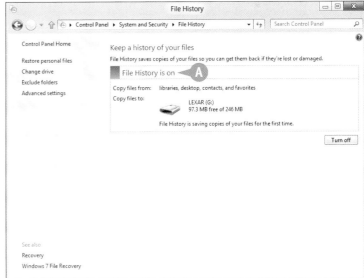

TIPS

How do you restore a backup?

To restore your backed up files and folders in the event of system failure or some other disaster, first attach, insert, or connect to the media on which the backup is stored. Then, in the File History screen of the Control Panel, click **Restore personal files**.

How do I back up my data to a network connection?

From the File History screen in the Control Panel, click the **Change Drive** link in the left pane. This opens the Change Your File History Drive window and you can click the **Add network location** button and specify a network resource for your backup.

Free Up Disk Space

In addition to storing files you create or save as you work on your computer, your laptop's hard drive stores many more files that Windows 8 creates, changes, and saves automatically. Over time, you can end up with a gigabyte or more of unneeded files, consuming valuable space on your hard drive. If your hard drive is low on free space, you can use the Disk Cleanup tool to find and remove these temporary files. This utility also empties the Recycle Bin. In fact, it is wise to run the Disk Cleanup tool regularly as part of standard disk management.

Free Up Disk Space

1 Open the Control Panel.

Note: You can right-click the bottom left corner from the Start screen or from the Desktop screen to view the same pop-up menu and choose **Control Panel**.

2 Click **System and Security**.

3 Under Administrative Tools, click **Free up disk space**.

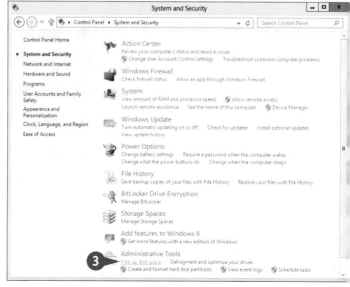

The Disk Cleanup: Drive Selection dialog box appears.

④ Click the **Drives** ⊡ and select the drive you want to clean.

Note: If you only have one drive, this dialog box will not appear.

⑤ Click **OK**.

Disk Cleanup scans your system to determine how much space can be freed.

Ⓐ When the scan is complete, the Disk Cleanup dialog box opens.

⑥ Click the check box (☐ becomes ✔) next to each type of file you want to delete.

⑦ Click **OK**.

Ⓑ Disk Cleanup prompts you to confirm the cleanup operation.

⑧ Click **Delete Files**.

Disk Cleanup deletes the unnecessary files, freeing up disk space.

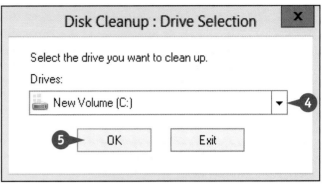

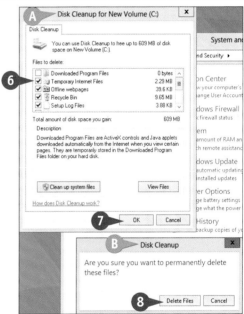

TIPS

How do you check the free space on your hard drive?

To quickly view the amount of free space on your hard drive, open File Explorer and right-click the name of the drive you want to check. The Properties dialog box opens displaying the amount of used and free space available on the chosen drive. See Chapter 9 to learn more about using File Explorer.

How can you find out more about the files that Disk Cleanup wants to delete?

To access more details about files that Disk Cleanup wants to delete, click **View Files** in the Disk Cleanup dialog box. These details include the size of the files, when they were created, and when you last accessed them.

Defragment Your Hard Drive

When you save a file on your laptop, Windows writes the data to a sector on the hard drive. If the sector is too small to hold the entire file, the extra bits are saved in the next available sector. Over time, your files may become quite fragmented, with bits spread across several sectors on the drive, meaning when you open a file, it takes Windows longer to find all the various pieces. To solve this problem, you can run Disk Defragmenter. This reassembles the files on your hard drive such that each one occupies as few sectors as possible.

Defragment Your Hard Drive

1 Open the Control Panel.

Note: You can right-click the bottom left corner from the Start screen or from the Desktop screen to view the same pop-up menu and choose **Control Panel.**

2 Click **System and Security.**

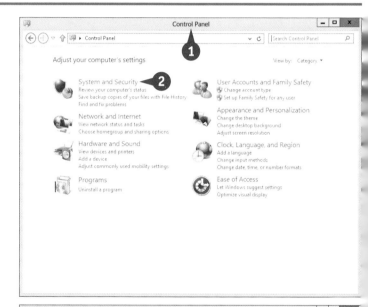

3 Under Administrative Tools, click **Defragment and optimize your drives**.

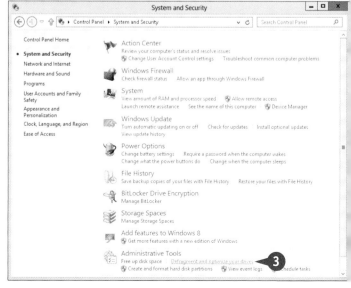

Windows launches the Optimize Drives utility.

④ Click the drive you want to defragment.

Ⓐ Before defragmenting a drive, you can click **Analyze** to determine how fragmented it is.

⑤ To defragment the disk, click **Optimize**.

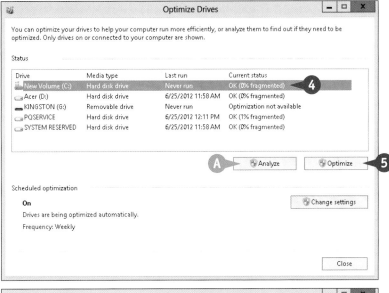

Disk Defragmenter defragments the disk. Note that the process can take several minutes or longer.

Ⓑ When the operation is complete, the drive is shown as 0% fragmented.

⑥ Click **Close**.

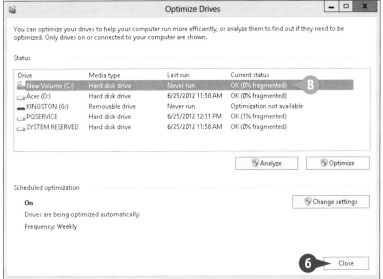

TIP

Can you set up Windows 8 to defragment automatically?

Yes. In fact, Windows 8 is set up to defrag your hard drive automatically by default. You can change the settings by clicking the **Change settings** button in the Optimize Drives window. You can specify a frequency, such as daily, weekly, or monthly, and specify exactly which drives to defragment. Click the **Frequency** drop-down arrow (⏷) and make your selection. Next, click **Choose** and select the disks you want to defragment; click **OK**, and click **OK** again to exit. To forego automatic defragmentation entirely, deselect the **Run on a schedule** check box.

Check Your Hard Drive for Errors

Problems with your hard drive can cause files to become corrupted. This can prevent you from running a program or opening a document. You can set up Windows 8's Check Disk program to look for and fix hard drive errors. Then, next time you restart your computer, Windows 8 performs a check. Check Disk runs two different types of checks: a basic hard drive check and a more thorough bad sector check. (A bad sector is one that can no longer reliably store data.) You should perform the basic check about once a week; perform the more thorough bad sector check once a month.

Check Your Hard Drive for Errors

1 From the desktop, open **File Explorer** (click the ▢ icon).

Note: See Chapter 9 to learn more about working with File Explorer.

2 Right-click the hard drive you want to check.

3 Click **Properties**.

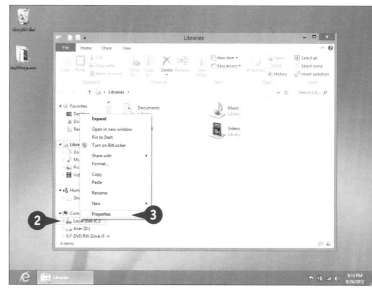

The Properties dialog box opens.

4 Click the **Tools** tab.

5 Click **Check**.

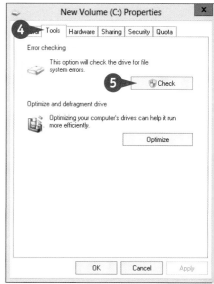

6 Click **Scan drive**.

Windows scans the drive. The process may take a few minutes, depending on your system.

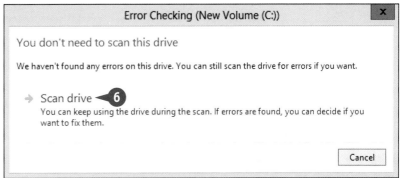

Error Checking (New Volume (C:))   x

You don't need to scan this drive

We haven't found any errors on this drive. You can still scan the drive for errors if you want.

→ Scan drive **6**
You can keep using the drive during the scan. If errors are found, you can decide if you want to fix them.

Cancel

When the scan is complete, Windows displays the results.

7 Click **Close**.

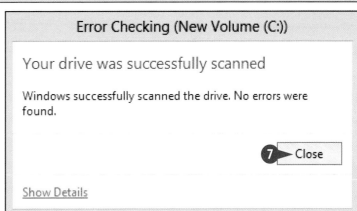

Error Checking (New Volume (C:))

Your drive was successfully scanned

Windows successfully scanned the drive. No errors were found.

7 Close

Show Details

TIPS

How do I refresh my laptop?
New to Windows 8, you can refresh your PC if you are having problems without losing all your personal files and settings. From the Start screen, open the PC Settings window and click **General**. Under **Refresh your PC without affecting your files**, click **Get started** and follow the prompts. To reset your laptop completely and start over with it, click the **Get started** button under the **Reset your PC and start over** heading.

How do I create a system repair disc?
Press ⊞+🅁 to open the Run command box. Type **recdisc** and press Enter to open the Create a System Repair Disc utility. Insert a blank CD or DVD into the optical drive and click **Create disc**. The utility then creates the necessary files for both 32-bit and 64-bit operating system editions.

Clean and Protect Your Screen and Keyboard

Laptop screens are typically of the liquid crystal display (LCD) variety. They are somewhat soft to the touch, and can be damaged rather easily. For this reason, you must take care to avoid scratching, poking, denting, or puncturing the screen; otherwise, it may become unusable. Although you can replace a laptop screen, doing so is expensive. Therefore, you should take good care of the laptop screen. The same is true for your laptop keyboard. You should clean your keyboard periodically to keep keys from becoming stuck or damaged.

Clean the Screen

Use a special microfiber cloth (usually made of polyester and nylon) to dust your screen. To avoid denting or otherwise damaging the screen as you clean it, do not press too hard on the screen with the cloth. If you use a liquid cleaning agent, be sure to remove the battery before cleaning your screen.

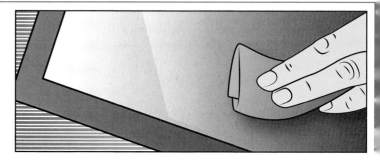

Cleaning Agents

Avoid ammonia-based cleaning liquids, such as Windex. These can damage your screen by removing antiglare and antistatic coatings on the surface. Instead, use isopropyl alcohol. Do not ever spray or pour a cleaner on the monitor surface; instead, coat a cloth or cotton swab with the cleaner and rub that gently on the screen.

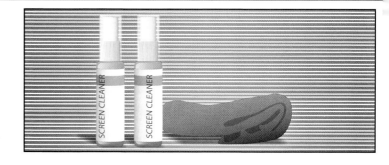

Protect Your Screen from Damage

When you are not using your laptop, close the clamshell lid. Consider purchasing a padded bag for your laptop for storing when not in use. Never place sharp objects, such as pens or your fingernail, against the screen. Be aware that exposure to extreme temperatures can cause problems with laptop displays.

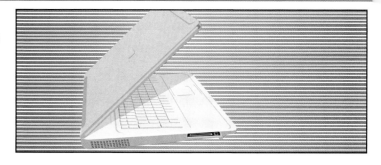

Avoid Spills

To avoid damaging your laptop, you should not eat or drink around your laptop. You can clean out spilled crumbs of food, but spilled liquids can be disastrous — especially to your keyboard. If you must eat while working on your laptop, try to keep any liquids at a safe distance.

Clean the Keys

You can clean the keys in a few ways. One is to run a handheld mini vacuum along the keys to pick up any dust or crumbs that have fallen in. You can also use a nonabrasive liquid cleaner to clean the surface of the keys. However, do not apply the cleaner to the actual keyboard; instead, spray it on a soft cloth and then wipe the keys with the cloth.

Clean Under the Keys

With some keyboards, you can easily remove the keys by gently popping them off with a screwdriver or coin. You can then use a nonabrasive liquid cleaner to clean underneath them. Again, do not apply the cleaner directly; instead, spray it on a soft cloth, and then use the cloth to clean under the keys. When you are finished cleaning under the keys, you can simply pop the keys back into place.

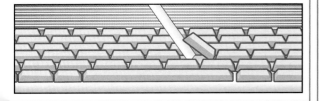

Replace a Damaged Key

If you break or otherwise damage a key, you may be able to replace it. Laptop keys are made of three components: the key cap, which is the visible portion of the key; a cup, which is a small rubber component; and a hinge, also called a retainer clip. You need all three pieces for the key to function properly. Be aware that removing and replacing larger keys such as the spacebar is slightly more difficult. You should check your owner's manual first to see if your manufacturer recommends replacing a key.

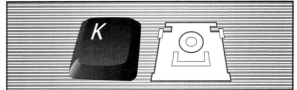

CHAPTER 17

Keeping Your Laptop Secure

If your laptop is connected to the Internet, it is vulnerable to any number of threats, including crackers, viruses, spyware, and more. Even an unconnected laptop can be compromised by someone who gains physical access to it. Fortunately, you can take certain steps to counter these threats, as covered in this chapter.

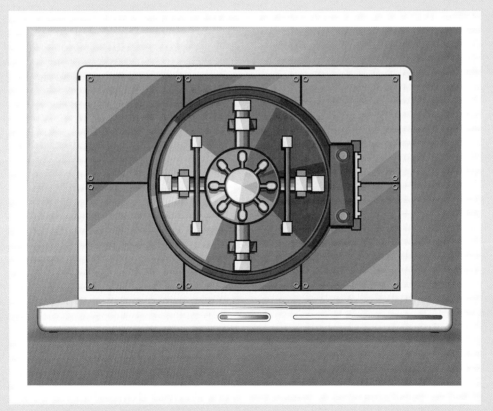

Using your laptop, especially online, gives you access to a great deal of information. That access, however, comes with a price: vulnerability to crackers, viruses, spyware, and so on. One of the best ways to protect yourself is to modify your own behavior. Just as you would not give personal information to a stranger on the street, you must learn to protect your identity and information online. In addition, tools are available to help you make your laptop secure. For example, you can set a password, install firewall software or an antivirus program, and so on.

Crackers

Crackers are constantly developing new ways to exploit the Internet for ill gain. Some create viruses—programs designed with some malicious intent; others use keystroke-tracking software to follow you around online or gather information that you contribute to blogs or social sites to steal your identity. Crackers should not be confused with hackers. Crackers exploit technology for criminal gain, while hackers simply enjoy the challenge of breaking into computer systems. True hackers subscribe to a strict code of "ethics" and frown upon crackers.

Viruses

A virus is a program created with malicious intent to copy itself and infect computers. Many viruses are distributed via e-mail or downloaded alongside other files. Viruses can destroy data on your hard drive, make changes in your operating system to open up a security gap, or make copies of a file until your laptop's memory is overwhelmed. The term *virus* is sometimes used to refer to other types of intrusive software, however only self-replicating programs can truly be called viruses.

Spyware

Spyware is a type of malicious software, or *malware*, that attaches to other software that you download and installs itself on your computer. Spyware can take control of your laptop without your knowledge, collecting little bits of information about you as you browse the Internet. Spyware can also perform such nefarious tasks as redirecting your browser to a bogus Internet site, where you might be prompted to enter personal information, or installing unwanted software on your laptop or unwanted pop-up ads.

Behavior

When using your laptop to surf the Internet, be careful where you go. Just as you do not walk in the worst part of town at midnight, so, too, should you avoid the unsavory parts of the Web. If you choose to register with a site and provide personal information, make sure that the site is secure. Submit information or purchase items online only at sites that you trust. Avoid posting personal information on a public blog or other site.

http://www.dangerous

Password

Use passwords to prevent others from logging in to your laptop and accessing your files. Be sure to set a strong password to prevent others from cracking it. Your password should be at least eight characters long, a mixture of uppercase and lowercase letters, and should not contain your username, your real name, your company's name, or any complete words. It is a good idea to periodically change your password. If you must write it down, store it somewhere safe.

User Name: blackcat13
Password: ********

Firewall

A firewall is a software program that stops certain types of data from passing from the Internet to your laptop (and vice versa) while still allowing other types of data to pass through. All data traveling between your laptop and the Internet passes through the firewall; the firewall examines each piece of data to determine whether it should be allowed to pass, blocking any data that does not meet the specified security criteria. Windows 8 includes its own firewall, called Windows Firewall.

Antivirus Software

Antivirus software, such as Norton AntiVirus, McAfee, and the free Microsoft Security Essentials, can be installed and set up to run regular scans for malware, including viruses, worms, and Trojan horses. Some antivirus software is also designed to scan for spyware and adware. (Adware is software installed on a computer, usually without the user's knowledge, that automatically displays advertisements.) Be sure to regularly run the Update Virus Definitions feature, because new viruses appear all the time.

Protect Your Laptop on the Road

Your laptop is especially vulnerable because of both its small size and the fact that you may take it with you to a variety of places and occasionally leave it unattended. There are several ways you can protect your laptop from theft and to protect your data from prying eyes. Start with faithfully using good passwords and password protection strategies. You can learn more about this later in this chapter. You can also employ the use of security devices and software to help keep your laptop safe, as outlined here.

Fingerprint Readers

Fingerprint readers do exactly as their name suggests. They read fingerprints. Some laptops even feature them as a selling point. Rather than use a password to gain access to your computer, you scan in your fingerprint. You can also buy external fingerprint readers that perform the same function. If you are on the road with your laptop a lot, this device or feature can be a valuable safeguard; if the computer is stolen, thieves cannot access your personal information.

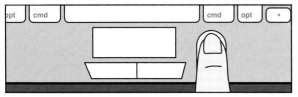

Cable Locks

Another device you can use to help prevent theft is a cable lock. A cable lock attaches your laptop to an external object, such as a chair or post. The cable end locks into a built-in lock slot, called a Universal Security Slot (USS), in the base of your laptop with a preset combination or key locking device. Once you insert the cable into the lock slot, you cannot remove it without entering the correct combination using the required key.

Tracking Software

Over a million laptops are lost or stolen each year, and less than 2% are ever recovered. Another way to protect your laptop is through tracking software. Tracking software, such as LoJack or GadgetTrak, helps you track your lost or stolen laptop. The software can be set up to email you with the location of your laptop, and allow you to remotely destroy data on it to keep people from accessing personal information.

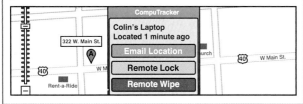

Insuring, Registering, and Engraving

You can insure your laptop by purchasing special laptop insurance that covers theft, accidental damage, or damage from a power surge. Some homeowner's policies may also cover laptops, but check to make sure yours does. Registering your laptop or having it engraved with your name can also make it difficult for thieves to resell it later. Engraving your name and phone number on the laptop can also help someone return it to you.

Protect Yourself Online

When using your laptop to surf the Internet, you can keep yourself safe by practicing a few simple guidelines: guard your personal information, be careful where you venture, and do business only with sites you trust. Just as you would not give personal information to a stranger out on the street, you must learn to protect your identity and information online. Be cautious about the Websites you visit, only doing business with reputable online stores and vendors. Take advantage of customer reviews, reading comments from others to find out about an online store's reputation.

Do Not Give Out Personal Information

Many sites request personal information from you to register a product or service. Before giving such information out, make sure the Website is secure and that they do not make your information public. Many social networking and blog sites make your profile publicly available by default; you have to change the default settings to make your information private. Refrain from posting information about your location, family, income, and activities; a predator can use this info to locate or stalk you.

> June 23 - Today we leave for two weeks in the Florida sun! We'll miss our neighborhood, Covington Corner, and most of all our cute little 2-story brick house, but hey, we'll only be gone one week! What can happen in just one week? As I said to our neighbor, Jane Summer, this is about the safest place to live. You could literally

Be Careful About Images You Post

Today many people are posting images on blogs and social networking sites. Posting images is fine, but be careful what they reveal. Is your street address or house visible in the image? Are you in a provocative pose? Is your daughter wearing a sweatshirt with her school name on it? Such images can be used to pinpoint your location, or may be modified and reposted on unsavory sites.

Be Wary of Scams

Common sense is your best defense regarding online scams. You have learned in your everyday life that nothing is free, and to suspect an offer that sounds too good to be true. The same applies online. Avoid promotions that offer you something for nothing; they are probably trying to collect your personal data to sell it or steal your identity. Ignore emails making unbelievable claims, such as promising you a hundred thousand dollars if you provide your bank account number for a transfer.

> Kind Sir,
> I represent the estate of Prince Dnai of Lualua. He has sadly passed on and directed that $12,000,000 be deposited immediately into your account. Please send account and routing number that we may carry out the late Prince's wishes. Best wishes on your very good fortune, and for your future.

Socialize Safely

There are numerous ways to interact with others online, including social networks, chat sites, and online gaming rooms. Be careful what you expose about yourself in such settings and practice good etiquette. Just remember, not everyone is who they say they are online. If you make a friend online, do not meet that "friend" in person unless it is in a very public place. You should also bring another person along for safety.

Improve Email Privacy

When you send and receive emails, you run the risk of errant messages wrongly addressed, spam, and viruses. You can also be vulnerable to people opening your email program if you leave your laptop unattended. There are several things you can do to improve your email privacy. Some email programs let you assign passwords to access accounts, which can prevent unauthorized usage. You can also encrypt messages, add digital certificates, and email signatures. To avoid spam, consider anti-spam software to block unwanted emails. Anti-virus programs can help protect your computer from harmful, hidden attachments, links, and programs.

Email Signatures

Most email programs have a feature for automatically adding a signature at the bottom of your email messages, such as your office contact information. Although this feature can be a convenient way to include important contact data with a message, it can also provide contact information to people you do not want to share it with if messages are forwarded or hacked. Either avoid using a signature or keep the information that it contains to a minimum.

Best wishes,
Colin Smith
Tel: 317-555-2969
Mobile: 617-555-7899
E-mail: CSmith@Silvercraft.com

SilverCraft

Encrypt Messages

When email is in transit, it can be intercepted by others. To avoid this, you can encrypt messages. Encrypting a message scrambles it in a way that makes its contents unreadable by anybody. Public-key encryption buries a key value in the message, and only somebody with the key can unscramble the message. Encrypted messages typically display a tiny lock icon. Most email programs, such as Microsoft Outlook, offer an encryption feature you can apply to messages.

```
sauigf648cng78ncigtfg76vbune561midbtyvw
ghaz576vr32mn$70,000insharesvxu3098nc6a
nbusvrlkamnllvt0qmnsiox68476halnvwig01h
gwqpmskvubefakjteqbkisnevxu3098nc6anbus
vrltradingthursday09:00x68476halnvwig01
hgwqpmskvubefaksauigf648cng78ncigtfg76v
```

Digital Certificates

Working along with encryption coding, you can use a digital ID or certificate. Digital certification is an electronic "credit card" of sorts that establishes your credentials when doing business online. Issued by a certification authority, a digital certificate is an email attachment that contains your name, a serial number, expiration date, and a copy of the holder's public key used for encrypting messages and digital signatures. It also includes the signature of the issuing authority to very its authenticity.

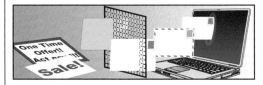

Filter Out Spam

Spam is unwanted email, sometimes from advertisers, sometimes from more malicious sources. Most email programs include tools for filtering out spam before you see it in your Inbox. Based on keywords, a spam filter uses a rule that pertains to certain words or phrases found in the subject line or body text of a message. Any mail found containing those words are sent to another designated folder. You can also install spam filtering software to further protect your Inbox.

You can use passwords to keep your laptop and data safe. Passwords deter intruders and keep out unauthorized users. However, passwords are often easy to forget. For this reason many people tend to favor the same password for many purposes, and easy passwords over more difficult ones. When choosing a password, it is important to use strong passwords that are difficult to guess or hack. A good password strategy can help you keep your system and data secure. If you do have to write down a password, make sure you keep it somewhere safe.

Bad Passwords

Passwords are not foolproof. Some, such as your birthdate, can be easily guessed by a person who has visited your blog or social network profile. Others can be found by people using special software that runs through millions of possible combinations of words and common words found in a dictionary in minutes. Names of pets, children, street names, or company names do not make good passwords. Text-based passwords, though simple to remember, are far too easy to hack.

> **User Name:** My Name
> **Password:** abc123

Good Passwords

The safest passwords use a combination of letters, numbers, and special characters, such as $, %, or *. These are not as vulnerable as text-based passwords, nor can they be easily guessed by those who know some personal facts about you. Another trick is to deliberately misspell words in your password. Even though random passwords are harder to remember, the inconvenience far outweighs having your identity, laptop, or data stolen.

> **User Name:** My Name
> **Password:** Kmle#4!08

Change Your Password Frequently

The best practice is to change your password regularly. If somebody has gained access to your password, changing it can protect you from future intrusions or breaches in security. It is tempting to use the same password for a variety of tasks, such as using the same password to access an online store as you use to access your banking system. This is never a good idea; if the password is discovered, it opens a security gap for all of your accounts.

> **NOTICE**
> It has been 90 days since you last changed your password. Changing your password frequently keeps your information secure.

Password-Protect Your Laptop

I f you care about keeping your files private, creating a password is crucial. Doing so prevents anyone who does not know the password from logging on to your account and accessing your files. Setting a strong password is important — that is, one that is at least eight characters long; does not contain your username or real name, or any complete words; and contains a mixture of uppercase and lowercase letters, numbers, symbols, and spaces. For an added layer of protection, change your password periodically. If you write down your password, be sure to store it somewhere safe and private.

Password-Protect Your Laptop

1 From the Start screen, swipe the right edge of the screen or move the mouse pointer to the lower-right corner.

Windows displays the Charms bar.

Note: You can also press ⊞+C to display the Charms bar.

2 Click **Settings** (⚙).

3 Click **Change PC Settings**.

The PC Settings window opens.

4 Click **Users**.

5 Click **Change Your Password**.

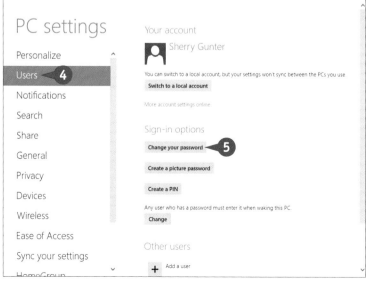

The Change your password screen appears.

6 Type the old password.

7 Type the new password.

8 Type the password a second time in the next field to confirm it.

9 Click **Next**.

Change your Microsoft account password

Sherry Gunter
swkgunter@yahoo.com

Old password _____ **6**

Forgot your password?

New password _____ **7**

Reenter password _____ **8**

9 [Next] [Cancel]

Windows changes your password.

10 Click **Finish**.

You changed your password
You've successfully changed your password!

Sherry Gunter

10 [Finish]

TIPS

What is a PIN?
Among the PC Settings options is a feature for setting a PIN instead of a regular password or picture password. A PIN uses 4-digits as a password Borrowing from smartphone setups, a PIN is a fast way to access Windows 8, especially for touchscreen users. To create a PIN, click the **Create a PIN** button on the PC Settings screen.

What if you forget your password?
If you forget your password, you must reset it using an Administrator account. If you forget the password for an Administrator account and no other Administrator accounts are on the laptop, you must reinstall Windows, which means you will lose all your files.

Set a Picture Password

N ew to Windows 8, you can use a picture password to create a unique login. Designed primarily for touchscreen technologies, you can also use the feature with a mouse. Using a gesture-based login, you can lock and unlock your computer by drawing a unique pattern on the screen using your finger or mouse. Commonly found among smartphones, this technology, also called pattern passwords, the Windows 8 picture password feature can help you add a layer of protection to your laptop.

Set a Picture Password

1 From the Start screen, swipe the right edge of the screen or move the mouse pointer to the lower-right corner.

Windows displays the Charms bar.

Note: You can also press ⊞+C to display the Charms bar.

2 Click **Settings** (⚙).

3 Click **Change PC Settings**.

The PC Settings window opens.

4 Click **Users**.

5 Click **Create a picture password**.

Note: You may need to identify yourself to the Windows 8 operating system by typing in your text password in order to continue creating a picture password.

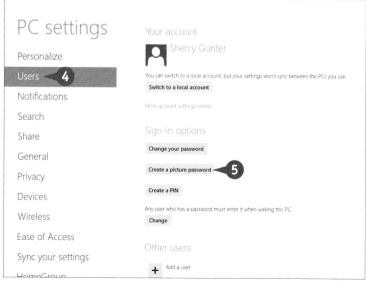

The Welcome to picture password screen opens.

6 Click **Choose picture**.

The Files screen opens.

7 Navigate to the folder containing the picture you want to use.

A Click here to move up in the folder heiarchy

8 Click to select the picture.

9 Click **Open**.

TIPS

Can I use a picture password without a touchscreen laptop?

Yes. Be mindful, however, of the need for accuracy when assigning gestures using the mouse and repeating the same gestures in the same places to log in again later. Mouse gestures include dragging the mouse in a straight line, dragging the mouse in a circle, or clicking in place to mimic a touchscreen tap.

Are picture passwords safe?

Picture passwords originated with mobile devices as a way of authenticating a user. Unlike regular text and number entries, malicious key logger programs cannot record and produce what is typed in with a picture password since there is no typing involved. The key to using it properly is making sure to always use the correct gestures in the correct order.

continued ▶

indows walks you through the process of setting up a picture password. The first step is to choose a picture. You can use any image file found on your computer. Next, you assign three gestures to the picture. Gestures are suited for touchscreen laptops, but you can also use the mouse to add gestures. Gestures can be circles, straight lines, or taps you draw directly on the screen, or in the case of a mouse, drag on the screen. Windows then prompts you to confirm the first three gestures by repeating them again. If you mess up, you can start again.

Set a Picture Password (continued)

The How's this look screen opens.

10 Click **Use this picture**.

B Optionally, if you are not satisfied with the picture placement, you can drag it to reposition it.

C You can click **Choose new picture** to return to the previous screen and select another picture to use.

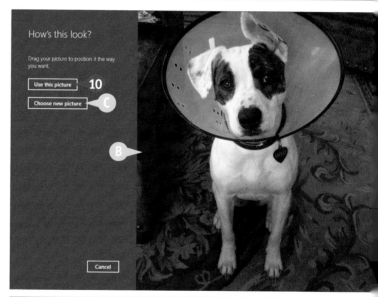

The Set up your gestures screen appears next.

11 Draw three gestures on the picture; draw lines, circles, or just tap.

D The countdown numbers indicate which gesture you are performing to make a total of three.

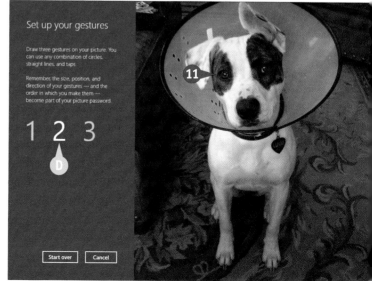

The next screen prompts you to confirm your gestures.

12 Confirm your gestures by repeating them again in the exact same way, order, and placement.

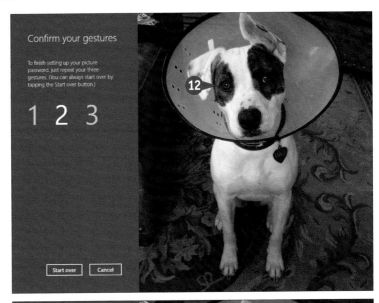

If you successfully duplicate the gestures, the Congratulations screen appears.

13 Click **Finish**.

The next time you sign in, you can use the picture password.

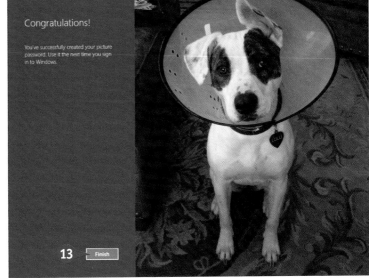

TIPS

How do I remove a picture password?
Return to the PC Settings screen and display the Users options. Under Sign-in options, click the **Remove** button. Windows deletes the password immediately and the buttons on the PC Settings screen change back to a **Create a picture password** button.

How do I change a picture password?
You can redo your password gestures to change the picture password, or assign a different picture. To do so, open the PC Settings screen again to the Users options. Click the **Change picture password** button. You can now go through the same screens you used to create the picture password to reassign a picture and redo the gestures.

Encrypt Your Data

I f someone gains access to your files via a network, you can prevent that person from viewing the files' contents by encrypting them. You can use the Windows 8 Encrypting File System, or EFS, to encrypt any files or folders that you store on your drive. With EFS, you choose what files and folders you want to encrypt. When you encrypt an entire folder, you automatically encrypt all of the files and subfolders within it. EFS works by issuing a file encryption key, which EFS then uses to encrypt and decrypt your data.

Encrypt Your Data

1 In File Explorer, right-click the file or folder you want to encrypt.

Note: See Chapter 9 to learn more about using File Explorer.

2 Click **Properties**.

Note: Not all files and folders can be encrypted. For example, compressed files or folders and system files that support your operating system cannot be encrypted.

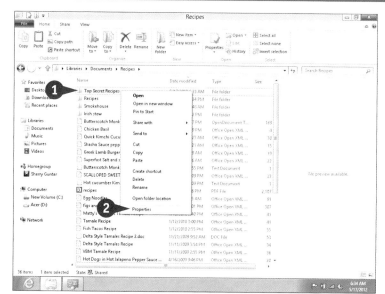

The file or folder's Properties dialog box opens.

3 If necessary, click the **General** tab.

4 Click **Advanced**.

Ⓐ The Advanced Attributes dialog box opens.

⑤ Click the **Encrypt contents to secure data** check box (☑) to select it.

⑥ Click **OK**.

⑦ Click **OK**.

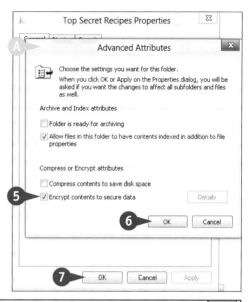

If you are encrypting a folder, the Confirm Attribute Changes dialog box opens, asking whether the encryption should be applied to the folder only or to subfolders and files in the folder.

If you are encrypting a file, the Encryption Warning dialog box opens, asking if you want to encrypt the file and its parent folder or just the file.

⑧ Select the desired option (⦿).

⑨ Click **OK**.

TIP

What if your encryption key is deleted or corrupted?
If your encryption key is deleted or corrupted, your data will be impossible to recover. For this reason, after you encrypt a file or folder, it is critical that you back up your encryption key; store the backup on removable media such as a USB flash drive, a CD or DVD, or an external hard drive; and keep this media in a safe place. You can also create a recovery certificate to recover files. For help backing up your encryption key and creating a recovery certificate, see the Help information in Windows 8 Help.

Thwart Intruders with Windows Firewall

I f your laptop is connected to the Internet, it is vulnerable to such dangers as identity theft, viruses, and more. To protect your system, you can enable Windows Firewall, which creates a barrier between your private computer files and outside connections. Windows Firewall monitors all programs that access the Internet from your computer or try to communicate with you from an external source and moves to block programs that may compromise your system's security. When this happens, Windows Firewall displays a prompt asking what you want to do; you can choose to continue blocking the software or stop blocking it.

Thwart Intruders with Windows Firewall

Enable Windows Firewall

1 Right-click the bottom left corner of the screen.

Note: You can right-click the bottom left corner from the Start screen or from the Desktop screen to view the same pop-up menu.

Note: You can also press ⊞+X to open the pop-up menu.

2 Click **Control Panel**.

3 In the main Control Panel window, click **System and Security**.

The System and Security window opens.

4 Click **Windows Firewall**.

The Windows Firewall window opens.

5 Click **Turn Windows Firewall on or off**.

The Customize Settings screen appears.

6 Under Private network location settings, select the **Turn on Windows Firewall** option button (⊙).

7 Deselect the **Block all incoming connections** check box (□).

8 Select the **Notify me when Windows Firewall blocks a new app** check box (□) if it is not already selected.

9 Repeat Steps **4** to **6** under Public network location settings.

10 Click **OK**.

Windows enables Windows Firewall.

What about physical threats?

Because of their small size and the fact that they are portable, laptops are especially vulnerable to physical threats such as theft as well as prying eyes. Various tools can protect your laptop from these threats. For example, you can install a fingerprint reader; that way, you can use your finger, rather than a password, to gain access to your system. To prevent theft, you can buy a cable lock. You can then use it to lock your laptop to a stationary object such as a chair. Another option is to install tracking software to help you track your lost or stolen laptop.

Sometimes, Windows Firewall works a little *too* well. That is, it blocks a safe program or connection. For example, the firewall may block the short-term connection made when you attempt to instant-message with someone. One way to deal with this is to temporarily disable the firewall. Doing so increases your system's exposure to various security threats, however. A better approach is to allow the problematic network connection or program as an exception. An *exception* is a program or connection that you want to allow so that it does not limit your ability to work or communicate.

Thwart Intruders with Windows Firewall (continued)

Manage Exceptions

1 Press ⊞+X to open the pop-up menu.

2 Click **Control Panel**.

3 In the main Control Panel window, click **System and Security**.

4 In the System and Security window, under Windows Firewall, click **Allow an app through Windows Firewall**.

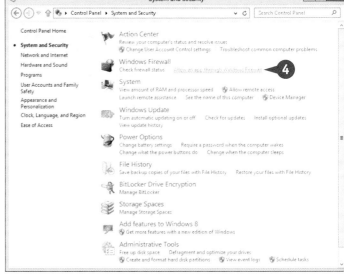

The Allow apps to communicate through Windows Firewall screen appears.

5 Click **Change settings**.

6 In the Allowed apps and features section, select a program or feature option (☐changes to ☑).

Note: To block rather than allow a program or feature, uncheck the check box next to the program or feature you want to block.

7 In the program's or feature's Private and Public section, select (☑) or deselect (☐) options to indicate whether the program or feature should be enabled on both types of networks.

8 Click **OK**.

TIPS

What other forms of protection does your system need?
In addition to Windows Firewall, you should run antivirus software and be careful when opening e-mail attachments or other files from any source, even a trusted one, to avoid inadvertently infecting your system with a virus. Norton and McAfee are two companies that sell reliable antivirus software.

What is Windows Defender?
Windows Defender is a program that runs automatically to scan for and uninstall spyware. *Spyware* is software installed on your computer, usually without your knowledge or consent, that can deluge your system with unwanted pop-up ads, and also monitor and record your Web-surfing activities and transmit this data to interested parties — including crackers. Learn more about using Windows Defender later in this chapter.

Enable Parental Controls

If you share your laptop with children, you can set up the Windows 8 parental controls. One way to use parental control is to limit children's use of the laptop to certain hours of the day on certain days of the week. If the child tries to log in at a restricted time, Windows blocks access; if the child is logged on at the commencement of the blocked time, Windows automatically logs him or her off. To implement the Windows parental controls, each child who uses your computer must have his or her own Standard user account.

Enable Parental Controls

1 Right-click the bottom left corner of the screen.

Note: You can right-click the bottom left corner from the Start screen or from the Desktop screen to view the same pop-up menu.

Note: You can also press ⊞+X to open the pop-up menu.

2 Click **Control Panel**.

3 In the main Control Panel window, under User Accounts and Family Safety, click **Set up Family Safety for any user**.

The Family Safety options appear.

4 Click the user account to which you want to apply parental controls.

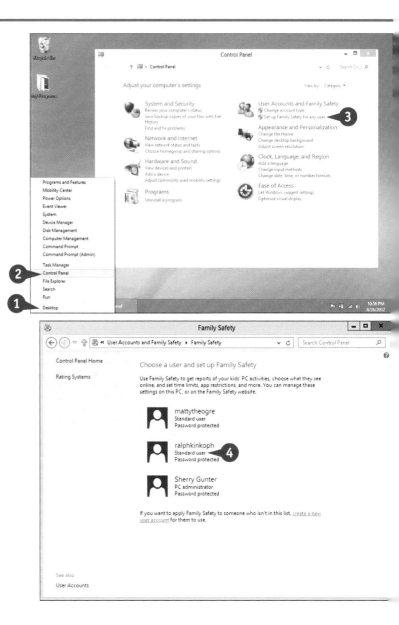

The User Settings options appear.

5 Under the Family Safety category, click the **On, enforce current settings** option (⊙) to select it.

Ⓐ Optionally, to record activity as reports you can check, activate the Activity reporting feature.

6 Click **Time limits**.

The Time Limits options appear.

7 Click **Set time allowance**.

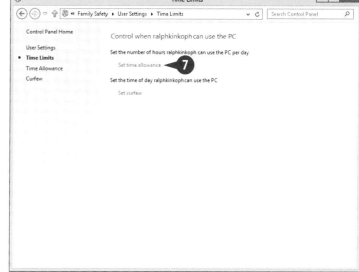

TIP

How do you create a Standard user account?

To implement the Windows 8 parental controls, children using your laptop must have their own Standard user accounts. To create a Standard user account, click the **Start** button and click **Control Panel**. Then, under **User Accounts and Family Safety**, click **Add or remove user accounts**. The Manage Accounts window opens; click **Create a new account**. In the Create New Account window, type a name for the new account, select the Standard account type, and click **Create Account**. Windows creates a Standard account. To log on to the account, click it in the Windows 8 Welcome screen.

continued ▶

You can also use Windows parental controls to restrict access to games on the computer. Games can be restricted by game rating, or on a game-by-game basis. In addition, parental controls can be used to restrict access to programs you might prefer to keep private. For example, you might choose to restrict access to a money-management program. In addition to using Windows parental controls to keep kids safe, you can use the Internet Explorer Content Advisor feature to prevent exposure to inappropriate subject matter, such as violent or sexually explicit Internet content.

Enable Parental Controls (continued)

The Time Allowance options appear.

8 Click the option for using the computer for the amount of time specified.

9 To specify weekday or weekend time amounts, click the ⊙.

10 Click the ⊡ and specify time amounts for each weekday or weekend day.

11 Click **Curfew**.

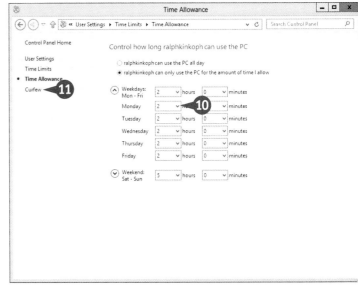

The Curfew options appear.

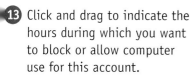 Click the option for using the computer for the time ranges specified.

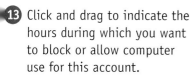 Click and drag to indicate the hours during which you want to block or allow computer use for this account.

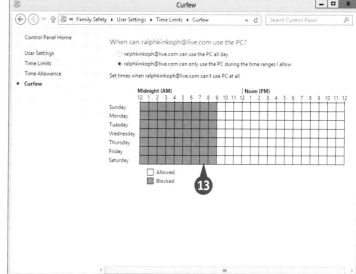

TIP

Are there other ways to protect kids?

In addition to using the Windows 8 parental controls to limit access to games and programs, you can also use the parental controls included with Internet Explorer 9, called Content Advisor, to prevent exposure to inappropriate subject matter, such as violent or sexually explicit Internet content. To enable Content Advisor, click the **Tools** button in Internet Explorer 9 and click **Internet Options**. The Internet Options dialog box opens; click the **Content** tab and, under Content Advisor, click **Enable**. The Content Advisor dialog box opens; adjust the settings in the various tabs as desired and click **OK**.

Filter Spam and Scams with Windows Live Mail

I n addition to being a real time-waster, spam e-mails often involve scams, making spam potentially dangerous. You can use Windows Live Mail's junk e-mail filter to divert spam from your inbox into a special Junk e-mail folder. The Windows Live Mail junk e-mail filter is enabled by default, but moves only the most obvious junk e-mail messages into your Junk e-mail folder. If you want, you can change the level of filtering. You should occasionally check your Junk e-mail folder to make sure no legitimate messages were diverted there by accident. E-mails that are not junk can be moved to your inbox.

Filter Spam and Scams with Windows Live Mail

Set the Junk Email Filter

1 Open Internet Explorer to Windows Live Mail.

2 Click the **Options** menu.

Note: See Chapter 12 to learn more about using Windows Live Mail.

3 Click **More options**.

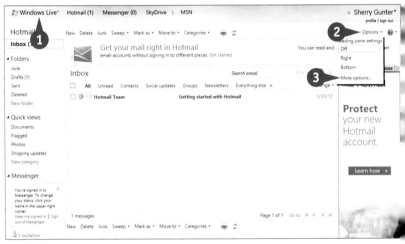

The Options window opens.

4 Click **Filters and reporting**.

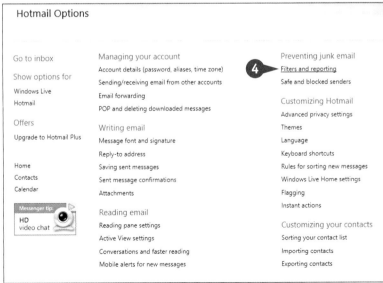

5 Select the desired filter.

A Click **Standard** to block most spam.

B Click **Exclusive** to block everything but trusted email sources.

6 Click **Save**.

Mark Mail as Junk

1 From the Inbox, click the message you want to mark as junk.

2 Click **Junk**.

The message is moved to your Junk folder and Windows Live Mail displays a message box.

3 Click **OK**.

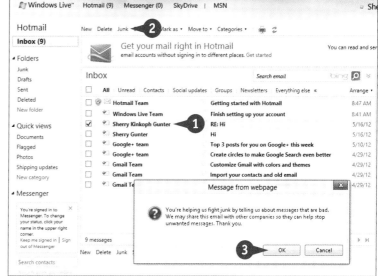

TIP

What is phishing?

Phishing is an attempt by a malicious party to obtain private information from computer users. Often, phishing involves an e-mail message that appears to be from a legitimate source such as a bank that contains links that direct users to a bogus Web site designed to steal personal information. If you use a Windows Live or Hotmail account with Windows Live Mail, the program automatically checks the sender ID of all incoming messages in an attempt to detect phishing messages. In addition, the Internet Explorer 9 SmartScreen Filter, enabled by default, helps detect fraudulent Web sites.

Check for Spyware with Windows Defender

indows Defender is an anti-spyware program you can use to protect your laptop from various types of spyware and malware. The term *malware* covers spyware, tracking cookies, and other malicious software that download and installs itself on your computer. Spyware can collect information about you as you browse the Internet, redirect your browser to a bogus Internet site, or install unwanted pop-up ads. You can use Windows Defender to scan your system for unwanted spyware and malware daily to keep your system running smoothly. Windows Defender is one of several apps you can monitor from the Windows Security Center.

Check for Spyware with Windows Defender

1 Right-click the bottom left corner of the screen.

Note: You can right-click the bottom left corner from the Start screen or from the Desktop screen to view the same pop-up menu.

Note: You can also press `Ctrl` + `X` to open the pop-up menu.

2 Click **Control Panel**.

The Control Panel window opens.

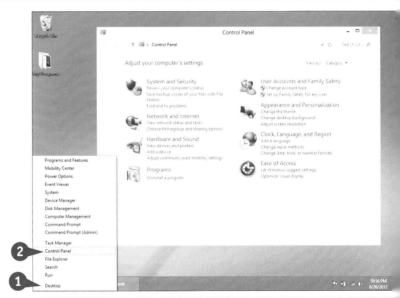

3 In the main Control Panel window, click the **View by** drop-down arrow (▾).

4 Click **Small Icons**.

The Control Panel displays all items as icons.

5 Click **Windows Defender**.

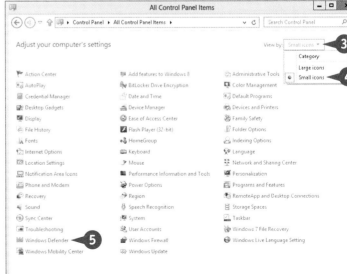

The Windows Defender window opens.

6 Click a scan option.

Ⓐ Click the **Settings** tab to turn real-time protection on or off.

Ⓑ Click the **Update** tab to download the latest virus and spyware definitions.

7 Click **Scan now**.

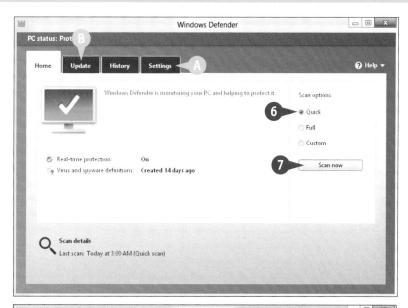

Windows Defender begins scanning your system for spyware.

Ⓒ When the scan is complete, Windows Defender posts a report.

8 Click **Close** to exit.

TIPS

Which scan option should I choose?
The Full scan option takes a lot longer to run than a Quick scan because more programs and system locations are checked. As such, it is a good idea to run a Full scan at the end of the day when you do not need to use the computer. You can use the Custom scan option to designate a specific drive to scan, including removable storage media such as flash drives or external hard drives.

How often should I update spyware and virus definitions?
Windows Defender works alongside Windows Update to keep your laptop up-to-date with the latest updates. You can also choose to manually update the definitions using the Update tab in the Windows Defender window. Click the tab and then click the **Update** button to install the latest information regarding viruses, spyware, and other types of malware.

Check Problems with the Action Center

You can use the Windows 8 Action Center to keep apprised of system problems and find solutions. The Action Center is a central spot to view alerts, address issues with the operating system that arise, and conduct maintenance tasks. If a problem with your computer does occur, such as a program crash, you can send a report to Microsoft and check for possible solutions. You can use the Action Center as a jumping off point for dealing with program issues, driver problems, corrupted files, and any updates you need to add to your system.

Check Problems with the Action Center

1 Right-click the bottom left corner of the screen.

Note: You can right-click the bottom left corner from the Start screen or from the Desktop screen to view the same pop-up menu.

Note: You can also press ⊞+☒ to open the pop-up menu.

2 Click **Control Panel**.

3 Click **System and Security**.

If the Control Panel is displaying Large icons or Small icons view instead of Category view, you can click the **Action Center** icon directly.

4 Click **Action Center**.

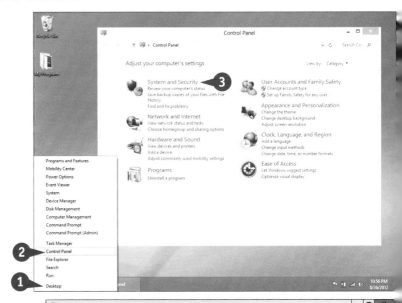

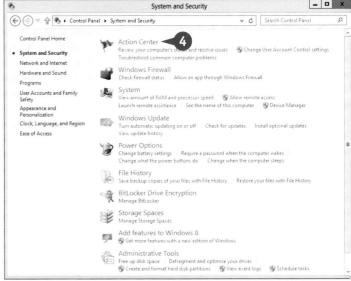

The Action Center displays any notifications and items for review.

Ⓐ You can view Security settings and make changes here.

Ⓑ You can view maintenance issues, such as when a program crashes, here and check for solutions.

Ⓒ If your problem is not listed, you can try the troubleshooting link to find and fix problems.

⑤ Click **Expand** (⊙).

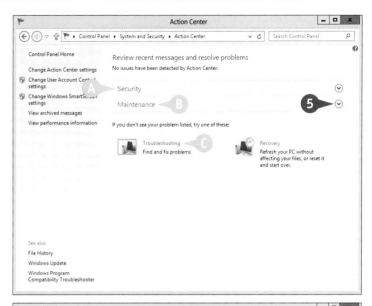

The Action Center expands the details for the issues.

Ⓓ You can click a link to change settings.

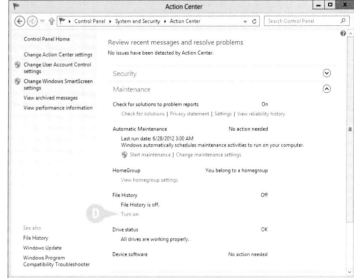

TIPS

How does Windows tell me there is a problem?

On the Desktop, you can view notifications on the Taskbar. A flag icon (🏳) appears in the far right edge of the Taskbar to signify any issues that arise. You can click the icon to view more details or address the issue. If you have a problem that does not involve a notification flag, you can check the Action Center to see if it has been identified there.

What does the Recovery feature do?

If something goes drastically wrong with your computer, you can use the Recovery link that appears in the Action Center window to reset your computer to your default system settings. The Refresh feature is similar to booting your laptop in safe mode. Personal data is not touched, but you may lose some apps when pursuing a system recovery.

Index

Index